Metaphysical Shadows

Metaphysical Shadows

The Persistence of Donne, Herbert, Vaughan, and Marvell in Contemporary Poetry

Sean H. McDowell

LEXINGTON BOOKS
Lanham • Boulder • New York • London

Jericho Brown, excerpts from "Cakewalk," "The Virus," "Monotheism," "A. D.," "Thighs and Ass," "The Microscopes," and "Duplex" from *The Tradition*. Copyright © 2019 by Jericho Brown. Excerpts "Another Elegy" and "To Be Seen" from *The New Testament*. Copyright © 2014 by Jericho Brown. All reprinted with the permission of The Permissions Company, LLC on behalf of Copper Canyon Press, coppercanyonpress.org.

Jericho Brown, excerpts from "Cakewalk," "The Virus," "Monotheism," "A. D.," "Thighs and Ass," "The Microscopes," and "Duplex" from *The Tradition*. Copyright © 2019 by Jericho Brown. Excerpts "Another Elegy" and "To Be Seen" from *The New Testament*. Copyright © 2014 by Jericho Brown. Reproduced with permission of the Licensor through PLSclear.

"Prayer of the Back Handed" and "Scarecrow" Copyright © 2008 by Jericho Brown. Reprinted by permission of New Issues Press.

"The Nunwell Letter" Copyright © 2019 by Maureen Boyle. Reprinted by permission of the author.

"Vaughan Variations" by Anne Cluysenaar (*Timeslips: New and Selected Poems*, 1997) are reprinted by kind permission of Carcanet Press, Manchester, UK.

"Resources" from *Tables* Copyright © 2013 by Alfred Corn. Reprinted by permission of Press 53.

Excerpts from *ARK* Copyright © 2013 by The Literary Estate of Ronald Johnson. Reprinted by permission of Flood Editions.

Brendan Kennelly, *Familiar Strangers: New & Selected Poems 1960–2004* (Bloodaxe Books, 2004) www.bloodaxebooks.com

Excerpts from "You, Andrew Marvell" from *COLLECTED POEMS 1917–1982* by Archibald Macleish. Copyright @ 1985 by The Estate of HarperCollins Publisher. All rights reserved.

Published by Lexington Books
An imprint of The Rowman & Littlefield Publishing Group, Inc.
4501 Forbes Boulevard, Suite 200, Lanham, Maryland 20706
www.rowman.com

86-90 Paul Street, London EC2A 4NE

Copyright © 2022 by The Rowman & Littlefield Publishing Group, Inc.

All rights reserved. No part of this book may be reproduced in any form or by any electronic or mechanical means, including information storage and retrieval systems, without written permission from the publisher, except by a reviewer who may quote passages in a review.

British Library Cataloguing in Publication Information Available

Library of Congress Cataloging-in-Publication Data

Names: McDowell, Sean H., author.
Title: Metaphysical shadows : the persistence of Donne, Herbert, Vaughan, and Marvell in contemporary poetry / Sean H. McDowell.
Description: Lanham : Lexington Books, [2022] | Includes bibliographical references and index.
Identifiers: LCCN 2021057316 (print) | LCCN 2021057317 (ebook) | ISBN 9781793635433 (cloth) | ISBN 9781793635457 (paperback) | ISBN 9781793635440 (ebook)
Subjects: LCSH: Poetry—21st century—History and criticism—Theory, etc. | Metaphysics in literature. | Donne, John, 1572-1631—Influence. | Herbert, George, 1593-1633—Influence. | Vaughan, Henry, 1621-1695—Influence. | Marvell, Andrew, 1621-1678—Influence.
Classification: LCC PN1281 .M33 2022 (print) | LCC PN1281 (ebook) |
DDC 808.1—dc23/eng/20211229
LC record available at https://lccn.loc.gov/2021057316
LC ebook record available at https://lccn.loc.gov/2021057317

Contents

Acknowledgments	vii
A Note to the Reader	ix
Metaphysical Shadows: An Introduction	1

PART I: VARIETIES OF SHADOWS — 19

1. Echo and Allusion: "The Extasie" Behind Seamus Heaney's "Chanson d'Aventure" — 21
2. The Answer Poem: Anne Donne on the Isle of Wight — 35
3. Shared Subjects: Andrew Marvell, Archibald MacLeish, and Brendan Kennelly — 57
4. Modal Resemblances: "Metaphysical," "Meditative," and the Poetry of Donne, W. B. Yeats, and Ronald Johnson — 73

PART II: LATE TWENTIETH- AND EARLY TWENTY-FIRST-CENTURY SHADOWS — 93

5. What Did Suffice: Scintillas of Vaughan in the Poetry of Anne Cluysenaar — 95
6. Donne, Heaney, and the Boldness of Love — 109
7. The Depth of Herbert's Voiceprint in the Poetry of Alfred Corn — 129
8. Verbal Relish in the Poetry of Donne and Kimberly Johnson — 143
9. *The Tradition* and the Individual Talent: Jericho Brown and the Donnean Note — 157

Shadow Instruction: An Afterword	175
Works Cited	183
Index	197
About the Author	203

Acknowledgments

An earlier version of chapter 1 was published as "Making the Present Speak: 'The Exstasie' Behind Seamus Heaney's *'Chanson d'Aventure*,'" *John Donne Journal* 30 (2011): 195–209, and a version of chapter 7 was published as "The Depth of Herbert's Voiceprint: Intentional and Unintentional Traces in the Poetry of Alfred Corn," *George Herbert Journal* 32.1-2 (Fall 2008/Spring 2009): 68–82. My thanks to the editors of these journals for permission to reprint. Chapter 6 was published in an earlier form as Sean H. McDowell, "Heaney, Donne, and the Boldness of Love," published in *John Donne and Contemporary Poetry*, edited by Judith Scherer Herz, 2017, Palgrave Macmillan, reproduced with permission of Palgrave Macmillan.

In addition, my thanks also to the following poets and presses for permission to reprint various poems and poetic passages throughout this book:

"The Nunwell Letter" Copyright © 2019 by Maureen Boyle, first published in *Poetry Ireland Review* 127 and forthcoming from Arlen House/Syracuse University Press in 2022. Reprinted by permission of the author.

Excerpts from "You, Andrew Marvell" from *COLLECTED POEMS 1917–1982* by Archibald MacLeish. Copyright © 1985 by The Estate of Archibald MacLeish. Reprinted by permission of HarperCollins Publishers. All rights reserved.

Excerpts from *Cromwell: A Poem* reprinted from Brendan Kennelly, *Familiar Strangers: New & Selected Poems 1960–2004* (Bloodaxe Books, 2004) by kind permission of the publisher Bloodaxe Books (www.bloodaxebooks.com).

Excerpts from *ARK* Copyright © 2013 by The Literary Estate of Ronald Johnson. Reprinted by kind permission of Flood Editions.

"Vaughan Variations" by Anne Cluysenaar (*Timeslips: New and Selected Poems*, 1997) are reprinted by kind permission of Carcanet Press, Manchester, UK.

"Resources" from *Tables* Copyright © 2013 by Alfred Corn. Reprinted by kind permission of Press 53.

Excerpts from *A Metaphorical God* (Persea Books) Copyright © Kimberly Johnson. Reprinted by kind permission of the author.

"Prayer of the Back Handed" and "Scarecrow" Copyright © 2008 by Jericho Brown. Reprinted by permission of New Issues Press.

Jericho Brown, excerpts from "Cakewalk," "The Virus," "Monotheism," "A. D.," "Thighs and Ass," "The Microscopes," and "Duplex" from *The Tradition*. Copyright © 2019 by Jericho Brown. Excerpts "Another Elegy" and "To Be Seen" from *The New Testament*. Copyright © 2014 by Jericho Brown. All reprinted with the permission of The Permissions Company, LLC on behalf of Copper Canyon Press, coppercanyonpress.org.

A Note to the Reader

Unless otherwise indicated, all quotations from the poetry of the metaphysical poets come from the following editions. In the case of John Donne's *Anniversaries*, *Divine Poems*, *Elegies*, *Holy Sonnets*, and *Verse Letters*, I quote from the following volumes of *The Variorum Edition of the Poetry of John Donne*:

Vol. 2: *The Elegies*, edited by Gary A. Stringer et al. Bloomington and London: Indiana University Press, 2000.
Vol. 3: *The Satyres*, edited by Gary A. Stringer et al. Bloomington and Indianapolis: Indiana University Press, 2016.
Vol. 5: *The Verse Letters*, edited by Jeffrey S. Johnson et al. Bloomington and Indianapolis: Indiana University Press, 2019.
Vol. 6: *The Anniversaries and the Epicedes and Obsequies*, edited by Gary A. Stringer et al. Bloomington and Indianapolis: Indiana University Press, 1995.
Vol. 7.1: *The Holy Sonnets*, edited by Gary A. Stringer et al. Bloomington and Indianapolis: Indiana University Press, 2005.
Vol. 7.2: *The Divine Poems*, edited Jeffrey S. Johnson et al. Bloomington and Indianapolis: Indiana University Press, 2020.
Vol. 8: *The Epigrams, Epithalamions, Epitaphs, Inscriptions, and Miscellaneous Poems*, edited by Gary A. Stringer et al. Bloomington and Indianapolis: Indiana University Press, 1995.

In the case of Donne's *Songs and Sonnets*, I quote from

The Complete Poetry of John Donne, edited by John T. Shawcross. Garden City, NY: Doubleday/Anchor, 1967.

George Herbert, *The Works of George Herbert*, edited by F. E. Hutchinson. Oxford: Clarendon Press, 1941.
Andrew Marvell, *The Poems and Letters of Andrew Marvell*, edited by H. M. Margoliouth; revised edition, edited by Pierre Legouis and E. E. Duncan-Jones. 3rd edition, 2 vols. Oxford: Clarendon Press, 1971.
Henry Vaughan, *The Works of Henry Vaughan*, edited by Donald R. Dickson, Alan Rudrum, and Robert Wilcher. 3 vols. Oxford: Oxford University Press, 2018.

I note the editions of the other poets whom I quote in the notes on a case-by-case basis.

Metaphysical Shadows
An Introduction

In his poem "Lecture upon the Shadow," possibly composed near the end of 1601, John Donne seizes upon the passage of the sun during a three-hour walk with his lover to "lecture" on the lifespan of love through a comparison with shadows. Early in their walk, the angled sunlight cast long shadows of their figures, and these shadows dogged their steps. Donne sees here an analogy with the early phases of their relationship, while their "infant loves did grow, / Disguises did, and shadows, flow, / From us, and our care" (ll. 9-11). But now, deep into their walk—and at the noon of their love—the sun shines directly above. Their shadows—and doubts—have disappeared underfoot ("We doe those shadowes tread," l. 7), and the lovers clearly see each other and their love, a degree of illumination the poet worries will end as the sun progresses into afternoon, and "new shadowes" will lengthen again, this time the "other way" (l. 15).

The likening of love to shadows, two startlingly unlike things, accords with Samuel Johnson's scornful definition of the metaphysical conceit as the "most heterogeneous ideas . . . yoked by violence together."[1] But such "violent" comparisons can be useful. They can illuminate what might have been obscure before. This book crafts its own metaphysical conceit by using shadows as an analogy for describing the diverse engagements of twentieth- and twenty-first-century poets with their seventeenth-century metaphysical predecessors. As with shadows, sometimes the presence of metaphysical poets or poems is obvious in the work of modern poets through allusion, echo, and direct response, the way shadows are obvious during mid-morning or late afternoon. But sometimes shadows seem nonexistent, hidden beneath the edges of shoes at noontime, just as the influence or inspiration of a metaphysical poet or poem might barely register when a modern poet follows a similar procedure but without any acknowledgment or perhaps even conscious awareness. By examining the work of an eclectic group of American, English, Welsh, and Irish poets, from T. S. Eliot and Archibald MacLeish at the start of the second phase of the "Donne Revival" to such contemporary poets as Seamus Heaney, Maureen Boyle, Brendan Kennelly, Ronald Johnson, Anne Cluysenaar, Alfred Corn, Kimberly Johnson, and Jericho Brown, this book explores a variety of shadows the older poets still cast today. In the process, it implicitly demonstrates their continuing relevance as we near the end of the first quarter of the twenty-first century.

This year—2021—is an auspicious time to take stock of the rich legacy of the metaphysical poets in the work of modern poets. For in addition to being the 400th anniversary of the births of Andrew Marvell and Henry Vaughan (both poets were born less than three weeks apart), it also marks the publication of Herbert J. C. Grierson's *Metaphysical Lyrics & Poems of the Seventeenth Century: Donne to Butler*.[2] This volume, which was reprinted seven times between 1921 and 1952, ignited a resurgence of interest not only in Donne but also in the work of other metaphysical poets, most notably Herbert, Crashaw, Vaughan, and Marvell, who together with Donne, defined the English metaphysical poets as a group for poets and academics throughout most of the past century.

Grierson, of course, sometimes still is mistakenly credited with initiating the "Donne Revival" through the publication of his two-volume edition of *The Poems of John Donne*.[3] But in truth, as Joseph E. Duncan, Raoul Granqvist, and Dayton Haskin have shown, a revival of interest in Donne's life and poetry began in the decades before through the biographies of William Minto, Augustus Jessopp, and Edmund W. Gosse; the editions of Alexander B. Grosart, James Russell Lowell/Mabel Burnett/Charles Eliot Norton, and E. K. Chambers; the anthologies of Felix E. Schelling and Frederic Ives Carpenter; and the inclusion of Donne in the curriculum of Harvard, Yale, and other universities.[4] Haskin summarizes the larger trajectory of the reception of Donne in the nineteenth century as one of growth and complication:

> as the aims of a self-consciously secular interpretive community collided with the interests of readers who were looking into the writings because they valued the Dr Donne mediated to posterity by Walton, a larger, more fluid interpretative community emerged. Its members found in Donne an intriguing site at which to explore their own cultural contradictions. The various interpretations of the poems now being reported in the *Variorum* [*Edition of the Poetry of John Donne*] attest to a struggle over the identity and significance of John Donne that took on an unprecedented urgency at the end of the nineteenth century. Because it involved a cultural investment that has continued to produce interest for more than a hundred years, that struggle has made the history of Donne's reputation a much more important subject than anyone could have imagined before it began.[5]

As the last event of this first phase of the Donne revival, Grierson's two-volume edition of Donne nevertheless made a substantial impact on multiple communities of readers and poets. So much so that John R. Roberts, the leading bibliographer in seventeenth-century studies during the last fifty years, began his coverage of Donne scholarship in his annotated bibliographies of modern criticism with Grierson's edition as the first entry. "Although all scholars are aware that the modern interest in Donne did not suddenly burst forth on the scene" in 1912, Roberts explains, "Grierson's edition was the first major effort in this century to deal with Donne in a thoroughly scholarly and serious way."[6] Grierson's also was the edition to which poets increasingly responded.

W. B. Yeats, for example, was a personal acquaintance of Grierson's. In fact, he was staying with Grierson at Grierson's home in Aberdeen when *The Playboy of the Western World* premiered at the Abbey Theatre in Dublin on Saturday, January 26, 1907.[7] Lady Augusta Gregory's telegram in the wee hours of the morning about the audience uproar that first night precipitated Yeats's early return to Dublin, thereby setting in motion one of the most storied confrontations in Irish dramatic history. In 1912, Grierson sent Yeats his edition of Donne, and Yeats expressed his gratitude in warm terms: "I have been using [your edition] constantly and find that at last I can understand Donne," Yeats wrote:

> Poems that I could not understand or could but understand are now clear and I notice that the more precise and learned the thought the greater the beauty, the passion; the intricacy and subtleties of his imagination are the length and depths of the furrow made by his passion.[8]

He wrote this letter from the comparative quiet of Lady Gregory's Coole Park estate, where he was convalescing and settling down to work again. "I shall fish for pike and plan out poems," he concluded. His immersion in Donne appears to have fed at least some of that planning. Wayne C. Chapman notes that several of the poems published in *Responsibilities* (1914), especially "Fallen Majesty" and "The Cold Heaven," evince Donne's influence. Yeats's "poetic mixing of the spiritual and the sensual (or outwardly sexual) in 1912 became, for the first time, recognizably Metaphysical and unmistakably Donnean in manner," Chapman explains. "In view of his characteristic affinity for imagery forged from contrarieties, such imagery became more fully developed, concentrated, and conspicuous under Donne's influence."[9] At times Yeats voices what seems like envy toward Donne's mastery.[10] Donne joined the ranks of Spenser, Milton, Blake, and other older poets toward whom Yeats felt a sense of kinship. In "To a Young Beauty," from *The Wild Swans of Coole* (1919), he remarks, "There is not a fool can call me friend, / And I may dine at journey's end / With Landor and with Donne" (ll. 16-18).[11] From 1912 on, Grierson's edition of Donne was the primary one Yeats consulted.[12]

While the 1912 edition stirred the imaginations of Yeats, Rupert Brooke,[13] and other notable poets, however, Grierson's 1921 anthology sparked a second phase of the revival, this time showcasing not just Donne but the other metaphysical poets as well. It proved a decisive influence on T. S. Eliot and through Eliot, on many others who followed. Indeed, as Eliot himself noticed, Grierson's volume was as much a work of criticism as an anthology, an attempt to define through both description and example metaphysical poetry as a distinctive literary mode rooted in but not necessarily bound to a historical period. All great poetry, Grierson believed, is "metaphysical" in the sense in which it "has been inspired by a philosophical conception of the universe and the rôle assigned to the human spirit in the great drama of existence."[14] He believed the term "metaphysical" defines their work better than any other because

> it lays stress on the right things—the survival, one might say the reaccentuation of the metaphysical strain, the *concetti metafisici ed ideali* as Testi calls them in contrast to the simpler imagery of classical poetry, of mediaeval Italian poetry; the more intellectual, less verbal, character of their wit compared with the conceits of the Elizabethans; the finer psychology of which their conceits are often the expression; their learned imagery; the argumentative, subtle evolution of their lyrics; above all the peculiar blend of passion and thought, feeling and ratiocination which is their greatest achievement. Passionate thinking is always apt to become metaphysical, probing and investigating the experience from which it takes its rise. All these qualities are in the poetry of Donne, and Donne is the great master of English poetry in the seventeenth century.[15]

By "right things," Grierson meant the essential stylistic and rhetorical characteristics of the poetry of Donne, Herbert, Crashaw, Carew, Vaughan, Marvell, et al. But he also suggested the rightness of these characteristics in his own historical moment, the 1920s. The English metaphysical poets infused their poetry with a passion, an intellectualism, a freshness, a playfulness, and an extravagance that contrasted sharply with the sentimentality of the Augustans. They thus had much to offer the post–World War I era, in Grierson's view.

Eliot, in his *Times Literary Supplement* review of Grierson's anthology and in a series of articles and lectures throughout the 1920s and early 1930s, greatly elaborated on the ideational and stylistic attributes of these poets. The *TLS* review especially became an early landmark of a substantial outpouring of criticism and scholarship on their lives and works. Twenty years later, John Crowe Ransom said of this review:

Its public effect has been to have just about upset the old comparative valuations of the great cycles of English poetic history: reducing the nineteenth century greatly and the Restoration and eighteenth century a little less, elevating the sixteenth and early seventeenth centuries to supreme importance as the locus of the poetic tradition operating at its full.[16]

In this review, Eliot, like Grierson, emphasized the blend of passion and thought—"felt thought"—in the work of the metaphysical poets as well as their propensity for fusing new wholes. Taking issue with Samuel Johnson's criticism of metaphysical wit in his *Life of Cowley*, he highlighted signature differences between the nineteenth-century poets and their seventeenth-century forebears:

> Tennyson and Browning are poets, and they think; but they do not feel their thought as immediately as the odour of a rose. A thought to Donne was an experience; it modified his sensibility. When a poet's mind is perfectly equipped for its work, it is constantly amalgamating disparate experience; the ordinary man's experience is chaotic, irregular, fragmentary. The latter falls in love, or reads Spinoza, and these two experiences have nothing to do with each other, or with the sound of a typewriter or with the smell of cooking; in the mind of the poet these experiences are always forming new wholes.[17]

Yeats also distinguished between the "bundle of accident and incoherence that sits down to breakfast" and the poet on the page who "has been reborn as an idea, something intended, complete," except that he thought of these as the same person at different moments.[18] By resuscitating what Johnson found objectionable about metaphysical conceits, Eliot suggested Donne was a truer poet than Browning or Tennyson. He also implied that the process of "forming new wholes" should be the principal activity of the modern poet in 1921 and implicitly indicted a view of poetry as the rendering of powerful emotion recollected in tranquility. Such reflection, he suggested, lacked the immediacy of Donne's dramatic intensity.

In a flurry of subsequent essays, reviews, and lectures,[19] Eliot thought through at least some of the ways he and his contemporaries could "draw instruction and encouragement" from the seventeenth-century poets.[20] At times, he comes across as a campaigner wholly committed to a cause. The most complete articulation of his ideas about the metaphysical poets emerged in the eight Clark Lectures he gave at Trinity College, Cambridge, in 1926 and the later Turnbull Lectures delivered at Johns Hopkins University in 1933.[21] Both sets of lectures captured the conclusions of a working poet "studying the work of dead artisans who have made better verses":

> The interest of the craftsman is centred in the present and the immediate future: he studies the literature of the past in order to learn how he should write in the present and the immediate future; and no matter how profound and disinterested his studies, they will always so to speak come out at the finger tips, and find their completion in the action of the chisel, the brush, or the typewriter.[22]

Eliot was impressed by the metaphysical poets' skillful fusion of sensation, thought, and feeling; their apt, eloquent phrasing; their knack for controlling even the most extravagant imagery so that it is "always deliberate" to "produce a deliberate pleasure"; and the exactitude with which "the object of feeling" in their poems "is always definite."[23] Most importantly for him, the manifestation of strong, even intense emotion within the process of thought distinguished Donne from most other authors as worthy of emulation. Heightened thought and feeling together informed Donne's judgments. Elsewhere, Eliot highlighted how the "profoundest thought and feeling" of the Elizabethans occurred in their dramatic blank verse, and how these qualities passed into the lyric poems of Donne and others.[24] Even in his prose, Eliot explained, Donne differs from Hooker and Bacon chiefly in the way he reasons "in emotion" while they reason "in tranquility."[25] What emerged in essay after essay was a consistent point of view that Eliot eventually planned to develop into a monograph on what he styled *The School of Donne*.

But such a book never came to be—at least, by Eliot. American scholar George Williamson, greatly inspired by Eliot's writings, published *The Donne Tradition: A Study in English Poetry from Donne to the Death of Cowley* in 1930 to wide acclaim.[26] In so doing, however, Ronald Schuchard, editor of Eliot's lectures, believes Williamson "stole some" of Eliot's "thunder."[27] The following year, when Theodore Spencer asked him to contribute to the tercentenary volume commemorating Donne's death in 1631, Eliot touted a few of the attributes that still fascinated him about Donne. For instance, he was still struck by how Donne "is interested in and amused by ideas in themselves, and interested in the way in which he *feels* an idea; almost as if it were something that he could touch and stroke."[28] But he also admitted that the subject of Donne and metaphysical poetry "has been so fully treated that there appears to me no possible justification of turning my lectures into a book."[29] He further expressed his belief that "Donne's poetry is a concern of the present and the recent past, rather than of the future."[30]

By the time Eliot's interest in Donne waned in the early 1930s, the metaphysical poets already had lodged in bedrock of Anglophone poetry. F. R. Leavis praised Eliot for returning "the seventeenth century to its proper place in the English tradition" and for showing modern poets how to learn from their seventeenth-century forbears: "what they will learn from him will be, as much as anything, how to learn from Donne."[31] Learn they did.

In seventeenth-century metaphysical poetry, poets and critics saw defined a style of writing worth modeling in whole or in part. They considered it advantageous for addressing the urgencies of their lives and times. As a result, by the end of the 1920s, critics believed a host of contemporary poets shared a kinship with the metaphysical poets. In *Poetry* magazine in 1929, Morton Dauwen Zabel mentioned the obvious "imprint" of these writers in the poetry of Alice Meynell, Allen Tate, Archibald MacLeish, Yvor Winters, Louise Bogan, Hart Crane, and Elinor Wylie.[32] Other critics added other names to the list of modern metaphysicals as the concentric circles of the metaphysical mode widened throughout Anglophone poetry: the later Yeats, C. Day Lewis, Wallace Stevens, Herbert Read, Stephen Spender, John Crowe Ransom, Robert Penn Warren, Anthony Hecht, Louis MacNiece, Edith Sitwell, William Empson, even the Dylan Thomas of "The Hand that Signed the Paper Felled a City," "And Death Shall Have No Dominion," and "The Force that Through the Green Fuse Drives the Flower."[33] Elizabeth Drew's still insightful handbook *Discovering Poetry* (1933) frequently cited Donne, Herbert, and others to illustrate various points about the skillful handling of forms and stanzas, the use of imagery, and the importance of verbal boldness.[34] Donne appeared regularly on the same level as other English exemplar poets: Chaucer, Milton, Dryden, Wordsworth, Keats, and Eliot. By the mid-1950s, the metaphysical influence was seen as the dominant one on Anglophone poets writing from the end of the World War I to the then present. "With the late nineteenth-century French Symbolists, the 'Metaphysicals' have had a more marked effect than any other of our ancestors on the work of the past four decades," Margaret Wiley declared in 1955.[35]

The present study enters this story at the far end of a curious development: beginning in the 1960s, the influence of the metaphysical poets on practicing poets appeared to have dissipated; but in fact, it had merely become more diffuse and more difficult to discern. In 1972, Denis Donoghue wrote that "it would be hard to name any substantial poet now flourishing to whom Donne's poems speak with unusual force."[36] A decade later, Roberts, in an assessment of modern criticism published in the inaugural volume of the *John Donne Journal: Studies in the Age of Donne*, agreed with Donoghue. He conceded that Eliot "was not entirely incorrect" in his tercentenary essay when he suggested the metaphysical poets would not be a "concern" of future poets.[37] "[W]ho among the poets of the 1970s and 1980s would one to choose to include" on the list of major poets who were "principal champions or even major adversaries" of Donne? Roberts asks.

> Therefore, although Donne continues to thrive and flourish in the halls of ivy and in library stacks from Texas to Tokyo and from Berkeley to Oxford, perhaps Eliot was not so terribly mistaken after all when he predicted nearly fifty years

ago that Donne's reputation in the years ahead would be something quite different from what it was in 1931.[38]

Subsequent scholars and poets, however, have demonstrated that while practicing poets from the 1960s to 2021 may not have talked as much about Donne and the other metaphysicals as they did in the 1920s, 1930s, and 1940s, many still read, admired, and learned from them. When she first encountered Donne as an undergraduate in the 1960s, Alicia Ostriker recalls, "I did not merely admire John Donne; I wanted to be him."[39] Poetic investment in the metaphysical poets had not ceased. Instead, due to the proliferation of practicing poets, the advent of creative writing programs at the undergraduate and graduate levels, and the blossoming of diverse literary communities that in effect created local and regional microclimates of reading and writing, these engagements had simply become harder to notice.

The same developments have made it difficult to label poets as members of various groups or movements. Gone are the days in which communities of poets can be easily classified as groups (e.g., the Imagists, the Fugitives, the Objectivists, the Black Mountain Poets, the Beats) widely known to the non-academic reading public. In the twenty-first century, one rarely sees the wholesale adoption of a "metaphysical" mode of writing. Instead, the turn to Donne or Herbert or Vaughan is more of a private affair than part of the dues one pays for group membership. Scholars have noticed such turns in the work of poets as diverse as Allen Ginsberg, Adrienne Rich, Paul Muldoon, Mark Jarman, Carl Phillips, Kate Bingham, and Brenda Hillman, none of whom seem to have much in common with each other at first glance.[40] The resulting interactions between the modern—or postmodern—and the metaphysical are as vibrant as they were decades ago, even if they are more localized. The unique 2017 collection *John Donne and Contemporary Poetry: Poems and Essays*, edited by Judith Scherer Herz, for example, features essays by poets about their own interactions with Donne, original poems in dialogue with or intertextually linked to Donne poems (with notes by the poets), and essays about other poets' similar forays.[41] Contributors include Heather Dubrow, Carl Phillips, Kimberly Johnson, Molly Peacock, Jonathan F. S. Post, Katie Ford, Alicia Ostriker, Rowan Ricardo Phillips, Stephen (Stephanie) Burt, Stephen Yenser, Mark Dow, Calvin Bedient, and Joseph Campana.

Given the diffuse nature of these more recent turns to the metaphysical poets and their personal character, this book is not meant to be an exhaustive or comprehensive account of every poet influenced by a seventeenth-century metaphysical poet from the 1920s to the present. The worlds of Anglophone poetry are too vast and the number of poets writing too many for any one person to notice, much less catalogue them all. But the ensuing pages illustrate a range of the forms of intertextuality resulting from these engagements. Along the way, this book also highlights a variety of delightfully unexpected and surprising twentieth- and twenty-first-century poems, worthy of notice in their own right. In accounting for how poets writing today make creative use of metaphysical poetry, often without any directives from the academy, this book additionally suggests how literary studies might better bridge reading poetry and making poetry in ways that can empower the next generation of poets more directly than the frequent siloing of creative writing typically allows.

Metaphysical Shadows is divided into two parts. Part I, "Varieties of Shadows," delves into four manifestations of poetic interactions, using different poets as the focal point for each. The chapters are arranged from the most to the least sharply defined metaphysical shadows. Chapter 1, "Echo and Allusion: 'The Extasie' Behind Seamus Heaney's 'Chanson d'Aventure,'" investigates Heaney's allusion to Donne's "The Extasie" in his poem about the ambulance ride to the hospital after his stroke in August 2006. For thirty-six hours, Heaney's left arm and leg were paralyzed before his ability to move gradually returned. During the ambulance ride, his physical closeness to his wife Marie, who held his seemingly lifeless hand, recalled the closeness of the lovers in Donne's poem. This chapter locates this instance of allusion within Heaney's habit of treating lines from poems as touchstone insights into the human condition that can be relied on during times of crisis. Echoes and allusions accomplish more than merely signal a poet's knowledge of prior poems; they enable the poet to communicate and build upon past insights in the present moment.

A second form of engagement—the poem as a direct response—also casts a fairly well-defined shadow. The response poem often presupposes a need to correct, add to, or alter the terms of a prior poem or poems. After surveying a few examples of response poems from *The Muse Strikes Back: A Poetic Response by Women to Men*,[42] chapter 2, "The Answer Poem: Anne Donne on the Isle of Wight," examines Maureen Boyle's "The Nunwell Letter," published in *Poetry Ireland Review* in 2019. The poem is a response to a famous episode that Donne's first biographer Izaak Walton connects to the composition of "A Valediction forbidding mourning." Donne wrote this poem, Walton speculates, before leaving on a trip to France with one of his patrons, Sir Robert Drury. Donne was reluctant to leave his then-pregnant wife Anne. But he had no choice. While he was away, Anne miscarried the baby but survived. Boyle's seven-part poem speaks from Anne's point of view as she recuperated from the miscarriage on the Isle of Wight. It is written as a letter to John in a mostly modern diction, and it complicates the presumption of critique within the genre of poetic response by assuming the veracity of Donne's poems of mutual love.

What happens when two poets from different time periods address the same subject, especially when the older poet's treatment is so famous it has become canonized? Chapter 3, "Shared Subjects: Andrew Marvell, Archibald MacLeish, and Brendan Kennelly," addresses this question by examining two instances in which twentieth-century poets ventured into territory Marvell previously explored. It begins with an analysis of MacLeish's "You, Andrew Marvell," most often seen as a poem in dialogue with Marvell's "To His Coy Mistress." But MacLeish's attention to the powers of the mind in contemplation suggests a dialogue with Marvell's "The Garden" as well. The chapter then compares Marvell's and Kennelly's very different poetic analyses of Oliver Cromwell in "An Horatian Ode upon Cromwell's Return from Ireland" and *Cromwell: A Poem*, respectively. Marvell's nuanced ode, with its lyrical treatment of the execution of Charles I—an oddly positive rendition for pro-Commonwealth Marvell—wrestles with Cromwell as an unstoppable force in the "arts of war." Meanwhile, Kennelly's *Cromwell: A Poem*, which many consider his masterpiece, is a book-length poem of many smaller poems that range freely in time from the seventeenth through the twentieth centuries. It draws upon a diverse range of genres (letter, newspaper article, history, legend, folktale, fantasy) to analyze the nature of human brutality. Marvell's poem is from an English perspective, Kennelly's, from an Irish perspective. Yet both complicate the story of Cromwell's time suppressing the Irish rebellion in the early 1650s in intriguing ways. Like painters who have propped their easels before the same scene but who nonetheless paint radically different paintings, both Marvell and Kennelly highlight recognizable features, despite their considerable differences in approach.

Chapter 4, "Modal Resemblances: 'Metaphysical,' 'Meditative,' and the Poetry of Donne, W. B. Yeats, and Ronald Johnson," the final chapter of part I, finds parallels between the meditative poems of Donne, the similarly meditative poems of Yeats, and the highly experimental work of American poet Ronald Johnson. Johnson's masterpiece *ARK*, which he began in 1970 and completed in 1990, has been described as a "metaphysical" poem. But while "metaphysical" captures some elements that Eliot valued in the seventeenth-century poets, this chapter posits that Martz's definition of the "meditative poem," also a descriptor of the work of Donne et al., more accurately captures the way in which individual beams, arches, and spires in Johnson's *ARK* unfold as poems within the larger whole. This modal resemblance—the shadow at noon—opens a space for discussing poets from different times and places who nonetheless share affinities in how they approach their art.

Part II of the book, "Late Twentieth- and Early Twenty-First-Century Shadows," explores the work of five Welsh, Irish, and American poets—Anne Cluysenaar, Heaney, Alfred Corn, Kimberly Johnson, and Jericho Brown—whose poetry exhibits the kinds of engagements elucidated in part I and enlarges our understanding of what we mean by "poetic influence" today. Chapter 5, "What Did Suffice: Scintillas of Vaughan in the Poetry of Anne

Cluysenaar," explains how the poetry of Henry Vaughan served as a practical source of inspiration for the Belgian-born, Irish-educated poet Cluysenaar, who spent the last decades of her life living in and writing about Wales. Her 1997 sequence "Vaughan Variations" is a set of twenty-three occasional poems that directly spark from Vaughan's poetry and prose. Vaughan's eloquence and wisdom aided Cluysenaar in working through a poetic impasse during a challenging time in her life. In Vaughan, she found an energizing presence. Cluysenaar's profound personal and imaginative connection to Vaughan through his poetry led her to collaborate with Peter Thomas and Angela Morton in the founding of both the Vaughan Association, which holds an annual Vaughan Colloquium each year, and the literary journal *Scintilla: A Journal of Literary Criticism, Prose and New Poetry in the Metaphysical Tradition*. This journal, which centers on the lives, works, and continuing influence of the seventeenth-century brothers Henry and Thomas Vaughan, juxtaposes scholarship on the Vaughans and on other Welsh writers with new poetry from a variety of poets, thereby promoting a sustained dialogue between past and present.

Chapter 6, "Donne, Heaney, and the Boldness of Love," traces parallels in the love poetry of the two poets. Apart from the "Glanmore Sonnets" and "Chanson d'Aventure," in which Heaney echoes or alludes to Donne's poems, Heaney does not answer, respond to, rewrite, or substantially appropriate Donne's poems. But in some of his love poems, the presence of Donne can be felt more palpably. One can detect a Donnean boldness in some Heaney's love poems as he uses three of the same techniques Donne does: beginning love poems in an abrupt, surprising fashion; constructing metaphysical conceits and striking, unforeseen comparisons; and rapidly shifting directions within a poem toward the conveyance of a precise, often unexpected insight about love. This chapter describes all three to explain why Heaney's love poems can seem like Donne's at times.

Chapter 7, "The Depth of Herbert's Voiceprint in the Poetry of Alfred Corn," invokes Herz's notion of the "voiceprint," the verbal residue of one poet within another poet's imagination, to describe the presence of Herbert in the poetry of Alfred Corn, the author of twelve well-received collections of verse and one of the strongest and most wide-ranging practitioners of formalist verse writing today. Corn's example is intriguing because one of his poems, "Resources," published in *Tables* (2013), offers an occasion for us to assess the distinction between the *conscious invocation* and the *unconscious intrusion* of a predecessor's work. During my correspondence with Corn in 2007–2008, it became apparent that while "Resources," then unpublished, contained intentional allusions to Herbert's "The Collar," the poem also contains *unintended* parallels with Herbert's "Love (III)" and with "The Thanksgiving." The unintended presence of these poems, products of Corn's "self-delighting inventiveness," results from the seepage of Herbert's language into Corn's in exactly the right place to reinforce the central gesture of the poem. A full treatment of Herbert's voiceprint in Corn's poetry must take into account both forms of intertextual entanglement.

Chapter 8, "Verbal Relish in the Poetry of Donne and Kimberly Johnson," describes a kinship in the stylistic richness of both poets. Johnson, a scholar of early modern literature as well as one of the most significant American poets writing today, openly dialogues with Donne's work in her three collections, *Leviathan with a Hook* (2002), *A Metaphorical God* (2008), and *Uncommon Prayer* (2014). The title of *A Metaphorical God* alludes to Donne's *Devotions upon Emergent Occasions*, and several of the poems therein anatomize Johnson's body like Donne anatomizes his body in *Devotions*. But in addition to these direct intertextual engagements, one can detect as well stylistic similarities, as both poets cram their lines with stressed syllables, vigorously specific nouns, and visually and sonically rich verbs. It is as if the example of Donne both inspires and gives Johnson permission to pull out all the stops of verbal relish within the slender confines of a lyric poem. One voice authorizes another that is nonetheless wholly distinctive.

The final chapter explores the influence of Donne on African American poet Jericho Brown, the author of three collections of poetry and the recipient of the American Book Award, the Anisfield-Wolf Book Award, the Thom Gunn Award, and the Pulitzer Prize for poetry. In an interview in 2016, Brown remarked, "I would not have been able to write my poems if Donne had not existed."[43] This chapter, "*The Tradition* and the Individual Talent: Jericho Brown and the Donnean Note," itself a play on Eliot's similarly titled classic essay, attempts to explain what Brown might have meant by exploring the parallels between his and Donne's approaches to poetry as prayer, and prayer as poetry. Both poets share a verbal boldness that Donne has in common with other poets considered in this book. But both also have a habit of interrogating received traditions in startling ways. The strong passions Donne dramatizes in his poems and religious prose often precipitate vehement, borderline blasphemous phrases and lines of thinking. In Brown's case, such interrogations of received traditions often defamiliarize episodes from the Bible that look very different when connected to the many forms of oppression experienced routinely by African Americans throughout the United States. While such a bold retellings can be shocking, they also allow for a necessary honesty about the truths of experiences some may not wish to hear.

The book concludes with a brief afterward, "Shadow Instruction," in which I highlight a few of the implications of the present line of inquiry in the teaching of metaphysical poetry today and make a case for the continued presence of the metaphysical poets in the twenty-first-century classroom, alongside the strong voices of other poets from other times and cultures.

At the end of "Lecture upon the Shadow," Donne looks ahead toward the westward declining movement of the sun and the lengthening of the lovers' shadows. He bemoans this progression because of what it portends metaphorically about love. "[O]h, loves day is short, if love decay," he says by way of conclusion. "Love is a growing, or full constant light; / And his first minute, after noone, is night" (ll. 24-26). From one perspective, the various crises in the humanities right now, including diminishing enrollments in English and literature departments across the world, the foreclosure of classics and related departments, and the drive toward professionalization and overspecialization at the expense of the liberal arts tradition, suggest that the heyday of the metaphysical poets has passed. But if the poets discussed in the second half of this book are any indication, this love affair is far from spent. We may have passed noon but we are still a long way from night.

My thinking about the poetry of Donne, Herbert, Vaughan, and Marvell, both by itself and in conjunction with the poems of others, developed over the course of many years. I have benefitted greatly from numerous conversations and exchanges with quite a few friends and colleagues, especially Gary A. Stringer, Judith H. Anderson, Joan Faust, Helen Wilcox, Anne Lake Prescott, Dayton Haskin, Dennis Flynn, R. V. Young, Ernest W. Sullivan II, George Klawitter, Nicholas von Maltzahn, Nigel Smith, Martin Dzelzainis, Steph Coster, Timothy Raylor, Sidney Gottlieb, Christopher Hodgkins, Angela Balla, Anne-Marie Miller-Blaise, Greg Miller, Michael C. Schoenfeldt, Graham Roebuck, Chanita Goodblatt, Jonathan Nauman, Joseph Sterrett, Tracy McLawhorn Hayes, Donald R. Dickson, Paul A. Parrish, Kate Narveson, Paul Dyck, Daniel Starza Smith, Tessie Prakas, Claire Falck, Arnaud Zimmern, Lara M. Crowley, Claude J. Summers, the late Ted-Larry Pebworth, and the late John R. Roberts. The fields of seventeenth-century English poetry are especially rich and abundant in no small measure because such wonderful, smart people work and tend them.

I owe another profound debt of thanks to those drawn, like me, to the task of describing the unmistakable presence of the metaphysical poets in modern poetry. Judith Scherer Herz, P. G. Stanwood, Heather Dubrow, Theresa M. DiPasquale, Raymond-Jean Frontain, and Jonathan F. S. Post all showed me much through their insights and their examples. Indeed, if it were not for their work and encouragement, I likely would not have undertaken this study. My conversations with them regularly reminded me why I became a scholar in the first place.

Much of this book assumes the poetry of Donne et al. continues to be relevant in the classroom in its own right and because of how it speaks to our historical moment. So I am grateful as well to my fellow teachers of early modern literature at Seattle University over the years—Bill Taylor, John C. Bean, Andrew Tadie, and Allison Machlis Meyer—for numerous chats and brainstorming sessions. Intrepid librarians Bryna Brown and Holly Sturgeon at the Lemieux Library managed to locate and bring forth quite a few hard-to-find books and articles—and during periods of lockdown as well. My thanks to them, too, for their diligence and their ingenuity.

I wrote most of this book during the COVID-19 pandemic of 2020 and 2021. While quite a few of us were painfully aware of Shakespeare's unbelievable writing productivity during the plague shutdowns of his time, the tremendous burdens of online teaching, the closure of libraries, the postponement of conferences, the cancellation of travel, and the pressures of weeks of working from home argued against imagining anything like the same. So I appreciate all the more the unstinting support of friends and compatriots who defied the conditions and through Zoom, email, and phone calls managed to bridge what might have seemed impossible distances to keep in close touch. Raymond again, Kirsten Stirling, Greg Kneidel, Jeanne Shami, Brent Nelson, Maria Salenius, Jeff Johnson, Kimberly Johnson, Dean Peterson, Jim Risser, Thorne Clayton-Falls, David Boness, Edwin Weihe, Sam Green, Tony Curtis, and Achsah Guibbory all kept the spirit of true community alive. Thanks, everyone, for the regular check-ins, encouragement, inspiration, and occasional laughter when all of us needed it. As Yeats says, "Think where man's glory most begins and ends / And say my glory was I had such friends."[44]

A huge thanks as well to Holly Buchanan, my editor at Lexington Books, for her keen eye, her sage advice, and her unshaking belief in the project from its early stages. And thanks also to Megan White, Vishnu Prasad R, Dominique McIndoe, and the other members of the copyediting and production teams for their close attention this book as an artifact. They all have been a pleasure to work with throughout this process. The anonymous readers for the press made a number of astute suggestions that strengthened greatly this final draft. I am grateful to them as well.

Finally, I owe my greatest debt of gratitude to my immediate family. My mother Virginia Lofendo continually renewed my faith in myself even during the most stressful times. Beth and Gib Rossing unfailingly offered encouragement throughout these many months. And my wife Andrea and our children Tessa, Kieran, and Jensen every day provided the love and support any author would be lucky to have as well as the 10,000 little things that made this book—and my life—possible. I dedicate this book to them.

NOTES

1. Qtd. in A. J. Smith, *John Donne: The Critical Heritage* (London and Boston, MA: Routledge and Kegan Paul, 1975), 218.

2. Grierson, *Metaphysical Poems & Lyrics of the Seventeenth Century: Donne to Butler* (Oxford: Clarendon Press, 1921). To mark the two quatercentenaries, the Vaughan Association held an online commemoration on April 25, 2021, that included the annual wreath laying ceremony on Vaughan's grave (www.vaughanassociation.org/22nd-annual-colloquium-programme/), and the Andrew Marvell Society held a conference on "Reimagining Andrew Marvell: The Poet at 400" from 6 to 8 May 2021 (marvell.wp.st-andrews.ac.uk/2021/03/04/reimagining-andrew-marvell-the-poet-at-400/).

3. *The Poems of John Donne*, 2 vols. (Oxford: Oxford University Press, 1912).

4. Haskin's magisterial study *John Donne in the Nineteenth Century* (Oxford: Oxford University Press, 2007) includes the most thorough treatment of the labors of the biographers and editors as well as the early educators at Harvard and Yale who assured Donne a place of prominence in the emerging discipline of English. Many of these efforts were published in the 1890s. Duncan remarks that despite common assumptions, "[i]n reality . . . Grierson's edition and the reviews that acclaimed it marked the end of the first stage of the metaphysical revival" ("The Revival of Metaphysical Poetry, 1872-1912," *PMLA* 68 [1953]: 658). This essay was reprinted in *The Revival of Metaphysical Poetry: The History of a Style, 1800 to the Present* (Minneapolis: University of Minnesota Press, 1959). See also Granqvist, *The Reputation of John Donne 1779-1873*, Studia Universitatis Upsaliensia, 24 (Stockholm: Almqvist and Wiksell, 1975) and "A 'Fashionable Poet' in New England in the 1890s: A Study of the Reception of John Donne," *John Donne Journal* 4 (1985): 337–349.

5. Haskin, *Donne in the Nineteenth Century*, 14.

6. Roberts, *John Donne an Annotated Bibliography of Modern Criticism 1912-1967*, 1.

7. R. F. Foster, *W. B. Yeats: A Life*, Vol. I: *The Apprentice Mage, 1865-1914* (Oxford: Oxford University Press, 1998), 360.

8. Yeats, *The Letters of W. B. Yeats*, ed. Allan Wade (New York: The Macmillan Company, 1955), 570.

9. Chapman, *Yeats and English Renaissance Literature* (London: Macmillan, 1991), 162. See also Duncan, *The Revival of Metaphysical Poetry*, 130–142.

10. Reflecting on the poets of his generation in *The Trembling of the Veil* (1922), Yeats envies what he perceives as the freedom of Donne's expression: "Donne could be as metaphysical as he pleased, and yet never seemed inhuman and hysterical as Shelley often does, because he could be as physical as he pleased." He also reflects on Donne in comparison with himself:

> I have felt in certain early works of my own which I have long abandoned, and here and there in the work of others of my generation, a slight, sentimental sensuality which is disagreeable, and does not exist in the work of Donne, let us say, because he, being permitted to say what he pleased, was never tempted to linger, or rather to pretend that we can linger, between spirit and sense. (*The Collected Works of W. B. Yeats, Vol. III: Autobiographies*, ed. William H. O'Donnell and Douglas N. Archibald [New York: Scriber, 1999], 251)

11. Yeats, *The Collected Works of W. B. Yeats*. Vol. I: *The Poems*. Ed. Richard J. Finneran, second ed. (New York: Scribner, 1997).

12. Chapman, *Yeats and English Renaissance Literature*, 161.

13. See Brooke, "John Donne," *Poetry and Drama* 1 (June 1913): 186; Walter de la Mare, "An Elizabethan Poet and Modern Poetry," *The Edinburgh Review* ccxvii (April 1913): 385; and Joseph Bristow, "Rupert Brooke's Poetic Deaths," *English Literary History* 81, no. 2 (Summer 2014): 663–692.

14. *Metaphysical Lyrics & Poems*, xxiii.

15. *Metaphysical Lyrics & Poems*, xv–xvi.

16. Ransom, "Eliot and the Metaphysicals," *Accent* 1 (1941): 148. The *TLS* review is where Eliot first posited his theory of the "dissociation of sensibility." He retreated from this theory fairly soon, but it continued to ripple through the scholarly discourse like a wave unspent for some time.

17. Eliot, "The Metaphysical Poets," *TLS* 20 Oct (1921): 669.

18. Yeats, *The Yeats Reader*, ed. Richard J. Finneran (New York: Scribner Poetry, 1997; rev. ed. 2002), 422.

19. Eliot, "Andrew Marvell," *Times Literary Supplement* (20 January 1921): 43; "The Metaphysical Poets," *Times Literary Supplement* (20 October 1921): 669–670; "The Metaphysical Poets," *Times Literary Supplement* (3 November 1921): 716; "The Prose of the Preacher: The Sermons of Donne," *The Listener* 2 (2 July 1929): 22–23; "Thinking in Verse: A Survey of Early Seventeenth-Century Poetry," *The Listener* 3 (12 March 1930): 441–443; "Rhyme and Reason: The Poetry of John Donne," *The Listener* 3 (19 March 1930): 502–503; and "The Devotional Poets of the Seventeenth Century: Donne, Herbert, Crashaw," *The Listener* 3 (26 March 1930): 552–553.

20. Eliot, "John Donne," *Nation and Athenaeum* 30 (9 June 1923): 332.

21. Both sets of lectures were published posthumously as *The Varieties of Metaphysical Poetry*, ed. Ronald Schuchard (New York: Harcourt Brace & Company, 1993).

22. Eliot, *Varieties of Metaphysical Poetry*, 44.

23. Eliot, *Varieties of Metaphysical Poetry*, 174, 202. He says of this last point about exactitude, "And this is perhaps one of the healthier reasons why their poetry is popular today; by a healthy reaction against vagueness."

24. Eliot, T. S. "Thinking in Verse: A Survey of Early Seventeenth-Century Poetry," *The Listener* 3 (1930): 441–443.

25. Eliot, T. S. "The Prose of the Preacher: The Sermons of Donne," *The Listener* 2 (2 July 1929): 22.

26. Williamson, *The Donne Tradition: A Study in English Poetry from Donne to the Death of Cowley* (New York: The Noonday Press, 1930). In his preface, Williamson notes that he "became absorbed in the Donne tradition through a contemporary poet": "But my debt to Mr. Eliot goes beyond enticement. His critical thinking on the 'metaphysical poets' has so influenced my own that I can only express my deep obligation to him, without trying to define its limits" (ix).

27. Eliot, *Varieties of Metaphysical Poetry*, 23.

28. Eliot, "Donne in Our Time," in *A Garland for John Donne 1631-1931*, ed. Theodore Spencer (Gloucester, MA: Peter Smith, 1931; repr. 1958), 12.
29. Eliot, "Donne in Our Time," 4.
30. Eliot, "Donne in Our Time," 5.
31. Leavis, F. R. "The Influence of Donne on Modern Poetry," *The Bookman* 79 (1931): 347.
32. *Poetry,* 34.3 (June 1929): 151–152. On MacLeish, Wylie, and Crane, see also Sona Raiziss, *The Metaphysical Passion: Seven Modern American Poets and the Seventeenth-Century Tradition* (Philadelphia: University of Pennsylvania Press, 1952), 212–241.
33. On Day Lewis, Spender, and Thomas, see Margaret Wiley, "The Poetry of Donne: Its Interest and Influence Today," *Essays and Studies* 7 (1955): 78–104. On Stevens, Read, Sitwell, and Empson, see Duncan, *The Revival of Metaphysical Poetry*, 182–202. On Hecht, see Jonathan F. S. Post, "Donne, Discontinuity, and the Proto-Post Modern: The Case of Anthony Hecht," *John Donne Journal* 26 (2007): 283–294. On the Fugitives (Tate, Ransom, and Warren), see P. G. Stanwood, *John Donne and the Line of Wit: From Metaphysical to Modern* (Vancouver, BC: Ronsdale Press, 2008) and Raiziss, *The Metaphysical Passion*, 184–211.
34. Drew, *Discovering Poetry* (New York: W. W. Norton & Company, 1933). See especially the chapters on "Form" (93–144), "Imagery" (145–161), "Words" (162–179), and "The Continuity of Poetry" (180–199).
35. "The Poetry of Donne: Its Interest and Influence Today," *Essays and Studies* 7 (1955): 79.
36. Donoghue, "Denis Donoghue Celebrates the Quatercentenary of John Donne," *Spectator* 229 (18 November 1972), 795.
37. Roberts, "John Donne's Poetry: An Assessment of Modern Criticism," *John Donne Journal* 1 (1982): 56.
38. Roberts, "John Donne's Poetry," 57.
39. Ostriker, "What's Done is Donne and How Can I Find God Now: Poems from *The Volcano Sequence*," in *John Donne and Contemporary Poetry*, edited by Judith Scherer Herz (London: Palgrave Macmillan, 2017), 85.
40. On Ginsberg, see Raymond-Jean Frontain, "Registering Donne's Voiceprint: Additional Reverberations," *John Donne Journal* 26 (2007): 295–312. On Adrienne Rich, see Helen B. Brooks, "A 'Re-Vision' of Donne: Adrienne Rich's 'A Valediction Forbidding Mourning,'" *John Donne Journal* 26 (2007): 333–362. On Muldoon, Jarman, Phillips, Bingham, and Hillman, see Judith Scherer Herz, "Tracking the Voiceprint of Donne," *John Donne Journal* 26 (2007): 269–282. All three of these essays appeared in the "More Signs of Donne" section the *John Donne Journal* publishes occasionally.
41. Herz, *Donne and Contemporary Poetry* (London: Palgrave Macmillan, 2017).
42. Ed. Katherine McAlpine and Gail White (Story Line Press, 1997).
43. http://lightboxpoetry.com/?p=516, accessed on 2 March 2020.
44. "The Municipal Gallery Re-visited," ll. 54–55.

Part I

VARIETIES OF SHADOWS

Chapter 1

Echo and Allusion

"The Extasie" Behind Seamus Heaney's "Chanson d'Aventure"

Recent studies of Donne's influence on modern poets, both those in the earlier twentieth century and those writing more recently, have developed the concept of the "voiceprint" as a way of "tracking" Donne's linguistic presence. Judith Scherer Herz defines this term as a profound immersion of one poet into the "psychology" and "linguistic system" of another.[1] The "later writer greets" Donne, she explains, "trying on his language and looking inside his imagination."[2] The ensuing "encounter" "happens less in the manner of a Bloomean agon or an overreaching than simply as a willingness to listen, to reimagine, to make over as one's own."[3] As Raymond-Jean Frontain notes, a "cultural tradition evolves—not through an anxiety of influence, as Harold Bloom would have it, strong poets competing to prove themselves against other strong poets—but through a sympathetic call and response, a system" of what Walter J. Ong calls "'reciprocating physical interiors,' one poetic voice reverberating in reply to a voice that sounded earlier, the nature of that response revealing something about the 'interior structure' of the instrument from which the new voice emerges."[4] When Donne's voiceprint appears in the work of subsequent writers, his language furnishes the imaginative spur, enabling the creation of new poems or at the very least "verbally color[ing]" them.[5] Readers may notice this form of Donne's afterlife most obviously through echo and allusion, those markers through which a poet establishes intertextual connections with the work of another. A remembered phrase or line might suddenly spring forth as part of a poet's meditation on a subject. But a voiceprint also registers through the incorporation of parallel logical or grammatical structures, reused stanza forms, or repeated words. It characterizes an intimate exchange between Donne and our contemporaries.

In the work of such diverse poets as John Crowe Ransom, Robert Penn Warren, Allen Tate, Anthony Hecht, Allen Ginsberg, Mark Jarman, Carl

Phillips, and Paul Muldoon,[6] Donne's presence becomes something to bounce off of as well as incorporate wholly or piecemeal. A poem from Seamus Heaney's last collection, *Human Chain* (2010),[7] showcases another way in which Donne's poems become useful for the modern poet: not just for their language or their approaches to subjects or even for the strong, engaging presence of Donne within them, but for the way they define specific experiences and for the truths they convey about them, truths the subsequent poet assumes as his or her own. Allusion in this sense does more than merely signal the alluding poet's knowledge of prior poems or cement an intertextual connection between present and past; it also enables the poet to communicate and rely upon a past insight into human life in the immediate moment. As a resource for defining experience, the prior poet—in this case, Donne—allows later poets to make their moments speak with greater force.

Unlike close friend Paul Muldoon, who in such poems as "Sillyhow Stride: *In Memory of Warren Zevon*" "swallow[s] Donne whole" to create a music heavily dependent on Donne's "beat,"[8] Heaney did not often engage Donne's verse as assiduously in the making of his own, though he wrote eloquently about the work of other seventeenth-century poets, most notably George Herbert.[9] Yet the few occasions when he does turn to Donne overtly in his poetry are revealing, especially in the poem "Chanson d'Aventure," composed to recall a day of personal crisis.

In August 2006, Heaney suffered a minor stroke. For thirty-six hours, it caused complete paralysis on his left side; he was unable to move his leg and arm. Gradually his mobility returned, though he spent five weeks in the stroke unit of the Royal Hospital in Dublin to undergo what he subsequently called a "rest cure."[10] He subsequently made a complete recovery. From his first collection, *Death of a Naturalist* (1966), onwards, Heaney gazed unflinchingly and yet unsentimentally at the major traumas of his life in a quest to come to terms with his experiences. His meditation on his stroke continued this work. In "Chanson d'Aventure," published in September 2010 in *Human Chain*, his twelfth collection, he recounts his ambulance trip to the hospital with Marie, his wife of then forty-one years. The poem consists of three parts, each of which explores the tenuousness of bodily presence in the face of physical paralysis. It begins with an epigram of two lines from the penultimate stanza of Donne's "The Extasie": "Loves mysteries in soules doe grow, / But yet the body is his booke" (71–72).[11] Rather than simply provide a jumping off point for the ensuing poem, however, these lines—and Donne's larger definition of a soulful love inclusive of the body—furnish Heaney with a means to speak powerfully of his relationship with his wife at a time when mortality threatened the dissolution of their connection and even his fundamental ability to feel his wife's presence:

I
Strapped on, wheeled out, forklifted, locked
In position for the drive,
Bone-shaken, bumped at speed,

The nurse a passenger in front, you ensconced
In her vacated corner seat, me flat on my back –
Our postures all the journey still the same,

Everything and nothing spoken,
Our eyebeams threaded laser-fast, no transport
Ever like it until then, in the sunlit cold

Of a Sunday morning ambulance
When we might, O my love, have quoted Donne
On love on hold, body and soul apart.

II
Apart: the very word is like a bell
That the sexton Malachy Boyle outrolled
In illo tempore in Bellaghy

Or the one I tolled in Derry in my turn
As college bellman, the haul of it there still
In the heel of my once capable

Warm hand, hand that I could not feel you lift
And lag in yours throughout that journey
When it lay flop-heavy as a bellpull

And we careered at speed through Dungloe,
Glendoan, our gaze ecstatic and bisected
By a hooked-up drip-feed to the cannula.

III
The charioteer at Delphi holds his own,
His six horses and chariot gone,
His left hand lopped

From a wrist protruding like an open spout,
Bronze reins astream in his right, his gaze ahead
Empty as the space where the team should be,

His eyes-front, straight-backed posture like my own
Doing physio in the corridor, holding up
As if once more I'd found myself in step

Between two shafts, another's hand on mine,
Each slither of the share, each stone it hit
Registered like a pulse in the timbered grips.[12]

This poem is the second in which Heaney calls to mind "The Extasie" in reference to his relationship with Marie. Twenty-nine years earlier, he alluded to it in the last of the "Glanmore Sonnets," written after the Heaneys moved out of Northern Ireland and settled into County Wicklow, where they lived from 1972 to 1975 in Glanmore Cottage, which they rented from J. M. Synge scholar Ann Saddlemyer. The early 1970s were a key period in Heaney's life. In 1972, the Bloody Sunday shootings occurred in Derry and the Bloody Friday bombings in Belfast. Many Northern Irish poets felt a keen pressure to respond to these terrible events and the sectarian violence that intensified in the aftermath. Heaney resigned his lectureship at Queen's University Belfast and started a new life as a full-time writer in the Irish Republic. In addition to the significance of physical relocation, the early years at Glanmore marked an artistic change. "Glanmore was the first place where my immediate experience got into my work," Heaney recalls. "Almost all the poems before that had arisen from memories of older haunts; but after a couple of years in the cottage, it changed from being just living quarters to a locus that was being written into poems."[13] He refers to Glanmore Cottage as a kind of "hedge row school" for learning a new way to make poetic use of his experiences. The "Glanmore Sonnets," dedicated to Saddlemyer, capture glimpses of that "immediate experience," and the last of these, number X, meditates on the nature of Heaney's union with his wife. It begins with the recollection of a dream that, as Donald W. Rude has noticed, recalls the initial set-up of Donne's poem[14]:

I dreamt we slept in a moss in Donegal
On turf banks under blankets, with our faces
Exposed all night in a wetting drizzle,
Pallid as the dripping sapling birches.
Lorenzo and Jessica in a cold climate.
Diarmuid and Grainne waiting to be found.
Darkly asperged and censed, we were laid out
Like breathing effigies on a raised ground. (ll. 1–8)[15]

Citing these lines, Helen Vendler views the allusions to famous literary lovers as evidence of Heaney's desire to "leave his level cottage ground" for more mythical territory: "The first, Shakespearean metaphor still lies within the positive dimension of pastoral, even if transmuted from the warmth of Venice to the chill of Wicklow; the second, Celtic one, however, comes within the aura of tragedy."[16] Yet a third literary couple reposes here, as these lines also quietly recall the lovers in Donne's "The Exstasie":

Where, like a pillow on a bed,
   A Pregnant banke swel'd up, to rest
The violets reclining head,
   Sat we two, one anothers best;

Our hands were firmely cimented
   With a fast balme, which thence did spring,
Our eye-beames twisted, and did thred
   Our eyes, upon one double string,

So to'entergraft our hands, as yet
   Was all the meanes to make us one,
And pictures in our eyes to get
   Was all our propagation. (ll. 1-12)

Donne's lovers lie like "sepulchrall statues" alongside a "Pregnant banke" (ll. 18, 1–4) in a manner similar to Heaney. Heaney and his wife are "Pallid," the color of "dripping sapling birches," which also is the color of sculpted marble, and they "were laid out / Like breathing effigies on a raised ground" (ll. 7–8). While the implied parallel may seem slight here, perhaps even coincidental, the resonance with Donne's poem builds as the dream of still, companionable lovers with drizzle-dampened faces leads to the memory of the Heaneys' wedding night:

And in that dream I dreamt—how like you this?—
Our first night years ago in that hotel
When you came with your deliberate kiss
To raise us towards the lovely and painful
Covenants of flesh; our separateness;
The respite in our dewy dreaming faces. (ll. 9–14)

"By inviting us to visualize the lovers similarly lying upon a bank," Rude explains, "Heaney may suggest that the pair had believed that the consummation which is recalled in the rest of the poem was based upon a comparable spiritual unity."[17] In the final lines of the poem, Heaney describes the physical, real-time aftermath of that wedding night encounter, the "first night" of their union as husband and wife. He attempts no larger metaphysical speculation the way Donne does. He does not speak of the "unperplex[ing]" character of spiritual (and/or sexual) ecstasy, the mysterious mixture of souls, or the way in which "soule into the soule may flow" ("The Extasie," ll. 29, 33–36, 59). Indeed, he does not have to: the echo of Donne's poem calls to mind the metaphysical unity Donne defined, and that recall creates an implicit suggestion for how to gloss the "Covenants" of flesh these lovers make to each other. After their elevation, their "separateness" merely marks the end of the lovemaking. The "respite in their dewy faces" suggests confidence and contentment, a result of their newfound understanding of their union, "[s]mall change" from the union that preceded it, now that they "are to bodies gone" ("The Extasie," l. 76).

As the preceding example suggests, Heaney implicitly sides with those scholarly readers of "The Extasie" who emphasize what they consider its consummate portrayal of what Achsah Guibbory calls its "celebration of the sacredness of sexual love," its treatment of loving as an experience of mutuality between lovers, made mysterious, even sacred, through the complex and indefinable relations between the body and, in Donne's terms, the soul.[18] Heaney thereby implicitly rejects other recent scholarly interpretations that resist the sense of mutuality, such as Sergei Lobanov-Rostovsky's, which views the image of the lovers' gaze as, finally, a reification of Donne's "masculine subject,"[19] as well as readings that treat Donne's definition of ecstatic love as merely rhetorical, a ploy for seduction.[20] This is for good reason: Heaney's purpose is not to rewrite or contradict or even answer Donne's poem in any way but to press it into service as he defines his own experiences of the dawning comprehension of union with his beloved wife (the tenth "Glanmore Sonnet") and of potentially losing that connection ("Chanson d'Aventure"). Although the seductive gesture of "The Extasie," however we construe it, has no place in the circumstances of either poem, Heaney can trust Donne's sturdy metaphysical description to carry great semantic weight.

In "Chanson d'Aventure," "The Extasie" once again offers Heaney supplemental meaning within the context of the otherwise uncertain ambulance ride. It also cements a connection with the earlier "Glanmore Sonnet." This time, Heaney depends on Donne's vision of soulful lovers on the verge of sexual consummation not simply to affirm the connection with his wife but to underscore the tenuousness of physical relationships, dependent as they are on the allowances of health and time. He explicitly invokes Donne here, both through the epigraph and direct allusion. Perfectly still, though not lying beside one another, and silent, their "eyebeams threaded laser-fast," Heaney and his wife had experienced "no transport / Ever like it until then" (ll. 8–9). Heaney's "eyebeams"—recalling Donne's lines, "Our eye-beames twisted, and did thred / Our eyes, upon one double string" ("The Extasie," ll. 7–8)—draw our attention to the particular way in which Heaney absorbs the work of other poets as encapsulations of experiential truths. Through the coinage of apt terms, phrases, and lines, poets add to the vernacular of human experience when they capture fine truths about experiences. In his interviews, essays, and poems, Heaney frequently introduced other poets' phrases when trying to describe, as accurately as he can, his meaning. He appeared to *think* intertextually. For example, when describing Ted Hughes in an interview with Dennis O'Driscoll, he again used a Donnean apt phrase, loaded with meaning:

> Ted was a chip off the Old English block, for sure, but in his own view of himself, he was a relict of Elmet, the old Romano-Celtic kingdom of the north-east; and he also had what John Donne called an hydroptical immoderate desire for learning.[21]

Likewise in "Chanson d'Aventure," the use of "eyebeams" also serves as shorthand, this time for the rapt, whole-person attentiveness of lovers transported. Meanwhile, the rest of Donne's "The Extasie" speaks to the poignancy of "love on hold, body and soul apart," in this case not from purposeful sexual restraint but because of a failure of the body.

Each section of "Chanson d'Aventure" draws upon a different work of art. As we have seen, the first borrows the definition of soulful connection from "The Extasie"; the second immediately conjures John Keats's "Ode to a Nightingale." Yet the ensuing dialogue with Keats does not replace Donne's definition, as if the poet has moved on to an acceptance of the melancholy plaguing the Romantic. Rather, part two counters the poetic logic of Keats in such a way as to preserve Donne's vision—again, within the context of Heaney's relationship with his wife. The lines of the first part move quickly, mimicking the rush of the ambulance. Where are they rushing to? Not just the hospital but also the possibility of permanent separation. It is here that Keats's "Ode" enters the poem, through allusion and grammatical parallel. Compare the opening lines of part two—

Apart: the very word is like a bell
That the sexton Malachy Boyle outrolled
In illo tempore in Bellaghy. (ll. 13–15)

—with the opening lines of the eighth stanza of "Ode to a Nightingale":

Forlorn! the very word is like a bell
  To toll me back from thee to my sole self!
Adieu! the fancy cannot cheat so well
  As she is fain'd to do, deceiving elf. (ll. 71–74)[22]

The notion that a single, two-syllable world can sound like a bell toll appears to signal a change in direction, as if thoughts of death threaten to overpower as they appear to do in Keats's poem (i.e., "Darkling, I listen; and, for many a time / I have been half in love with easeful Death, / Call'd him soft names in many a mused rhyme . . ." [ll. 51–53]). We might be tempted to say that the Donnean ecstasy born of the lovers' experience of connection has ceded to the lonesome "ecstasy" of the Nightingale, "pouring forth" its "soul abroad" near the close of midnight (ll. 56–58). Then, too, "Apart," the first word of the second section, emphasizes a key difference between the Heaneys and the lovers in Donne's poem. For Donne, the soulful mingling preludes a physical joining. For Heaney, "locked" in place, the future holds no such certain promise. "Apart," he writes, "the very word is like a bell." Like "Forlorn," which for Keats sounds a return to isolation, "Apart" sounds an almost funereal finality.

Yet we should resist these temptations, for, the focus of part two undermines a straightforward endorsement of Keatsian melancholy. In the "Ode," the Nightingale's song seduces the speaker partly because its beauty encourages forgetfulness of present pains. Keats even demands the bird flee from the sight of human suffering:

Fade far away, dissolve, and quite forget
   What thou among the leaves hast never known,
The weariness, the fever, and the fret
   Here, where men sit and hear each other groan;
Where palsy shakes a few, sad, last gray hairs,
   Where youth grows pale, and spectre-thin, and dies;
Where but to think is to be full of sorrow
   And leaden-eyed despairs,
Where Beauty cannot keep her lustrous eyes,
   Or new Love pine at them beyond to-morrow. (ll. 21–30)

By contrast, rather than seek escape from past and present, Heaney dives into memory to explain the resonance of the current moment. In this sense, the "bell" of "Apart" might remind us of another bell, which carried the invalid Donne of December 1623 into, not away from, an understanding of community (". . . who bends not his *eare* to any *bell*, which upon an occasion rings? but who can remove it from that *bell*, which is passing a *peece of himself* out of this *world*? No Man is an *Iland*, intire of it selfe; every man is a peece of the *Continent*, a part of the *maine* . . .").[23] Heaney remembers a sexton, Malanchy Boyle, ringing "*In illo tempore* in Bellaghy" and the heft of the college bell he once tolled "in Derry in [his] turn / As college bellman" (ll.

14–17), both memories of active participation within the life of a community. These memories contrast sharply with Keats's response and lend poignancy to Heaney's current crisis—his lack of feeling in his "once capable / Warm hand, hand that I could not feel you lift / And lag in yours throughout that journey / When it lay flop-heavy as a bellpull" (ll. 18–21). Heaney here conjures a different Keatsian moment through direct allusion to the fragment, "This living hand, now warm and capable," a poem in which Keats urges an unnamed addressee (possibly Fanny Brawne) to grasp his hand while it still lives.[24] Likewise, for Heaney, the struggle is not to escape, as in the Nightingale ode, but to remain rooted in the life he shares with his wife. Small wonder, then, that Heaney returns to the Donnean gaze in the following lines, this time to show, through the intrusion of medical equipment, how the stroke threatens the connection symbolized by their "threaded" "eyebeams": a "hooked-up drip-feed to the cannula" "bisect[s]" their gaze. The instrument blocks their uninterrupted view of each other. They career "at speed" toward the hospital and the uncertainty of their future together and how long that future might last.

As if the recourse to memory were not enough to keep at bay the Keatsian escape into solitude, Heaney's choice of art work in the third section—the *Charioteer of Delphi* (470 BCE), the ancient Greek bronze statue that is missing its left arm—presents another contrasting image of fortitude. Unlike Keats, who eschews the chariot of "Bacchus" (wine) in favor of another intoxicant, the "viewless wings of Poesy," as a means of coping with lingering illness (ll. 32–33), Heaney, like the ancient charioteer, stands fast, even after his chariot and horses have crumbled away:

The charioteer at Delphi holds his own,
His six horses and chariot gone,
His left hand lopped

From a wrist protruding like an open spout,
Bronze reins astream in his right, his gaze ahead
Empty as the space where the team should be,

His eyes-front, straight-backed posture like my own
Doing physio in the corridor, holding up
As if once more I'd found myself in step

Between two shafts, another's hand on mine,
Each slither of the share, each stone it hit
Registered like a pulse in timbered grips. (ll. 25–36)

Just as the idea of ecstasy provides the associationistic link between "The Extasie" and "Ode to a Nightingale" in the first and second parts, the paralyzed left hand, "flop-heavy as a bellpull," in part two leads naturally to the missing left hand of the charioteer in part three. Heaney seems to marvel at what seems the charioteer's resilience, made all the more suggestive by the subtractions of time and the oxidation and rubble that have claimed the horses, chariot, and hand. In spite of a "wrist protruding like an open spout," the charioteer holds onto the "[b]ronze reins astream in his right" hand. Heaney sketches a parallel between the charioteer's "eyes-front, straight-backed posture" and his own during recovery, "[d]oing physio in the corridor" as he reclaims his mobility. He, too, will persist in spite of all. By ending the poem with the solidity of the gaze and of handholding ("another's hand on mine"), Heaney leaves open the possibility of future contact and eyebeam threading with his wife, thereby returning to Donne's definition of true lovers' union.

Heaney's use of Donne in "Chanson d'Aventure" is distinctive from that of other contemporary poets. One cannot call Heaney's poem a rewriting or refashioning or corrective of Donne's poem because Heaney's purpose is not to address Donne in the slightest; rather, Donne's poem becomes instrumental in helping Heaney define the poignancy of the ambulance trip, how and why there had been "no transport / Ever like it until then" (ll. 8–9). He relies on Donne's poem to carry the weight of defining the "transport" of the moment, the depth of the love he feels toward Marie; yet the full cognizance of this reliance belongs only to those who know "The Extasie" as a poem defining an experience. Curiously, by assuming Donne's definition and by not positing his own, Heaney manages to introduce a sense of privacy in what is otherwise a public poem because of Heaney's popularity.

The distinction I am drawing involves the poet's motivation. Is the inclusion of Donne the result of a desire to engage Donne's language, Donne's wit, Donne's personality, or all of these as a means to measure one's poetic abilities or contribute to centuries-old poetic conversations or merely have a little fun? Or does the poet turn to a Donne poem out of an emotional urgency, emergency, or even crisis? Does the poem become a need because of what it accomplishes within the poet? In other words, is the poet's desire related to the same impulse that causes "The Good-Morrow" to be read at weddings and "Death be not proud" at funerals? These are not simple questions. They have stakes. They force us to remember the noncreative justification for reading poetry in the first place: for its capacity to function as, in Ezra Pound's words, the "news that stays news,"[25] the message that is always relevant, regardless of time. Heaney's engagements with Donne's "The Extasie" prove the verity of Pound's description within the ongoing story of Donne's poetic afterlife. They also show there is more to echo and allusion than a simple display of erudition.

NOTES

1. Herz, "Under the Sign of Donne," *Criticism* 43, no. 1 (2001): 31. This essay is the first stage of Herz's "tracking of Donne's voiceprint." Stage two was published later as "Tracking the Voiceprint of Donne," *John Donne Journal* 26 (2007): 269–282. The later installment appeared in a cluster of essays in *John Donne Journal* on Donne's influence, along with contributions by Jonathan F. S. Post ("Donne, Discontinuity, and the Proto-Post Modern: The Case of Anthony Hecht," 283–294) and Raymond-Jean Frontain ("Registering Donne's Voiceprint: Additional Reverberations," 295–312).
2. Herz, "Under the Sign of Donne," 31.
3. Herz, "Under the Sign of Donne," 31.
4. Frontain, "Registering Donne's Voiceprint," 295–296. The relevant passage about "interior structures" comes from Ong, *The Presence of the Word: Some Prolegomena for Cultural and Religious History* (Minneapolis: University of Minnesota Press, 1981), 125.
5. Frontain, "Registering Donne's Voiceprint," 297.
6. On Hecht, see Post; on Ginsberg, see Frontain; on Jarman, Phillips, and Muldoon, see Herz, "Tracking the Voiceprint of Donne"; and on Ransom, Warren, and Tate, see P. G. Stanwood, *John Donne and the Line of Wit: From Metaphysical to Modernist*, the 2008 Garnett Sedgewick Memorial Lecture (Vancouver, BC: Ronsdale Press, 2008).
7. Heaney, *Human Chain* (New York: Farrar, Straus and Giroux; London: Faber and Faber, 2010).
8. Herz, "Tracking the Voiceprint of Donne," 270–271. "Sillyhow Stride: *In Memory of Warren Zevon*" is the last poem in *Horse Latitudes* (London: Faber and Faber, 2006). Within Herz's musical analogy, apropos for the musically attuned Muldoon, Donne is the "left hand of the stride piano, his words set the rhythm, they offer a deep structure, while Muldoon with the right hand makes melodic improvisations against those Donne chords." Muldoon establishes this "beat" through the inclusion of Donne's words, "half lines," and "whole lines." According to Herz, the words remain Donne's rather than become subsumed: Even as they "move through this new medium, they unspool old meanings and new, but also remain intact as a challenge to the pityings and self pityings which they evoke, ironize, and comment on and this is largely because, sorrows aside, Donne's words handle so well" (272).
9. For Heaney's comments on Herbert, see the eponymous essay in *The Redress of Poetry* (New York: Farrar, Straus and Giroux, 1995), where he sees Herbert as an important example of a poet who treats "poetry *as* poetry" and who therefore "redresses" poetry from the anti-aesthetic charge that poetry lacks value if it is not directly engaged in political action (1–16). In Chapter 6, I explore how Heaney's description of Herbert's verbal inventiveness offers an insight into the nature of how Herbert's voiceprint operates in the work of American poet Alfred Corn.
10. Dennis O'Driscoll, *Stepping Stones: Interviews with Seamus Heaney* (London: Faber and Faber, 2008), 461–462. During his stay Heaney received a surprise visit from former president Bill Clinton.

11. Heaney modernizes the spelling of the two lines of Donne's poem in his epigraph.
12. Heaney, "Chanson d'Aventure," in *Human Chain: Poems* (New York: Farrar, Straus and Giroux; London: Faber and Faber, 2010), 14–16.
13. O'Driscoll, *Stepping Stones*, 198.
14. Rude, "Seamus Heaney and John Donne: An Echo of 'The Ecstasy,'" *John Donne Journal* 22 (2003): 255–257.
15. Heaney, "Glanmore Sonnet X," in *Field Work* (London: Faber and Faber, 1979), 42.
16. Vendler, *Seamus Heaney* (Cambridge: Harvard University Press, 1998), 68–69.
17. Rude, "Seamus Heaney and John Donne," 256.
18. See Guibbory, "Donne, Milton, and Holy Sex," *Milton Studies* 32 (1996): 3. Like Guibbory, other recent interpreters think nothing of speaking of the poem in religious terms. For Eleanor J. McNees, "The Extasie" proceeds like a eucharistic ceremony by shifting from an "emphasis on the physical presence of the elements—the two bodies—to the spiritual union of souls" (*Eucharistic Poetry: The Search for Presence in the Writings of John Donne, Gerard Manley Hopkins, Dylan Thomas, and Geoffrey Hill* [Lewisburg, PA: Bucknell University Press, 1992], 40). See also Harold Bloom, who remarks that the "sophistication" of Donne's "erotic meditation" "touches upon sanctification" (*Genius: A Mosaic of One Hundred Exemplary Creative Minds* [New York: Warner Books, 2002], 264). "For Donne," according to Catherine Gimelli Martin, the "simultaneously physical and mental 'testing' of the lovers' purity," in addition to being deeply learned in Renaissance Neoplatonic discourse, "meant looking through the grossly physical bodies of mortal humans to see the blinding miracle of the incarnation and resurrection experienced here below in the anticipatory ecstasy of fully requited love" ("The Erotology of Donne's 'Extasie' and the Secret History of Voluptuous Rationalism," *SEL* 44, no. 1 [2004]: 141).
19. Lobanov-Rostovsky, "Taming the Basilisk," in *The Body in Parts: Fantasies of Corporeality in Early Modern Europe*, ed. David Hillman and Carla Mazzio (New York and London: Routledge, 1997), 208–209.
20. Eugene R. Cunnar, for example, says that the "speaker's argument ultimately turns on the control and fulfillment of his desire, which, in turn, marginalizes the woman" ("Fantasizing a Sexual Golden Age in Seventeenth-Century Poetry," in *Renaissance Discourses of Desire*, ed. Claude J. Summers and Ted-Larry Pebworth [Columbia: University of Missouri Press, 1993], 198). Similarly, Don Beecher, in "Eye-Beams, Raptures, and Androgynes: Inverted Neoplatonism in Poems by Donne, Herbert of Cherbury, Overbury, and Carew," claims that Neoplatonic love in the poem is simply an "outlandish" conceit added to the "libertine invitation to sex" (*Cahiers Elisabéthains: Late Medieval and Renaissance Studies* 65 [2004]: 5–7). David W. Shaw, meanwhile, considers Donne's speaker's metaphysical argument as casuistical, in that it is "carefully rehearsed, and proceeds logically to its foregone conclusion," the need for the lovers to have sex ("Masks of the Unconscious: Bad Faith and Casuistry in the Dramatic Monologue," *ELH* 66 [1999]: 442).
21. O'Driscoll, *Stepping Stones*, 298.

22. All quotations from Keats's "Ode to a Nightingale" are from the poem as it appears in *The Poetical Works of John Keats*, ed. H. W. Garrod, 2nd ed. (Oxford: Clarendon Press, 1958), 257–260.

23. Donne, *Devotions upon Emergent Occasions*, ed. Anthony Raspa (Oxford and New York: Oxford University Press, 1987), 87.

24. I am grateful to Seamus Heaney for noting this allusion in a private note. "This living hand" appears on p. 553 of the Garrod edition of Keats's poetry.

25. Ezra Pound, *ABC of Reading* (New Haven, CT: Yale University Press, 1934), ch. 8.

Chapter 2

The Answer Poem
Anne Donne on the Isle of Wight

Echoes and allusions enrich and enlarge a new poem by tapping into the charge of literary predecessors. We have seen how referring to Donne's "The Extasie" allows Seamus Heaney in a compressed space to call forth a powerful set of associations that resonate strongly during and after the ambulance ride to the hospital. They energize the experience and render it more comprehensible. In this way, echoes and allusions attest to, depend on, and translate the ongoing energy of prior lines, phrases, or bright particulars into a new context. Additionally they cement the new poem to established poetic traditions and ground the poet's imagination in the lives and artistry of those who came before. An enlargement occurs in two directions simultaneously: in the expansion of the present in light of the past and of the past in light of the present. In this fashion, allusion and echo demonstrate the continuity of human existence for as long as cultural memory persists.

By contrast, the answer poem often presupposes a need to critique, correct, add to, or alter the terms of a prior poem or poems. Rather than treat a lyric poem as a one-off, one person's cry against the dark, a discrete artifact removed from time and circumstance, the answer poem often issues from a poet's desire to have a last word. It assumes the lyric is occasional, inviting exchange, and that the act of writing is conversation and in some contexts—that of coterie verse, for example—competition.[1] It draws its energy, its inspiration, its subject matter, and often its form from an identifiable precursor its author presumes requires response. Without this precursor, it cannot exist.

We may never know fully how many of Donne's mostly occasional poems answer directly or obliquely those of his contemporaries. But his most obvious answer poem, "The Baite"—and the exchange to which it responded—offers insights into the range of possibilities modern poets so far have explored in answering Donne, from feminist critiques of individual lyrics (poems by Mary Holtby and Karen Donnelly, for example) to one of the most intriguing responses in recent years, Maureen Boyle's "The Nunwell Letter," an oblique sequel, of sorts, to Donne's "A Valediction forbidding Mourning." First published in *Poetry Ireland Review* in 2019, Boyle's poem is a seven-part, 153-line letter to Donne from his wife Anne, purportedly written on April 12, 1612, to break the news of her miscarriage the previous January.[2] It is a remarkable poem that creates, in a mostly modern idiom, a three-dimensional Anne in terms consistent with what we can deduce about the exceptionally close bond she shared with her husband. It also follows Donne in its approach to poetic answering.

"The Baite," as readers of Donne know well, is one of many poems that followed what may be the most famous poem-and-answer exchange in Elizabethan literature: Christopher Marlowe's "The passionate Sheepheard to his love" and Walter Ralegh's response "The Nymph's reply to the Sheepheard." Marlowe's poem probably was composed in 1588; Ralegh's, likely sometime in the early 1590s.[3] Both poems circulated in manuscript at the height of the courtier pastoral craze in the 1590s before being published together as companion pieces in the miscellany anthology *Englands Helicon* in 1600. So successful is Ralegh's rebuff of the argument of Marlowe's poem that modern readers who know no better risk thinking of the bad boy, boundary pusher Marlowe as hopelessly naïve. Yet such a judgment mistakes what seems Marlowe's intention. Marlowe based his poem on Theocritus's eleventh idyll, either directly from the Greek or from a prior English translation in *Six Idillia* (Oxford, 1588) or via Book 13 of Ovid's *Metamorphoses*.[4] Following this classical lead, he attempts to corner the market, so to speak, on the pastoral seduction poem—to craft the quintessential poem of this kind for his place and time in much the same way that Horace's Ode iii.30 ("Exegi monumentum aere perennius") was the quintessential encomium of poetry's immortalizing power for Augustan Rome, or Tu Fu's "Chūn Wàng" ("Spring Scene") was the quintessential *lü-shih* meditation on the state for Tang Dynasty China, or Herrick's "To the Virgins, to Make Much of Time" and Marvell's "To His Coy Mistress" were the quintessential *carpe diem* poems for seventeenth-century England. Marlowe dials back his mighty line, which helped power the unstoppable Tamburlaine onstage, to create a lovely euphonious tone that serves as part of the poem's argument:

Come liue with mee, and be my loue,
And we will all the pleasures proue,
That Vallies, groues, hills and fieldes,
Woods, or steepie mountaine yeeldes.

And wee will sit vpon the Rocks,
Seeing the Sheepheards feede theyr flocks,
By shallow Riuers, to whose falls,
Melodious byrds sing Madrigalls. (ll. 1-8)[5]

These opening lines, along with the remaining four stanzas, flow as evenly as a burbling stream. Marlowe's shepherd sweet-talks his would-be mistress with pleasing words and a sensual rhythm intended to influence her soul in his favor. He offers her an idealized life of timelessness; naturally rich attire (i.e., "cap of flowers," embroidered "kirtle," fine woolen gown, and a belt of straw and ivy with "Corall clasps and Amber studs," ll. 11-18); an endless series of days brimming with poetry, singing, and dancing; and the presumed banishment of earthly work and suffering.

In the close match of style, content, and memorable phrasing, Marlowe's poem is a tour de force—but only if one accepts its pastoral premises. Quite a few Elizabethan imitators did, but not Ralegh. To check the university wit with a courtier's prerogative, Ralegh's "The Nymph's reply" rejects Marlowe's idealizations while still retaining the fiction of pastoralism. It is the classic answer-poem-as-corrective. Its form signals its status as a direct response: the same iambic tetrameter line and the same six-quatrain length as the version of Marlowe's poem published in *Englands Helicon*. Ralegh seizes on Marlowe's poetic occasion by positing his poem as the nymph's immediate point-by-point refutation of the shepherd's suit, delivered as if the shepherd had just finished speaking. Even Marlowe's euphony receives correction. After mimicking (mocking?) her suitor's tone in the first stanza, the nymph counters with her own more emphatic phrasing in the second. Note the stylistic contrast between the first two stanzas:

If all the world and loue were young,
And truth in every Sheepheards tongue,
These pretty pleasures might me moue,
To liue with thee, and by thy loue.

Time driues the flocks from field to fold,
When Riuers rage, and Rocks grow cold,
And *Philomell* becommeth dombe,
The rest complaines of cares to come. (ll. 1-8)

The nymph starts by aping her suitor's smooth speech even as she dismisses his offered pleasures as "pretty." Then she strikes out more forcibly on her own. The spondaic "Time driues" beginning to line five and the heavier reliance on stressed alliterated syllables in lines six and eight ("Riuers rage, and Rocks grow cold" and "The rest complaines of cares to come") emphasize the strength of temporal change and intemperate forces that no amount of wishing can prevent. The nymph speaks with the sassy authority of experience.

The opening lines also convey the vehemence of what will be the nymph's nearly categorical rejection of the shepherd's suit. The rest of Ralegh's poem corrects the shepherd's offer point-by-point, starting with the supposed timelessness of floral beauty:

The flowers doe fade, & wanton fieldes,
To wayward winter reckoning yeeldes,
A honny tongue, a hart of gall,
Is fancies spring, but sorrowes fall. (ll. 9-12)

Stanza by stanza, the nymph then devalues each of the shepherd's promised goods as prone to either break or decay. They are incapable of causing her to love him. Through her words, she comes across as adult and worldly wise, and the shepherd, young and silly. She would have nothing to say aside from a straightforward "no," however, if she lacked the shepherd's lines to draw upon. Ralegh's invention hinges on Marlowe's, alters prior assumptions and terms of engagement, and provides a thorough corrective. By the end, the nymph—and Ralegh—claim the last word. Within the fiction of this exchange, it is hard to imagine how the poor, rejected passionate shepherd could respond.

So definitive is Ralegh's answer poem that it leaves little room for others to answer Marlowe by way of correction. Ralegh has cornered *this* market. Indeed, the poem immediately following the Marlowe-Ralegh pair in *Englands Helicon*, "Another of the same nature, made since," is not an answer to Ralegh but an eleven-stanza imitation of Marlowe that echoes the first line ("Come liue with mee, and be my deere"), adopts the same meter and stanza form, and offers a catalogue of rustic pleasures with special emphasis on lying in the shepherd's embrace in some undisclosed bower.[6] After Ralegh, what can a poet do but offer "[a]nother of the same"?

Yet Donne advanced his own response poem, one that is *not* "[a]nother of the same." Eugene Cunnar considers "The Baite" a "witty and ironic attack on the pastoralism and Petrarchism so prominent in Renaissance courtly lyrics and their wider social contexts."[7] In his characteristic way, Donne surpassed the Ralegh creative impasse undaunted. The path he chose was to make the rustic seduction poem entirely new, neither corrective of predecessors nor too heavily dependent on them. His habit of responding to poetic occasions with originality grounded in tradition endeared him to the modern metaphysicals,

T. S. Eliot especially. Yet in this case, his response poem, "The Baite," was so memorable that it joined Marlowe's and Ralegh's as a frequent manuscript flyer, making the rounds in various miscellanies.[8] Indeed, one scribe, Edward Brookes, copied into his commonplace book the three poems together as a set.[9] Strangely, he titled Marlowe's poem "The Milke Maids Song" and Ralegh's response "The Milk Maids Mothers Answers." Donne's poem, however, he left untitled and alone, as if to suggest Donne had said the last word in this pastoral interlude.

One can readily see why the "The Baite" stands out. Donne creates a different possibility for the answer poem: the poem that answers by waving good-bye to its predecessor and by traveling into the poet's own field of play, there to render experience in the poet's own unmistakable idiom. "By changing the trope of the piscatorial as well as that of 'The Passionate Shepheard,'" M. Thomas Hester explains, "Donne rejects the benign—and fictional—relationship of protecting shepherd and protected sheep to that of *deceptive* fisherman and *betrayed* fish."[10] "The Baite" outdoes its predecessors through its striking originality. It is a making new, in a Poundian sense, through a making of one's own. In defining this form of response, I am reminded of Heaney's definition of "technique" as opposed to "craft" in his essay "Feeling into Words":

> Technique, as I would define it, involves not only a poet's way with words, his management of metre, rhythm, and verbal texture; it involves also a definition of his stance towards life, a definition of his own reality. It involves the discovery of ways to go out of his normal cognitive bounds and raid the inarticulate: a dynamic alertness that mediates between the origins of feeling in memory and experience and the formal ploys that express these in a work of art. Technique entails the watermarking of your essential patterns of perception, voice and thought into the touch and texture of your lines; it is that whole creative effort of the mind's and body's resources to bring the meaning of experience within the jurisdiction of form. Technique is what turns, in Yeats's phrase, "the bundle of accident and incoherence that sits down to breakfast" into "an idea, something intended, complete."[11]

Donne escapes the impasse of the Marlowe-Ralegh exchange by "watermarking" his "essential patterns of perception, voice and thought into the touch and texture" of the pastoral seduction poem. His "whole creative effort" entails bringing his characteristic modes of argument and metaphorical reasoning to bear on an implicit appeal to the intelligence of his would-be mistress. "The Baite" is still an answer poem in dialogue with Marlowe's, yet it is just as much Donne's own poem as "The good-morrow," "The Sunne Rising," "The Extasie," and "The Canonization." It illustrates Donne's characteristic technique, its Donnean watermark clear for all to see.

Like Ralegh and the Marlowe imitators, Donne connects his poem to Marlowe's by adopting the same rhyming couplet quatrains and by echoing Marlowe's first line:

Come live with mee, and bee my love,
And wee will some new pleasures prove
Of golden sands, and christall brookes:
With silken lines, and silver hookes. (ll. 1-4)

This first line marks the poem unmistakably as an answer. It says, come see how *I* approach the pastoral seduction poem. Donne begins his watermarking as early as line two, when he embarks on his own direction: on offer is not the entire pastoral world but "*some* pleasures" (my emphasis), those enjoyed beside a riverbank. It is as if we have been transported to the setting of "The Extasie," yet in the company of those who have not yet become lovers:

There will the river whispering runne
Warm'd by thy eyes, more then the Sunne.
And there the'inamor'd fish will stay,
Begging themselves they may betray.

When thou wilt swimme in that live bath,
Each fish, which every channel hath,
Will amorously to thee swimme,
Gladder to catch thee, then thou him.

If thou, to be so seene, beest loath,
By Sunne, or Moone, thou darknest both,
And if my selfe have leave to see,
I need not their light, having thee. (ll. 5-16)

Much here is typically Donne. In line six, for example, Donne insinuates praise of his mistress's beauty within his energetic description of the riverbank scene, a sudden flattering glance sideways to note the source of his attraction: the riverbank is "Warm'd by thy eyes, more then the Sunne." He makes the same flattering move when dissing the sun in "The Sunne Rising":

> Thy beames, so reverend, and strong
> Why shouldst thou thinke?
> I could eclipse and cloud them with a winke,
> But that I would not lose her sight so long: (ll. 11-14)

A direct, albeit playful, address to the sun shifts unexpectedly to praise of the mistress. Similar instances of collateral flattery occur at the end of the first stanza of "The good-morrow": "If ever any beauty I did see, / Which I desir'd, and got, t'was but a dreame of thee" (ll. 6-7). And again at the end of "The Relique": "These miracles wee did; but now alas, / All measure, and all language, I should passe, / Should I tell what a miracle shee was" (ll. 31-33). With a single line, "The Baite" connects with other *Songs and Sonets* epideictically and imagistically.

Meanwhile, the "inamor'd fish" are certainly hyperbolic in their begging to be caught. But gone are the trappings of shepherds and nymphs. One imagines the speaker of this poem attired like a courtier, floating praise with a courtier's eye. The way the fish quickly become metaphors for suitors also accords with a courtly aesthetic, as does the danger implied in the metaphor (being caught is usually fatal for a fish). Also typically Donne is the distinctive way he foregrounds his mistress's luminosity as a central power of attraction. He figures the radiance of beauty in cosmological terms, even referencing the debate about whether the heavenly bodies, aside from the sun, shine by their own or by borrowed light.

The last movement of "The Baite" (stanzas five through seven) creates a new non-pastoral catalogue of kinds of fisherfolk as hapless lovers:

Let others freeze with angling reeds,
And cut their legges, with shells and weeds,
Or treacherously poore fish beset,
With strangling snare, or windowie net:

Let coarse bold hands, from slimy nest
The bedded fish in banks out-wrest,
Or curious traitors, sleavesilke flies
Bewitch poore fishes wandring eyes.

For thee, thou needst no such deceit,
For thou thy selfe art thine owne bait;
That fish, that is not catch'd thereby,
Alas, is wiser farre then I. (ll. 17-28)

Donne's courtier does not say which of these fishermen he considers himself to be. Clearly Marlowe's shepherd, at least when juxtaposed with Ralegh's nymph, is one of those freezing with his angling reed. Presumably Donne's courtier intends to share with his mistress the joke of making fun of recognizable stereotypes of male suitors, like people watchers somehow distanced from the social tragicomedy of love. The remaining three of these four stereotypes—the fisherman/suitor who strangles fish with "snare, or windowie net," the one who snatches unsuspecting fish with "coarse bold hands," and the one who bewitches "poore fishes wandring eyes" with deceptive "sleevesilk flies"—are dangerous to any attractive lady. They suggest a dark undercurrent of rape culture within the court. Eva Feder Kittay finds implicit in Donne's bait metaphor a suggestion that

> in courtship too we move from the pleasant activity of flirtation through the struggle of real sexual encounters and conflicts and sometimes to the extremes of brute force, rape, and the more subtle violence, the cunning and villainy of seduction.[12]

Donne's courtier distinguishes himself from courtly types by attributing the most effective power of fishing only to his mistress—"For thee, thou needst no such deceit, / For thou thy selfe art thine owne bait"—and then by figuring himself, as humbly as he can, as a fish she has already caught. Anthony Low considers this last stanza a "mock retraction" that "does not exonerate the mistress from treachery, violence, or intimidating sexuality, but simply relieves her from having to destroy her victims covertly": her "sexuality is so powerful that she need neither conceal nor idealize it."[13] But it is also true that the concluding gesture of the poem, like many of Donne's, is a sophisticated rhetorical appeal. He communicates his love without naming it and asks without asking for his mistress's attention. His implicit acknowledgment of her intelligence is an appeal all by itself. In sum, "The Baite" finds its way out of the impasse of Ralegh's last word by forgoing the answer poem-as-corrective in favor of the answer poem-made-new, the poem that creates its own new field of play by responding not to the text of an original per se but to its occasion or circumstances in an effort to make a better poem.

The Marlowe-Ralegh-Donne exchange, well-known within the coterie of early seventeenth-century manuscript scribes and their readers, offers a useful distinction for making sense of twentieth- and twenty-first-century poets answering seventeenth-century metaphysical poets. In this scenario, poems by Donne, Herbert, Marvell, and Vaughan occupy the Marlovian position. Themselves inspired by and intertextually connected to notable predecessors, they survived a waning readership in the mid-to-late eighteenth century. Now, enshrined in the canon thanks to the editions and anthologies of Grierson and many others, they are the exempla to learn from, connect with, engage, compete with, overcome (in a Bloomean sense), or even pointedly ignore. Many modern poets answering poems by Donne, Herbert, and Marvell critique their originals in a Raleghian manner, often by asserting twentieth- and twenty-first-century perspectives as superior, much like Ralegh's nymph exposing the naiveté of her suitor's pastoralism. Fewer poems, like Boyle's, follow in the way of Donne in responding to metaphysical poems by making new, by abandoning the original textual parameters in favor of new territory.

Two of the three poems answering Donne in the intriguing 1997 anthology *The Muse Strikes Back: A Poetic Response by Women to Men*, edited by Katherine McAlpine and Gail White,[14] strike back at Donne mostly in the Raleghian vein. These two draw upon the forms of the poems to which they respond and confine their answers within a fairly narrow scope. They thus introduce a modern almost epigrammatic concision. Mary Holtby's "To Donne Rhyming" is a ten-line poem adapting the form of a single stanza of Donne's "The Sunne Rising." It functions as a fourth stanza of Donne's poem—a direct answer, like "The Nymph's Reply." The mistress responds to Donne's confident, enthusiastic, sweeping reconfiguring of the universe as a microcosm of bed and bedroom: "Shine here to us, and thou art every where; / This bed thy center is, these walls, thy spheare" (ll. 29-30). Strangely, though, Holtby's speaker ignores this bold declaration and Donne's cosmological description of the perspectival effects of soulful love and even his aforementioned praise of the mistress's beauty at the end of the second stanza. Instead, she treats "The Sunne Rising" as merely an elaborate invitation to have sex again. She checks Donne's amorousness and makes fun of his language. "Busy young fool, unruly Donne," she begins. Donne, not the sun, is a fool this time, not old but young and still unruly. Holby's reference to Donne by name raises an interesting question: Is the speaker of her poem Anne? Not likely. Why would Anne refer to her husband by her last name? Is she some anachronistically placed mistress? Possibly she is Holtby herself, critiquing Donne's libido across the centuries and thereby fulfilling the feminist intent of the anthology's subtitle.

Indeed, most of Holtby's ten-line poem answers through critique. Donne's participation in and appropriation of the aubade tradition is a "fuss" (l. 3), no more than a "poet's fantasies" (l. 6). The mistress/Holtby has no time to dally for sex. Both she and Donne "have other business" to attend to, an implicit rewriting of the situation informing another of Donne's aubades "Breake of Day." They best get to this "other business" while the day is young, for, the poem concludes, "Love has its proper season—as does rhyme. / (The afternoon might be a better time.)" (ll. 9-10). The witty turn in the last line softens the immediate rejection as merely a postponement as well as asserts female desire both through direct statement and through echoing the last two lines of Donne's first stanza: "Love, all alike, no season knows, nor rhyme, / Nor houres, dayes, moneths, which are the rags of time" (ll. 9-10). She agrees with Donne about the all-season durability of desire. She just isn't in the mood that morning.

If Holtby's answer poem plays ambiguously with the identity of Donne's mistress to craft a feminist response, Karen Donnelly's "The Dead Flea" offers an even more full-blown critique by trouncing the male speaker's seductive gesture in "The Flea." Like "To Donne Rhyming," "The Dead Flea" adopts the form of a single stanza of Donne's original and similarly presents itself as fourth stanza answering Donne. "Dead" here refers both to the murdered flea and to the man's prospects of sexual bliss. The mistress speaker gleefully takes pleasure in the gore of crushing the flea between her fingernails, as if killing the flea were tantamount to crushing her suitor's hopes. She "flick[s]" away the "bits of flesh" and "wipe[s] the blood" on an "unsullied" "linen square" (ll. 4-5). This, she tells him, "will be the only stain you'll see." Yet in the act of calling out the desperate urgency of male desire and the absurdity of Donne's argument from a modern perspective, the poem runs counter to the dramatic unfolding of Donne's original. In "The Flea," the mistress murders the flea in the white space between the second and third stanzas. At the same time, she apparently celebrates her action as proof against her suitor's claims. As he subsequently replies, "thou triumph'st, and saist that thou / Find'st not thy selfe, nor mee the weaker now" (ll. 23-4). Her reaction, as implied by these lines, suggests she is playing along, flirtatiously disproving the description of flea as marriage bed and repository of vital spirits by demonstrating no loss of vitality as a result of the flea's destruction. There is little likelihood either party ever accepted the suitor's argument or that the argument by itself would persuade the mistress to have sex. But that hardly seems the point. The game in this poem appears to matter more than any consummation.

By contrast, Donnelly's lady has no interest in flirtation. She begins, "'Tis true I am not weakened by this death," as if this point were her suitor's first and not her own. This remark issues from a seemingly different person from the one implied by Donne's lines. This lady likely would not have checked her hand the first time between stanzas one and two. Her opening line makes little sense as an immediate response to her suitor's concluding comments about feminine honor. Instead, it initiates a new tact and introduces a new context. Somehow we are now at the mistress's bedside, and she seems to be either in the process of lying down or already in bed. Her suitor, meanwhile, is standing there fully clothed "with bulging eyes and pants" (l. 2). A suitor with Donne's verbal acumen likely would have worn breeches, not pants. And if his mistress were so adamant against their union, how did he end up in her bedroom? Such quibbles likely pick too many nits, however. The central purpose of this answer poem-as-corrective is to send up, even lampoon the original, to tell it, like the suitor, "Go scratch your itching in some other place" (l. 10).

As much fun and Holtby's and Donnelly's poems are as critiques of masculine desire, however, neither one achieves the creative autonomy of

Donne's "The Baite." Both are bound intertextually to their originals in the same manner as Ralegh's response to Marlowe. By contrast, the third poem answering Donne in *The Muse Strikes Back*, Katherine McAlpine's "Ann Wishes She'd Taken a Little More Heed," follows a more Donnean path of answering with a new autonomy. It begins with Anne's simple acknowledgment of how pleasurable she finds lying with Donne "indiff'rent to the'unruly sun" (l. 2). But "guess what?" she tells him, "Th'eleventh's on the way. / Yes, once again we've been undone" (ll. 3-4). The second line echoes the first line of "The Sunne Rising," thereby signaling the poem's status as an answer to that poem. The two lovers are still lying abed. But as a single quatrain rhyming abab, it departs from "The Sunne Rising" stanza, a first step in giving Anne—this time, clearly identified through the title—her own voice. The poem creates an Anne who holds her husband dear but who also is her own person—intelligent, playful, and also as brooding as her husband.[15] In addition to echoing "th'unruly sun" of Donne's original, she alludes in line four to the famous punning epigram Donne purportedly wrote after signing off a "sad Letter" to Anne after Lord Thomas Egerton dismissed him from Egerton's service in the aftermath of the Donnes's clandestine marriage in 1601: "*John Donne, Anne Donne, Vn-done.*"[16] This time, Anne wittily explains, they are "undone" in the present sexual sense because "Th'eleventh's on the way"; but the line also introduces an undoing in a future sense as well. By referring to the eleventh of Anne's pregnancies, McAlpine plays loosely with chronology: Robin Robbins suggests the summer of 1604 as the likely date of "The Sunne Rising"[17] rather than 1615–1616, when Anne was pregnant with her eleventh child Elizabeth. But the implicit later dating creates a poignant dramatic irony. On August 15, 1617, Anne died of complications while delivering their twelfth child. By placing this poem later in the Donnes's marriage, McAlpine introduces an intimation of that future fatal parting, made all the more poignant in light of the common knowledge of how devastated Donne was after Anne's death.[18] While neither John nor Anne could have known the nearness of that parting in 1615, Anne's response dampens Donne's exuberance with a reminder of the transience of sexual pleasures. Four lines is not much to go on in the construction of a personality. Yet McAlpine creates enough of one here for her Anne to emerge as distinctive. One might call this accomplishment McAlpine's watermarking of the answer poem.

Maureen Boyle's "The Nunwell Letter" creates a more full-bodied Anne at much greater length, thereby also following Donne's lead in claiming the poetic occasion as wholly hers. Written in free verse, this seven-section poem takes the form of a serial letter to Donne following a long epistolary silence in the late winter and spring of 1612. The poem resulted from a commission Boyle received from the inaugural Ireland Chair of Poetry Travel Bursary in 2017. As Boyle explains,

The award allowed me to travel to the Isle of Wight where John Donne's wife Ann spent the winter of 1611 and the spring of 1612, while Donne travelled to Europe with Robert Drury and his wife. Ann lost a child during this absence, and I wanted to attempt to give her a voice partly in response to Donne's "Valediction Forbidding Mourning," the poem he gave her by way of consolation on leaving, and partly because she's a silent presence known only from his love poems.[19]

Izaak Walton's biography of Donne, of course, is our primary source associating "A Valediction forbidding mourning" with the 1611–1612 Continental trip. His account of the episode is full of inaccuracies. Sir Robert Drury received a license to travel for three years, not for two months as Walton indicates; the Drury entourage, Donne included, was in Amiens, not Paris, from December 1611 until March 1612; the Donnes did not move into a cottage at Drury House until after Donne's return, and Ann and her children resided not in London but with her younger sister's family on the Isle of Wight that winter.[20] Yet the main theme of Walton's account—the *sympathy of souls*—backgrounds Boyle's portrayal of Anne and the Donne marriage.

In addition to quoting a full text of Donne's valediction, Walton conveys the soulful connection of John and Anne through the famous story of Donne's ghostly vision of seeing his absent wife carrying a dead child in her arms. Two days after the arrival of the Drury entourage in Paris, Walton tells us,

> Mr. *Donne* was left alone, in that room in which Sir *Robert*, and he, and some other friends had din'd together. To this place Sir *Robert* return'd within half an hour; and, as he left, so he found Mr. *Donne* alone; but, in such an Extasie, and so alter'd as to his looks, as amaz'd Sir *Robert* to behold him: insomuch that he earnestly desired Mr. *Donne* to declare what had befaln him in the short time of his absence? to which, Mr. *Donne* was not able to make a present answer: but, after a long and perplext pause, did at last say, *I have seen a dreadful Vision since I saw you: I have seen my dear wife pass twice by me through this room, with her hair hanging about her shoulders, and a dead child in her arms: this, I have seen since I saw you.* To which, Sir *Robert* reply'd; *Sure Sir, you have slept since I saw you; and, this is the result of some melancholy dream, which I desire you to forget, for you are now awake.* To which Mr. *Donne's* reply was: *I cannot be surer that I now live, then that I have not slept since I saw you: and am, as sure, that at her second appearing, she stopt, and look'd me in the face, and vanisht.*[21]

Walton acknowledges the wondrousness of this story. To justify its legitimacy, he claims he heard it from a reliable source. He also provides a short catalogue of similar instances of ghostly visitations from Roman history, the Bible, and Augustine's *Confessions*. Moreover, in a move that would have appealed to both Donne and Herbert, he offers the analogy of musical instruments in harmony as a way of explaining how two souls can be in sympathy with each other:

> 'Tis most certain, that two Lutes, begin laid upon a Table at a fit distance, will (like an Eccho to a trumpet) warble at a faint audible harmony, in answer to the same tune: yet many will not believe there is any such thing as a *sympathy of souls*; and I am well pleas'd, that every Reader to injoy his own opinion.[22]

Even though he considered Donne's clandestine marriage the great error of Donne's life, Walton nonetheless credited Donne's expressions of soulful love as accurate in defining the bond he shared with Anne.

This same consideration informs the dark foreshadowing in Walton's telling of the Donnes's reluctance in parting from each other at the start of the episode. When Anne, "Who was then with Child, and otherways under so dangerous habit of body," first heard about this trip, Walton explains, she "profest an unwillingness to allow" her husband "any absence from her; saying, *her divining soul boded her some ill in his absence*."[23] Donne decided against the trip but then changed his mind in response to Drury's counterarguments. "Mr. *Donne* was so generous, as to think he had sold his liberty when he received so many charitable kindnesses" from Drury, Walton says, "and told his wife so; who did therefore with an unwilling-willingness give a faint Consent to the Journey."

Subsequent interpreters disagree about the extent of Donne's willingness to accompany the Drurys to the Continent. R. C. Bald and Edward Le Comte accept Walton's account of Donne's reluctance, waffling, and subsequent resolution at face value.[24] John Carey, after commenting on Anne's reluctance, treats her husband's decision to travel matter-of-factly as a cost of clientage: "but since he was living off Sir Robert he had little choice."[25] John Stubbs quotes freely from Walton's account but emphasizes how Donne broke the news to Henry Goodyer before his wife and later seemed to be relieved to be away from their "draughty" house at Mitcham.[26] Regardless, Boyle's "The Nunwell Letter" assumes both husband and wife had misgivings about the trip; that their separation placed a strain on their relationship; and that they both believed in the harmony of souls as both Donne and Walton described it.

The church register at Brading on the Isle of Wight records the burial of Anne's still-born child on January 24, 1612.[27] Walton claims Donne had his vision of Anne on "the same day, and about the very hour" of the delivery.[28] But in truth, months passed before Donne learned the news. After writing to

Anne from Amiens via his brother-in-law Sir Robert More in February, he still had not heard news of Anne's delivery by mid-April.[29] "The Nunwell Letter" breaks Anne's "islanded silence" with a stark declaration of her most salient news:

John

It has been untenably long winter
and our baby died.

There, I have told you,
though you may heard in other ways by now.
This ends my islanded silence
just as spring comes in.
I had not thought to keep it
out of any spite but
I have been more of body John,
than soul, one of those you felt inferior,
sub-lunary, that thin airy chain
made heavy and lowered,
brought to earth by loss. (ll. 1-14)

As with Donne's echo of Marlowe in "The Baite," Boyle posits her poem as an answer through direct allusion near the start. Anne's reference to "sublunary" connects this poem to Donne's valediction, the presence of which is felt throughout the ensuing lines. The distinction between "sublunary" lovers "whose soul is sense" and soulful lovers who experience an enduring nonmaterial connection is crucial for Donne's famous compass conceit. Here, though, it weighs heavily on Anne, who, like the "airy chain," has been "brought to earth by loss." Her difficult delivery and subsequent grief and recuperation caused her to withdraw into herself and her immediate circumstances. With this letter, however, she seeks to return to life. "I know you feel that letters link souls," she writes at the end of the first section, "let this be a mending link in ours" (ll. 23-24).

The ensuing six sections convey this return to life, as Anne shares her experiences with vividness and economy. Each section features a series of bright particulars grounding family life on the island—her effort to share something of this life with her husband from afar. Boyle gives voice to Anne's "silent presence" first by rendering the island's most memorable features with special attention to her children's reactions. The Donne children are fascinated by the daily rhythms of rural life. They rise "with the dew" (l.

34) each day to accompany Frances as she makes the rounds with her chores. They love watching the pigs being fed "in their darkened byres" (l. 30). The "little ones especially loved to be lifted up / to gaze into the rank, rich space," Anne says, "Lucy's eyes lightening / in awe at the sow lolling in the mud" (ll. 31-33). The Oglander crest, a stork, is "everywhere," which prompts Anne to tell the children of the storks their father talked about seeing in Strasbourg during his previous Continental trip (l. 57). The house where they are staying contains a distinctive staircase that "delights" both Anne and the children:

It rises like three branches of the vast tree it was hewn from
and makes the house feel simultaneously light and weighted.
From underneath, it looks like the rigging of a great ship
and going to bed we joke that we are climbing the mainsail,
George and Francis playing pirates on its steps and newel posts. (ll. 50-54).

This passage chimes with possible echoes of other Donne poems, suggesting Anne's deep familiarity with her husband's writings. The simile of a great ship's rigging and mainsail calls to mind Donne's attention to rigging a ship in "Confined Love" (ll. 14-15) and to the becalmed tackling in "The Calme" (l. 16). Meanwhile, the phrase "going to bed" cannot help but recall Donne's lascivious elegy "To his Mistress going to bed," a sharp contrast to the present separation of husband and wife. Anne's readiness for images and conceits suggests a poetic and intellectual affinity with her husband. Her wit proves as expansive as his as well.

Yet Anne is clearly her own person. Her personality emerges most strongly in her poignant descriptions of her intense experiences during the last phase of her pregnancy and its aftermath. She conveys to her husband why she has felt "more of body . . . than of soul" these past weeks and attends to the relationship between the feminine body, the present, and the past. In section six, a description of her delivery, she connects this birth process to her previous ones. As her labor pains took hold, she tells her husband,

I found that place I've told you of
in my other labours where time stops
and I'm contracted into myself
even as the body convulses. (ll. 108-111)

This thought flows to a childhood memory when Anne used to go into her grandfather's library at Losely Hall to read books "in a puddle of sun by the tall windows" (l. 114). Her learning shows in her account of the birth itself:

In the worst pain,
almost as if knowing what I faced,
I was Niobe turned to stone in grief
or Rhea, smeared with the soilure of birth,
her after-blood seeping into a dry river bed,
commanding the earth mother to create
a new stream to clean her and her god-child.

And then it was as if I had two souls
and two sets of eyes,
those of the child, for whom this was all story
and those of the woman
whose cold child is placed in her arms –
a still, ever-sleeping girl
who I will never know. (ll. 116-29)

In response to this heart-rending experience, Anne confesses to have considered suicide and refers to her husband's *Biathanatos*, which she clearly has read, but she resisted this desire out of a concern for God's reaction to the abandonment of her children.

In another section, Anne describes the postpartum ministrations of the midwife, who "covered" her with a sheepskin to "help" her "heal / along with bay-leaves, rupture-wort and chamomile / that she'd smear as lovingly as you on my poor torn body" (ll. 101-103). The same attention to detail she devotes to rendering her embodied experience applies as well to the burial place of her lost child:

They took her to Brading to bury her the next day
in an Oglander grave. I was too sick to go
but I have been since and planted it
with hellebore and winter aconite
for the season when she came. It is a little plot
by the sea-wall of St Mary-the-Virgin, where every day
she is by sea-spray newly christened. (ll. 90-97)

Through these and other like descriptions, Anne, no longer silent, becomes a memorable presence the way Donne is in his poems.

As may be apparent, the seven sections of "The Nunwell Letter" skip around chronologically. Anne's story builds through the juxtaposition of bright particulars. But by the end of the poem, we discover that not only do the seven parts enact a process of Anne's healing even as they relate it, but also that each one becomes a "mending link" in the chain binding Anne's soul with her husband's. The aforementioned last lines of the first section, with their slant allusion to Donne's verse letter "To Mr. Henry Wotton" ("Sir, More than kisses Letters mingle Souls"), establish the power of letters to mingle separated souls; the letter as a whole is meant to be a link in the "airy chain" connecting wife and husband. But each section within the letter becomes a link within this larger one. At the end of each section, Anne addresses John or remembers some part of their lives together or makes some resonant allusion to their love as a means of finding closure. It is as if Boyle were closing each section link with pincers until the letter as a whole becomes complete. At the end of the second section, Anne contrasts her "good" but "dull" brother-in-law with her livelier husband: "I miss the wit of your writing and your speech / our little house at Mitcham with its own smells / and our bed" (ll. 43-45). In the last two lines of section three, she refers to the "little room" where "one of the older children" slept with her until her "confinement," "little room" here a slant reference to the sonnet, as in "we'll build in sonnets pretty roomes" ("The Canonization," ll. 32) as well as, perhaps, to the bedchamber at Mitcham—witness Donne's account of the awakening of soulful love in "The Good-morrow": "For love, all love of other sights controules, / And makes one little roome, an every where" (ll. 10-11).

Another declaration of missing John concludes the fourth section, which digests previous separations. In contrast to John's last Continental trip, which Anne views as "a line break or lacuna in a poem," this time the separation "is hard": "even with our children here, / it is only a half-life without you" (ll. 73-76). Thoughts of this "half-life" give way to considerations about how love binds those it touches. Anne ends the fifth section with another allusion to "A Valediction forbidding mourning" as she worries about leaving her buried child behind: "I worry that we will leave her here so far from us / but pray my soul and hers can endure just such / an expansion as you imagined" (ll. 104-106). In so worrying, she expands Donne's original conceit to include their children as well as themselves, soulful love here redefined as more than amorous.

The last two sections of "The Nunwell Letter" bear witness to Anne's return to life. In section six, the penultimate link within this restorative epistolary chain, Anne follows her account of her difficult birthing experience by relating how, "in the days of fever afterwards," she recalled the days of their courtship more than a decade before:

              I was betimes
in our waking days of first glances at dinner
the thrill of passing one another close in busy corridors,
first words, the hours of fascinated talk
and then nights it seemed we hardly needed sleep
and the quickening sense that I had found my life. (ll. 136-141)

As with "little room," the phrase "waking days" connects again to the soulful awakening Donne refers to in the second awakening stanza of "The goodmorrow": "And now good morrow to our waking soules / Which watch not one another out of feare" (ll. 8-9). Here, too, is an impressionistic glimpse of the blooming compatibility of wife and husband—the thousand little moments that constitute a bringing together. Remembering these early days and the sense of life found brings Anne to life again. She concludes the final section and "The Nunwell Letter" as a whole with an almost formal declaration of the end of her period of mourning:

You cannot mourn one child too long
when there are others to care for
and so it is spring and I am looking to return.

This must be the longest time my body has had to rest
since we met—neither nursing nor pregnant.

Come home when you can and we will begin again.

Ann (ll. 149-53)

As so often in Donne's most famous poems of mutual love, the realization of soulful love, that *sympathy of souls*, departs from the purest Neoplatonic trajectory through its grounding in sexual expression, here with the notion that the Donnes "will begin again" as soon as John returns.

These few pages can do only a little justice to the full experience of reading "The Nunwell Letter" for those familiar with what we know of the Donnes' life story together. But I trust they do show the extent of Boyle's achievement in this poem. Boyle succeeds in ending Anne's silence by crafting a believable presence that accords with what we can deduce about the Donnes' marriage. She makes vivid Anne's time on the Isle of Wight with an admirable depth of perception and feeling. In so doing, her poem more than simply answers "A Valediction forbidding mourning"; it reinforces the idea that there are more ways to answer metaphysical poems than mere correction or critique. In this, The Nunwell Letter follows Donne's own approach to watermarking a poem in such a way that it is made new and capable of inspiring further acts of poetic making.

NOTES

1. As Arthur F. Marotti explains of answer poems and parodies, "Such poetry at the Inns of Court . . . was sometimes more directly the product of a game of literary

competition between friends, a manifestation of a spirit of competition that permeated most of the activities of Inns members." See *John Donne Coterie Poet* (Madison: University of Wisconsin Press, 1986), 85. In addition to Marotti's book, for more on the circulation of Donne's verse and his original readership, see Achsah Guibbory, "A Sense of the Future: Projected Audiences of Donne and Jonson," *John Donne Journal* 2, no. 2 (1983): 11–21; Dennis Flynn, "Donne and a *Female* Coterie," *LIT: Literature Interpretation Theory* 1 (1989): 127–136; Ted-Larry Pebworth, "John Donne, Coterie Poetry, and the Text as Performance," *Studies in English Literature* 29 (1989): 61–75 as well as his essay "The Early Audiences of Donne's Poetic Performances," *John Donne Journal* 15 (1996): 127–137; Ernest W. Sullivan II, *The Influence of John Donne: His Uncollected Seventeenth-Century Printed Verse* (Columbia: University of Missouri Press, 1993); Gary A. Stringer, "The Composition and Dissemination of Donne's Writings," in *The Oxford Handbook of John Donne*, ed. Jeanne Shami, Dennis Flynn, and M. Thomas Hester (Oxford: Oxford University Press, 2011), 12–25; Daniel Starza Smith, *John Donne and the Conway Papers: Patronage and Manuscript Circulation in the Early Seventeenth Century* (Oxford: Oxford University Press, 2014); Lara M. Crowley, *Manuscript Matters: Reading John Donne's Poetry & Prose in Early Modern England* (Oxford: Oxford University Press, 2018); and Joshua Eckhardt, *Religion Around John Donne* (University Park: The Pennsylvania State University Press, 2019).

2. Boyle, "The Nunwell Letter," *Poetry Ireland Review* 127 (April 2019): 36–40.

3. R. S. Forsythe, *"The Passionate Shepherd*; And English Poetry," *PMLA* 40, no. 3 (Sept. 1925): 701.

4. Forsythe, "*Passionate Shepherd*," notes Marlowe's "English poem resembles more closely the Ovidian passage than the Greek pastoral or its English version" (695). He also notes that there are "fourteen passages in Marlowe's plays in which 'The Passionate Shepherd' is suggested, in material, in purpose, and at times in metre," surely a testament to Marlowe's interest in the "formula for the invitation poem" (701).

5. My text of Marlowe's poem and Ralegh's "The Nymph's reply" come from *Englands Helicon*, printed by I. R. for John Flasket (London, 1602).

6. The third and fourth stanzas of this poem sketch a riverside scene in which fish are willing caught by nymphs. Helen Gardner suggests these lines may have inspired Donne in "The Baite." See her edition of *The Elegies and the Songs and Sonnets* (Oxford: Clarendon Press, 1965), pp. 155–156.

7. Cunnar, "Donne's Witty Theory of Atonement in 'The Baite,'" *SEL: Studies in English Literature, 1500-1900* 29 (1989): 77.

8. In calling Donne's poem "a frequent manuscript flyer," I do not mean to suggest Donne was an active, real-time participant in the Marlowe-Ralegh exchange but that his poem was a later response that acquired a lively manuscript circulation like theirs. I agree with M. Thomas Hester that "Donne's poem seems to be more of a *response to* those poems than part of a literary game in which he directly participated with the two 'court' poets" ("'Like a spyed Spie': Donne's Baiting of Marlowe," in *Literary Circles and Cultural Communities in Renaissance England*, ed. Claude J. Summers and Ted-Larry Pebworth [Columbia and London: University of Missouri Press, 2000]: 28).

9. Folger Shakespeare Library ms. V.a.169.

10. Hester, "Like a spyed Spie," 35. Hester contends Donne's poem additionally satirizes the anti-Catholicism of Marlowe and the Ralegh circle through its fishing terminology:

> One needs only to peruse Harrison's *Elizabethan Journals* or Erasmus' *Colloquies* to hear English Catholics associated with fish, or to peruse the Public Records Office correspondence of Walsingham's network to hear of the "angling" after "big fish" upon discovery or capture of a Catholic "traytor." Catholic records use the same terms. (36)

11. *Preoccupations: Selected Prose, 1968-1978* (New York: Farrar, Straus and Giroux, 1980), 47.

12. Kittay, "Semantic Fields and the Structure of Metaphor," in *Metaphor: Its Cognitive Force and Linguistic Structure* (Oxford: Clarendon Press, 1987), 274–275.

13. Low, "The Compleat Angler's 'Baite'; or, The Subverter Subverted," *John Donne Journal* 4, no. 1 (1985): 9.

14. *The Muse Strikes Back: A Poetic Response by Women to Men* (Brownsville, OR: Story Line Press, Inc., 1997).

15. The spelling of Anne's name is not consistent in modern scholarship. No extant signatures of hers exist, so we do not know how she spelled her name. Furthermore, Donne nowhere calls her by name in his extant writings. Like M. Thomas Hester, the editor of *John Donne's "desire of more": The Subject of Anne More Donne in His Poetry*, I choose to include the terminal "e" throughout for two of the same reasons: because Anne's mother and namesake spelled *her* name this way and because this spelling is repeated in references to Donne's purported quip "John Donne, Anne Donne, Un-done." In spelling her name *without* an "e," however, McAlpine and Boyle are in good company with other scholars who also prefer "Ann" to "Anne," including Marotti in *John Donne, Coterie Poet* (1986), Dennis Flynn in *John Donne and the Ancient Catholic Nobility* (1995), Jeffrey Johnson in *The Theology of John Donne* (1999), and Ann Hollinshead Hurley in *John Donne's Poetry and Early Modern Visual Culture* (2005).

16. Both quotes in this sentence come from Izaak Walton's *The Life of Dr. John Donne*, our most widely known source for this story (*Walton's Lives*, ed. S. B. Carter [London: Falcon Educational Books, 1951], 12). Right after quoting Donne's alleged epigram, Walton almost jauntily concludes, "God knows it proved too true." Ernest W. Sullivan II calls this famous punning quip "Donne's Epithalamion for Anne." See his essay so titled in *John Donne's "desire of more": The Subject of Anne More Donne in His Poetry*, ed. M. Thomas Hester (Newark: University of Delaware Press, 1996), 35–38, for the most up-to-date account of Walton's source for it.

17. *The Complete Poems of John Donne*, edited by Robin Robbins (London and New York: Routledge, 2010), 245.

18. Hester, in his explication of Donne's Latin epitaph on Anne, calls attention to the tremendous, life-changing force of Donne's grief when he notes that "[t]o be *Iohannes Donne* on 15 August 1617 is to sacrifice oneself to Anne, to 'God's blessing,' to die for the truth of the eternal Marriage that she and their fifteen years of

loving union mirror" ("'Fæminæ lectissimæ': Reading Anne Donne" in *John Donne's "desire of more": The Subject of Anne More Donne in His Poetry*, ed. M. Thomas Hester (Newark: University of Delaware Press, 1996), 28. See also the essays by Kate Gartner Frost, Theresa M. DiPasquale, Frances M. Malpezzi, Achsah Guibbory, Maureen Sabine, and Graham Roebuck in this same collection.

19. Boyle, "The Nunwell Letter," *Poetry Ireland Review* 127 (April 2019): 40. All subsequent quotations from Boyle's poem come from this publication.

20. Compare R. C. Bald's account of these details (*John Donne: A Life* [Oxford: Oxford University Press, 1970], 241–250) with Walton's (*Life of Donne*, 22). See also Bald's more detailed account of the Continental trip in *Donne and Drurys* (Cambridge: Cambridge University Press, 1959), 85–103.

21. Walton, *Life of Donne*, 22.

22. Walton, *Life of Donne*, 23.

23. Walton, *Life of Donne*, 21.

24. Bald, *John Donne: A Life,* 242; Le Comte, *Grace to a Witty Sinner: A Life of Donne* (New York: Walker and Company, 1965), 134–135.

25. Carey, *John Donne: Life, Mind & Art* (New York: Oxford University Press, 1981), 84.

26. Stubbs, *John Donne: The Reformed Soul* (New York and London: W. W. Norton & Company, 2006), 274.

27. Bald, *John Donne: A Life*, 252.

28. Walton, *Life of Donne*, 23.

29. Bald, *John Donne: A Life*, 249–253.

Chapter 3

Shared Subjects
Andrew Marvell, Archibald MacLeish, and Brendan Kennelly

Allusions, echoes, and answers all highlight the metaphysical poems occupying the attention of later poets. In such cases, the older poems cast clearly defined shadows during a reading of the newer ones. Modern poets depend on such stark definition for signaling affinity or contrast with their own poetic expression. But what happens when two poets, one modern and one seventeenth-century, write about the same subject without reference to each other? This question leads to another distinctive form of poetic engagement. Possibly worlds apart in worldviews, life circumstances, expressive styles, and/or cultural, political, and religious affinities, poets from different time periods who write about the same subjects nonetheless share a point of connection through their mutually chosen subject. The ensuing relationship between their poems may not be as clearly defined, the metaphysical shadow less distinct. But it exists in the minds of any readers well-read enough to perceive it. And it may, or may not, be part of later poets' intentions, depending on the degree of their awareness. This time, Andrew Marvell, not Donne, provides a convenient way in to explore this phenomenon.

At first blush, Archibald MacLeish's poem "You, Andrew Marvell" appears to be an answer poem in the Donnean vein. Published in his seventh collection *New Found Land* (1930)—the book title echoes line 27 of Donne's eighth elegy "To his Mistress going to bed": "Oh my America, my newfound land"—MacLeish wrote, "You, Andrew Marvell," within the first decade after the publication of Grierson's anthology and during the period of Eliot's greatest advocacy for the metaphysical poets as worthy of notice.[1] Within his own oeuvre, however, "You, Andrew Marvell" attests to MacLeish's fascination with answering or commenting on other writers. In this sense, it belongs in the same sub-group as "Mark Van Doren and the Brook," "Reply to Mr. Wordsworth," "Cummings," "Hemingway," "Edwin Muir," "Whistler in the Dark" (a poem on the death of Dylan Thomas), and "You Also, Gaius Valerius Catullus." MacLeish's direct address in the title—"You, Andrew Marvell"—unambiguously introduces what follows as an answer. In light of its concentration on geography and the passage of time, readers have considered it more particularly an answer to the *carpe diem* poem "To His Coy Mistress," especially the first paragraph, which begins:

Had we but World enough, and Time,
This coyness Lady were no crime.
We would sit down, and think which way
To walk, and pass our long Loves Day.
Thou by the *Indian Ganges* side
Should'st Rubies find: I by the Tide
Of *Humber* would complain. (ll. 1-7)[2]

Though he forgoes Marvell's rhyming couplets in favor of quatrains rhyming abab, MacLeish uses iambic tetrameter, Marvell's favorite meter. His geographic exploration similarly begins in Asia: while Marvell first imagines his lover in India beside the Ganges river, MacLeish begins by visualizing night darkening the leaves in Iran.

Yet unlike Donne's "The Baite," MacLeish's poem forgoes the central gesture of the poem it purportedly answers: an attempt at seduction. There is no mistress in "You, Andrew Marvell," willing or unwilling. Her absence says less about MacLeish's poetry as a whole—he treats multiple dimensions of desire in other poems—than it does about the speaker's urgencies in this poem. It is as if MacLeish fixated on Marvell's preoccupation with time but without the impatience evinced in Marvell's poem. Marvell's lines about time and its effects throughout "To His Coy Mistress" attracted the attention of other early to mid-twentieth-century American poets. Kenneth Rexroth, for example, in his *The Dragon and the Unicorn* (1952), his long poetic account of traveling through post-World War II America and Europe, recalls lines from the second verse paragraph of "To His Coy Mistress" as he describes the decrepit red light district of late-1940s Chicago: "I know / What Marvell meant by desarts / Of vast eternity" (ll. 87-87).[3] MacLeish's interest in Marvell's poem is not surprising.

But the arrested motion, if we can call it that, of MacLeish's attention raises the possibility that his use of the "To His Coy Mistress" tetrameter line does not in fact mark "You, Andrew Marvell" as an answer to that poem alone. Instead, the poem might be better described as a meditation on contemplation, the Marvell in the title not the sometime love poet but the poet of "The Garden." Both "You, Andrew Marvell" and "The Garden" focus on each poet's immersion in a natural space and reveal how a process of sensual feeling readily initiates a contemplative state. In "The Garden," the immediate pleasures of green leaves, flowers, fragrances, and fruit causes an intoxication that first elicits a sense of connection with Greek mythology but then advances to a higher, more transcendent contemplation. The poet, "[s]tumbling on Melons," falls onto the grass, and in this posture describes the shifting disposition of his mind:

Mean while the Mind, from pleasure less,
Withdraws into its happiness:
The Mind, that Ocean where each kind
Does streight its own resemblance find;
Yet it creates, transcending these,
Far other Worlds, and other Seas;
Annihilating all that's made
To a green Thought in a green Shade. (ll. 41-48)

The mind loses its tether to its immediate surroundings to roam a vaster space in a process of creation that is also a process of annihilation.

In a similar way, MacLeish starts with an emphasis on his body outside, receptive to the influence of natural surroundings. Though he does not describe his surroundings as effusively as Marvell, he twice emphasizes how he lies "here face down beneath the sun," once in the opening line and again in line thirty-four.[4] He already has fallen onto the grass, so to speak, and his mind already has launched a process of creation. In this case, creation proceeds from feeling that "night" is "always coming on" (ll. 3-4). He feels the ground beneath his face starting to cool as the sun advances toward the West:

To feel creep up the curving east
The earthly chill of dusk and slow
Upon those under lands the vast
And ever climbing shadow grow (ll. 5-8)

"[V]ast" recalls Marvell's description of vegetable love in "To His Coy Mistress": "Vaster than Empires, and more slow" (l. 12). But the passage of time here seems much faster, more in accordance with the sweeping speed of imaginative creation in "The Garden." MacLeish roams those "under lands," half-circumnavigating the globe through a series of imagined details that together create a broad landscape of the lengthening shadows. In place after place, these shadows presage the "flooding dark" of oncoming night. He imagines shadows claiming the trees leaf by leaf at Ecbatan in Western Iran (ll. 9-12), then moving westward to the "withered grass" near a gate in Kermanshah (ll. 13-16); a darkening bridge in Baghdad (ll. 17-20); a "wheel rut in the ruined stone" in Palmyra, Syria (ll. 21-22); and fading Lebanon and Crete (ll. 23-24). He imagines "landward gulls" "[s]till flashing" over Sicily (ll. 25-26); Spain "go[ing] under" (l. 27); and the "gilded sand" of the West African shore disappearing along with the evening (ll. 28-30), before he crosses the "long light on the sea" in a single line before winding up where he started, "face downward in the sun" (l. 34). The feeling of the swift spread of night persists, and the poem ends in an ellipsis as the "shadow of the night comes on" (l. 36).

Though he addresses Marvell, MacLeish answers neither "To His Coy Mistress" nor "The Garden" per se. But he does probe, in his own way, the passage of time and the sweep of geography in a process and a posture with which Marvell would have been familiar. Time does pass swiftly, he seems to say, if you pay attention to the world around you. Meanwhile, the mind is capable of a greater range of imaginative motion than we might credit in our humdrum, everyday lives.

The choice of a shared subject (the passage of time), in MacLeish's case, conveys a modern poet's affinity with the early modern poet. But revisiting a subject also can occasion a powerful demonstration of divergence, of sharp contrasts and amplifications, even of historically responsive corrections. Brendan Kennelly, a longtime fixture at Trinity College, Dublin, and the author of more than thirty collections of poetry, was one of the most popular and respected Irish poets of roughly the same generation as Seamus Heaney. Many Irish poets consider his 1983 book *Cromwell: A Poem* Kennelly's masterpiece. This collection is a book-length poem composed of many smaller poems that range freely in time from the seventeenth to the twentieth centuries. It draws upon a number of discursive modes (letter, newspaper article, history, legend, folktale, fantasy), yet maintains a constant, often sardonic and sometimes angry focus on the nature of human brutality. As Kennelly says, the "poem tries to present the nature and implications of various forms of dream and nightmare, including the nightmare of Irish history."[5] While the fictitious "hero" of the poem "M. P. G. M. Buffún Esq." serves as a mouthpiece for Kennelly, the poet also adopts the personae of a number of other characters, including Edmund Spenser and Cromwell himself, to describe the relationship between Irish and English history, a "relationship that has produced a singularly tragic mess."

The mere mention of Cromwell in the context of Anglophone poetry cannot help but recall the most famous poem in English about Cromwell: Marvell's "An Horatian Ode Upon Cromwell's Return from Ireland."[6] I cannot say for certain whether Kennelly had Marvell's *Horatian Ode* expressly in mind while writing *Cromwell: A Poem*. He does not address Marvell in any obvious way (á la MacLeish), nor does he allude to the Horatian ode or adopt any of its distinctive formal markers. The closest he comes is a reference to the power of the righteous God as lightning: "I saw Heaven's lightning descend on England / And burn up idle luster in a night" ("Praise the Lord," ll. 7-8).[7] Compare these lines to Marvell's likening of Cromwell to three-forked Lightning that burns his "fiery way" through his own "Side" (ll. 13-16). Yet like Marvell, Kennelly felt compelled to address the complexity of his subject—Cromwell's controversial actions and seemingly supernatural success in war—and of its historical occasion—how to make sense of the brutal suppression of the Irish in 1649–1650. In so doing, he had to work through the challenges arising from both in light of his own historical position, much as Marvell had done before him.

The Horatian ode exhibits one of Marvell's most intriguing qualities as a poet: his almost Yeatsian capacity to imagine how historical events might be perceived after his time. The Horatian ode is to Marvell's oeuvre what "Easter, 1916" is to Yeats's: an encapsulation of a defining moment or series of moments with far-reaching consequences for the history of a nation. This species of truth-telling arises from a desire to cast the final word on a subject, what might be a consensus historical judgment in a later time. Because of its anticipated futurity, it is fundamentally an act of imagination, an imaging of how events might look from a wider, even posthumous perspective.

Within the span of two years—from the summer of 1648 to the summer of 1650—Cromwell led parliamentary forces to a resounding victory against the Scots at Preston, thereby bringing to a close the Second English Civil War. He also suppressed the royalist-led rebellion in Ireland.[8] Now, returning to England and in the words of Nicholas von Maltzahn "[v]ery much in the ascendant," Cromwell was poised to take full command of the army to follow the Council of State's resolution to invade Scotland. This same resolution caused Sir Thomas Fairfax to resign his commission as Lord General, thus paving the way for his subordinate, Cromwell. During that same June and July, 1650, Marvell was about to join Fairfax's household as tutor to his daughter Mary. It was during this period of tumult and changes that Marvell paused to follow the example of Horace in taking stock of the national situation.

Pierre Legouis notes the degree to which Marvell's ode "has the merit of complete independence, nay, of an almost inhuman aloofness," the product of one who, with clear sight, was moving toward acceptance of the Republican government in light of what seemed to many the providential force behind it.[9] Blair Worden similarly sees the poem as a first move toward an embrace of a post-royalist world: the poem "explicitly set a royalist past against a Cromwellian future," he explains, and it "also set, implicitly, a Cromwellian future against a parliamentary present."[10] In writing the ode, however, which Legouis suggests he might have done for himself rather than for a wider readership, Marvell had to navigate between what Anabel Patterson characterizes as two imperatives, the "social responsibility of 'speaking well' . . . and the other responsibility of 'speaking true' which can also arise out of social or political circumstances."¹¹ The two are often in conflict:

> Far from being a merely rhetorical problem, the choice between speaking well and speaking true is what connects the writer to society. In a "world all furnished with subjects of praise, instruction and learned inquiry" there is no problem in supplying positive demonstrations of idealism. But in the "degenerate" times of civil war or the "age loose and all unlac't" which followed it, the poet who insists on speaking well must either look for exceptions or keep silent. The other alternative is to try and justify the satirist's destructive accuracy. The tension between alternative modes is not then governed by the pull of public needs against personal integrity, but rather by the changing nature of society itself, and the occasions it offers the poet.¹²

Speaking well of Cromwell's gathering power and speaking true required a measure of selectivity to counter its less savory aspects. Meanwhile, still smarting from the execution of Charles I the previous year, Marvell could not have been oblivious to the many mistakes and incompetent decisions of that fateful monarch's reign. Marvell's choice of Horace as a model and its ready-made analogies with the Caesars necessitated that he address both sets of complications in an attempt to arrive at a new understanding.

Most of Marvell's ode concerns Cromwell. Rather than freight his description of Cromwell with copious contemporary references, he relies on selective images and on a central simile to describe the larger-than-life dimensions of Cromwell's swift rise. He frames his account with a quick sketch of a "forward youth" forsaking poetry (and by extension, all leisure) and oiling armor and corslet in preparation for further warfare (ll. 1-8). Cromwell then enters, a man who has set aside the "inglorious Arts of Peace" and instead "through adventrous War / Urged his active Star" (11-13). We never see Cromwell in any discrete scene. Instead, Marvell telescopes the previous few years (Cromwell's military victories, the end of the Civil War, Cromwell's involvement in Pride's Purge of Parliament, and the ensuing trial and execution of the king) by likening Cromwell to lightning. Cromwell

>   like the three-forked Lightning, first
> Breaking the Clouds where it was nurst,
>   Did thorough his own Side
>   His fiery way divide.
> (For 'tis all one to Courage high,
> The Emulous or Enemy;
>   And with such to inclose

Is more than to oppose.)
Then burning through the Air he went,
And Pallaces and Temples rent:
  And *Caesars* head at last
  Did through his Laurels blast.
'Tis Madness to resist or blame
The force of angry Heaven's flame: (ll. 13-26)

This aerial view of Cromwell as lightning obscures any specific casualties he may have left on the ground. It also naturalizes the Machiavellian nature of Cromwell's ambitions. By his "industrious Valour," Marvell tells us, Cromwell could "ruine the great Work of Time, / And cast the Kingdome old / Into another Mold" (ll. 33-36). He credits Cromwell's strength of will in the victorious general's accomplishments. Nevertheless, here and elsewhere in the poem, Cromwell also functions as an agent of Fate. "Justice," Marvell tells us, "complain[s]" and "plead[s] the antient rights in vain" (ll. 37-38). The truth is those ancient rights of kings, prelates, and members of the nobility "do hold or break, / As men are strong or weak" (ll. 39-40). No one can deny Cromwell's incomparable strength. One would be mad to "resist" or even "blame" it.

John Malcolm Wallace remarks that when Marvell "decided to cast his ode in the form of a political oration he committed himself first to arguing a case—not to saying everything—and second to a certain order of proof."[13] His strategy of using selective details and relying largely on similitudes allows him to avoid any sustained commentary on the Irish campaign, including the siege of Drogheda in September, 1649, and the sack of Wexford the following October, both of which incurred substantial loss of civilian life. Cromwell's overarching military successes allow the poet to present him as the Scourge of God in general terms.

When Marvell comes to accounting for the king's demise, however, he adopts a different approach. No such case for success can be made for Charles. Instead, Marvell latches onto and dramatizes a single highly sympathetic episode: the doomed king's exemplary behavior during his execution. Marvell presents Charles on the scaffold with a lyricist's eye for poetic beauty and a playwright's eye for the dramatic. Cromwell

  wove a Net of such a scope
  That *Charles* himself might chase
  To *Caresbrooks* narrow case.
That thence the *Royal Actor* born
The *Tragick Scaffold* might adorn:
  While round the armed Bands

>   Did clap their bloody hands.
> *He* nothing common did or mean
> Upon that memorable Scene:
> >   But with his keener Eye
> >   The Axes edge did try.
> Nor call'd the *Gods* with vulgar spight
> To vindicate his helpless right,
> >   But bow'd his comely Head,
> >   Down, as upon a Bed. (ll. 50-64)

Later, Marvell employed the same strategy in *The Last Instructions to a Painter* when describing the death of the Scottish Captain Archibald Douglas, who perished while defending the English ship *Royal Oak* during the Dutch attack on the Medway in June 1667.[14] The lyrically rendered death of Douglas, a Scot and a Catholic, who stayed at his post even while his ship burned around him, provides a sharp contrast with English commanders who showed little courage or competence that day.

Back on the scaffold outside Whitehall Palace, Marvell's shift into this lyric sketch captures the sympathetic feelings of many on January 30, 1649, when Charles was executed. Eyewitness reports of the king's behavior concur on the salient details: how he wore an extra shirt so as not to shiver on the scaffold that frigid January morning, how he calmly addressed the crowd kept too far back to hear his words clearly, how he asked the executioner whether his hair would be in the way (and how the executioner helped him tuck his hair into a white night cap), how he lay his neck upon the block, and how he said his last prayers before stretching his arms wide to signal his readiness for the axe. Though he does not present all of these details, Marvell captures well Charles' ethos as he "bow'd his comely Head, / Down, as upon a Bed." Marvell calls Charles the "*Royal Actor*," a nod to Charles' love of court masques, and presents him succeeding in an admirable performance of courage and dignity. The passage cannot help but elicit sympathy for the fallen king as it bears witness to the feelings of those who opposed the execution.

The last section of the poem frames this death within the context of the rise of a strong man to power: "This was that memorable hour, / Which first assur'd the forced Pow'r" (ll. 65-66). Ensuing conflicts are inevitable. Marvell then swiftly summarizes subsequent events that prove the inevitability and efficacy of Cromwell. But the speed, brevity, and selectivity of his descriptions result in what have to be the most disingenuous lines of the entire poem: his description of the Irish campaign. Though Cromwell's victorious return from Ireland is the occasion of the ode, Marvell allows the campaign itself only eight lines:

And now the *Irish* are asham'd
To see themselves in one Year tam'd:
  So much one Man can do,
  That does both act and know.
They can affirm his Praises best,
And have, though overcome, confest
  How good he is, how just,
  And fit for highest Trust: (ll. 73-80)

Many people, Irish and English, then and now would take issue with lines 77–80 especially. While Cromwell may have shown a measure of restraint in slaughtering the people of the surrendered city of Clonmel, the same cannot be said of other engagements, especially Drogheda. Marvell's eight-line description of the rebellion and the Irish reaction to it greatly strain credibility in light of the antipathy many Irish people still have for Cromwell. Yet it accords with the English perspective of the time. Marvell's synoptic strategy manages to grasp and render the seemingly supernatural inevitability of Cromwell in such a way that his epideictic requirement to praise can lacquer over uncomfortable truths while at the same time it preserves a self-protective ambivalence. Without this approach, the *Horatian* ode would lose complexity just as much as if the lyrical, near real-time description of Charles I's dignified end on the scaffold were excised. As Worden remarks, the Horatian ode, "rather than taking neither side, takes both," royalist and parliamentary.[15] Marvell's balancing act manages to render how Cromwell must have seemed to political realists at the time.

    Kennelly's *Cromwell: A Poem* differs most dramatically from Marvell's ode in sheer size and scope: Marvell's single poem focuses on one occasion, Cromwell's return from Ireland, with a brief recall of the royal execution; Kennelly's *Cromwell: A Poem* is comprised of 254 poems that range across the entirety of the English imperial occupation of Ireland from the time of the Tudors to the Troubles. Yet like Marvell, Kennelly seizes on a perception that Cromwell acted as a kind of eerie cosmic force capable of otherworldly military success. In contrast to Marvell, he amplifies greatly the consequences of this success by showing in often gory detail the havoc and barbaric ferocity the English wrought upon the Irish directly and through collateral damage. He does not stop there: he presents as well atrocities committed by the Irish rebels against the Protestant English in the same stark light. It is as if Marvell's strategy of presenting Charles I in real-time were extended across the Irish campaign as a whole, the need to tell truths outweighing any epideictic imperative to speak well of the book's titular subject and the imperialistic forces behind it. Kennelly's perspective is informed by English and Irish scholarship uncovering the depth and extent of the atrocities Cromwell and his army perpetrated against the Irish populace.[16] It has the benefit of more than 300 years of hindsight and thus is not an attempt to render a future judgment; rather, *Cromwell: A Poem* suggests the reverberations of this dark history on the present.

Kennelly's conception of his book as a form of dream-as-nightmare informs his method: he describes it as "imagistic, not chronological."[17] Many of the poems are anecdotal. They tell small stories that pixelate the larger events in the English-Irish struggle. Buffún (pronounced "Buffoon"), an Irishman often stuck in Cromwell's company, narrates the whole. But Cromwell speaks in his own voice in quite a few poems, his words in quotation marks, often framed as parts of an ongoing conversation with Buffún. Sometimes he speaks as a seventeenth-century contemporary, but also he floats freely through time, his perspective ranging across the entire nightmare history of English brutality in Ireland, from the days of Edmund Spenser onward.

Kennelly unblinkingly describes English efforts to suppress, punish, and otherwise control the colonized Irish and the resulting counter-violence. Throughout, Cromwell operates as an agent of destruction, an explanation for murderous conflict even decades or centuries after his death. "Men die their different ways," he informs his brother in a letter,

And girls eat cherries
In the Christblessed fields of England.
Some weep. Some have cause. Let weep who will.
Whole floods of brine are at their beck and call.
I have work to do in Ireland. ("Oliver to His Brother," ll. 23-8)

The nature of that work becomes clear in other poems, as "Blood continues to run in the streets / Warmer now than ever it ran in human veins / Because the soldiers have set fire to the city" ("The Soldiers," ll. 12-14). These same soldiers desecrate Catholic churches. Many poems concern specific atrocities. Soldiers rip off the wooden leg of Sir Arthur Aston and beat him to death with it because they were disappointed to find it empty of gold ("That Leg"). Thomas à Wood rescues an Irish lady from a church, only to witness her stabbed with a pike before robbing her ("A Bad Time"). "Massacres, my best men tell me, are fun," Cromwell explains, "The only fun a common soldier has / After six months or a year in the wastes" ("Ghouls," ll. 5-7). In this same poem, he recalls how his soldiers laughed as they rampaged a town: "They had a ball / Splitting the women" (ll. 11-12).

As we read of English horses stabled in Catholic churches, public executions, ritual humiliations, babies ripped from wombs, women half-hung and then buried alive, and the casual way in which a pathological perception of

God's favor can be used to justify all, another theme emerges, one that resonates with readers of Marvell—the notion that Cromwell not only embodies the foibles of a faith-blinded man but also rides some macrocosmic force like the crest of an ocean wave. "Only a man of faith will do," Cromwell tells Buffún, "will rise and do

What he must do, be it smooth or rough.
A man of faith is a ready blade
Cutting through the bluster of himself, his time,
Friends, enemies. He lives for what is true
In himself. I am such a man, not more, not less.
Some say my faith is lies, my best deeds crimes.
I believe in God Who believes in what I do. ("A Man of Faith, ll. 7-14)

Cromwell's English contemporaries are shown to espouse a similar belief:

May God bring Cromwell safe to Dublin
To propagate the Gospel of Christ
Among the barbarous, bloodthirsty Irish
Whose cursing, swearing, drunken ways
Dishonour God by sea and land.

Visit them, Oliver, like God's right hand.
("According to *The Moderate Intelligencer*," ll. 9-14)

Visit them he does, and with an uncanny, deadly success.

Repeatedly the poem references the controversial sieges of Drogheda and Wexford (September and October of 1649), where thousands of troops and civilians were massacred after the towns no longer could defend themselves. While historians debate the extent to which Cromwell was responsible for what some have called the genocidal treatment of the Irish in the 1649–1650 campaign, Kennelly's poem locates the blame squarely within the providential vision espoused by *The Moderate Intelligencer*. Cromwell refers to it numerous times. "At Drogheda," Cromwell explains,

    I saw His judgment executed
Upon these barbarous wretches
Whose hands were thick with innocent blood.
As well as that, God's judgment meant
Less blood would be shed in the future.
The sword is an expert teacher
Like a drowning cry or the smell of burning.

Blood shed in proper quantities prevents
More shedding. Men are quick at learning. ("An Expert Teacher," ll. 6-14)

In another poem, he describes this bloodshed as a kind of surgery, guided by God's hand ("Praise the Lord").

But such wounding, it becomes clear, never ends, nor does it heal. In one of the most poignant poems, "To Think They All Become Silence," Kennelly notes that silence can never be a permanent outcome during partisan strife:

To think the silence can erupt
And battles spill again in a quiet street
And the swelling smell of blood guzzle the air
And the earth drink all, trying to forget
But failing and being forced to stand in the dock
Accused, found guilty, sentenced again to suffer, suffer. (ll. 9-14)

Cromwell's severity, his role in the perpetuation of suffering, predominates in such poems as "A Condition," "Severest Friend," "A Part to Play," "Gas," "Oliver's Prophecies," and "Honest to God, Oliver." As the book progresses, Cromwell comes across both as a righteous and dogmatic seventeenth-century Puritan and a late twentieth-century sociopath who would be perfectly at home in Cormac McCarthy's *Blood Meridian*. At times, Kennelly imagines him in completely ahistorical contexts. In "Manager, Perhaps?" Cromwell speaks like an English capitalist who claims his own "little estate in Kerry" and speculates he might become the manager of an Irish football team called "Drogheda United" (ll. 9-14).

Amid these descriptions of violence, Cromwell and Buffún exchange complaints and meditations as part of what Buffún characterizes as their "fear" / "hate" relationship. "The murderous syllables of your name"—the same name Cromwell celebrates as music elsewhere —"Are the foundation of my nightmare," Buffún says during an extended rant ("A Relationship," 5-6). He offers a candle of resistance in a windstorm of violence, empathy where it all-too-often has ceased to be. In this, he is a stand-in for Kennelly himself. In "The Crowd," Buffún / Kennelly imagines himself as woven through the long history of sectarian strife:

One moment I was nothing to the crowd
The next so helplessly a part of it
I had lost what I had come to regard
As myself. I was drowning in a river of hate
I was a jockey on a serpent's back
I was a grub half-way down a sparrow's throat

I was the look Judas threw at the tree
I was fingers fit to handle a pound-note
I was a voice and a sickness of voices
I was a hunger-striker wrapped in a Union Jack
In the rain on a slippery roof of the city
I was crying out to be judged I was
The crime I was the hangman the rope
I was a prisoner longing for love and pity.

Irish poet Michael Hartnett, in his poem "A Farewell to English," which he dedicated to Kennelly, famously declares that the "act of poetry / is a rebel act" (5.20-21).[18] The "rebel act" of "The Crowd" is, in part, an act of sympathetic engagement, an imagining of all sides of a conflict. But the poem resists Cromwell in another way, too: by rooting itself in a decidedly Irish, not English, poetics. Its structure hearkens to one of the most famous early Irish poems, "The Song of Amergin," in which the ancient Milesian poet Amergin imagines himself as all of Ireland.[19] In Robert Graves' translation, the series of "I am" statements (e.g., "I am a wind of the sea," "I am a wave of the sea," etc.) allow the poet to project his consciousness outward in an act of mystical identification with the land.[20] For Buffún / Kennelly, the analogous "I was" statements enable a similar identification, except this time with a land and people in pain. By the end, the poet becomes the hangman, the noose, and the condemned prisoner longing for a "love and pity" that likely never comes. The form of this poem is an act of resistance; yet in the collection as a whole, any resistance to the Cromwellian nightmare is short-lived. By the end, Cromwell's name has become a verb for sectarian violence even long after his lifetime.[21]

By revisiting a subject famously treated elsewhere, a poet can weigh in on a topic of importance, confident that the subject choice by itself will carry a literary resonance available to educated readers. Readers then can triangulate between that subject and the poets who write about it. In the process, a field of comparison and contrast opens. In Marvell's Horatian ode, written by one who eventually would work for Cromwell, the Irish are "ashamed" to see themselves in "one year tamed" and somehow consider Cromwell "good" and "just." Kennelly's *Cromwell: A Poem* corrects this facile description through a sustained portrayal of the Irish nightmare of history, a nightmare from which Buffún cannot awake. Yet the technique he adopts is similar to the one Marvell uses in his description of Charles on the scaffold: a scenic rendering of episodes in real or nearly real time. The difference, of course, is that Kennelly draws attention to the horrific actions Marvell's account of Cromwell lacquers over. One could call his work a dramatic filling in from the postcolonial margins.

But *Cromwell: A Poem* is also Irish in the way it presents Irish stoicism in the face of ceaseless partisan violence. The book was published in 1983, fifteen years before the Good Friday Agreement of 1998 formally ended hostilities in Northern Ireland. There were five major IRA bombings that year. Kennelly would not have been alone in thinking the conflict would never end. In "A Relationship" Buffún calls himself a "fucked-up Paddy" whose "loathing" for Cromwell (and all he stands for) will never afford him any "rest" (ll. 9-11).

"I sympathize with your plight," Cromwell responds, smiling. "You're fine, though, so / Long as you get it off your chest" (ll. 12-14).

To which Buffún replies, "You really are an understanding / Son-of-a-bitch, Oliver" (ll. 15-16). He then imagines a time when his nightmare finally ends, and he and Cromwell will sit together "Outside a pub on a June afternoon / Sipping infinite pints of cold beer." But as he broods on this strangely idyllic scene, he concludes, echoing Wordsworth, "Our destinies are mingled, late and soon. / But the prospects are not good, I fear." It is a decidedly Irish conclusion that Marvell could never have reached on his own. And it illustrates the expressive potential latent in revisiting a poetic subject from a completely different vantage point.

NOTES

1. Archibald MacLeish, *New Found Land* (Boston, MA: Houghton Mifflin Company, 1930).
2. Andrew Marvell, *The Poems and Letters of Andrew Marvell*, 3rd edition, vol. 1, ed. H. M. Margoliouth, rev. ed. Pierre Legouis and E. E. Duncan-Jones (Oxford: Clarendon Press, 1971).
3. Kenneth Rexroth, *The Complete Poems of Kenneth Rexroth*, ed. Sam Hamill and Bradford Morrow (Port Townsend, WA: Copper Canyon Press, 2003).
4. Archibald MacLeish, *Collected Poems, 1917-1982* (Boston, MA: Houghton Mifflin Company, 1985).
5. Brendan Kennelly, *Cromwell: A Poem* (Newcastle upon Tyne: Bloodaxe Books, 1983, 1987), 6.
6. First printed in Marvell's posthumous *Miscellaneous Poems* (1681), the Horatian ode was cancelled from the majority of copies, most likely for political reasons.
7. All quotations from *Cromwell: A Poem* come from *Familiar Strangers: New & Selected Poems 1960-2004* (Bloodaxe Books, 2004).
8. Nicholas von Maltzahn, *An Andrew Marvell Chronology* (New York: Palgrave Macmillan, 2005), 33–34.
9. Pierre Legouis, *Andrew Marvell: Poet, Puritan, Patriot* (Oxford: Oxford University Press, 1965), 14–15. In *The Poems of Andrew Marvell* (London and New York: Routledge, 2013), Nigel Smith describes Legouis's perspective as the "most resilient and far-sighted judgment in the last sixty years" (271).

10. Blair Worden, *Literature and Politics in Cromwellian England* (Oxford: Oxford University Press, 2007), 12. See Worden's fourth chapter "Marvell in 1650" for an astute account of Marvell's discernment about his political loyalties at the time of writing the ode.

11. Legouis, *Andrew Marvell*, 15; Patterson, *Marvell and the Civic Crown* (Princeton: Princeton University Press, 1978), 57–58.

12. Patterson, *Marvell and the Civic Crown*, 59. The quoted phrases come from the second part of Marvell's *The Rehearsal Transpros'd*. See The Rehearsal Transpros'd *and* The Rehearsal Transpros'd: The Second Part, ed. D. I. B. Smith (Oxford: Oxford University Press, 1971), 160–161.

13. John Malcolm Wallace, *Destiny His Choice: The Loyalism of Andrew Marvell* (Cambridge: Cambridge University Press, 1969), 101–102.

14. Marvell included this same account in the later satire *The Loyal Scot*.

15. Worden, *Literature and Politics*, 86.

16. In addition to various unnamed archival accounts, Kennelly cites the following books as the primary sources of his understanding of Cromwell's Irish campaign: J. H. Merle D' Aubigné, *The Protector: A Vindication* (Edinburgh: Oliver and Boyd, 1847); Thomas Carlyle, *Oliver Cromwell's Letters and Speeches: With* Elucidations, 5 vols. (London: Chapman and Hall, 1870); Denis Murphy, *Cromwell in Ireland: A History of Cromwell's Irish Campaign* (Dublin: M.H. Gill and Son, 1883); W. E. H. Lecky, *A History of Ireland in the Eighteenth Century* (London: Longmans Green and Company, 1896); C. H. Firth, *Cromwell's Army: A History of the English Soldier During the Civil Wars, the Commonwealth, and the Protectorate* (London: Methuen & Co., 1902); Dorothy MacArdle, *Tragedies of Kerry* (Dublin: The Emton Press, 1924); and Christopher Hill, *God's Englishman: Oliver Cromwell and the English Revolution* (London: Weidenfeld & Nicholson, 1970). See Kennelly, "Note," *Cromwell*, 6.

17. Kennelly, *Cromwell: A Poem*, 6.

18. Michael Hartnett, *Collected Poems* (Loughcrew, Ireland: The Gallery Press, 2001).

19. For an extended account of this poem, see Robert Graves, *The White Goddess* (New York: Farrar, Straus and Giroux, 1948; ren. 1975), 205–222.

20. John Montague notes that Graves' translation of Amergin's poem incorporates elements from a similar poem by the Welsh bard Taliesin. See *The Faber and Faber Book of Irish Verse* (London: Faber and Faber, 1974), 44. Taliesin's poem, "The Battle of the Trees," has been newly translated by Gwyneth Lewis and Rowan Williams in *The Book of Taliesin: Poems of Warfare and Praise in Enchanted Britain* (London: Penguin Classics, 2019).

21. See "The Voice of Us All" and "Vacancy."

Chapter 4

Modal Resemblances

"Metaphysical," "Meditative," and the Poetry of Donne, W. B. Yeats, and Ronald Johnson

Any shadows cast when a modern poet revisits a subject well-known in a metaphysical poem is bound to vary in intensity, depending on how overtly the modern poet nods to the prior poet or poem. Marvell's shadow, for instance, is more obvious in MacLeish's "You, Andrew Marvell" than in Kennelly's *Cromwell: A Poem*. Partly this variance is a consequence of poetic intention and/or compositional circumstance: consideration of Marvell's poems more obviously precipitated the kind of reflection MacLeish wanted to do, whereas Marvell's Horatian ode lacked that same engendering spark for Kennelly. If anything, the Irish poet would have considered the ode a product of English imperialistic discourse. As a result, Marvell's shadow registers less distinctly in his poem. Indeed, a reader unfamiliar with Marvell's poem would not perceive any shadow at all. Chapter 1 began with the most obvious manifestations of a modern poet's engagement with seventeenth-century poetry: direct reference through allusion and echo. This chapter will explore the opposite end of this intertextual spectrum: the modern poet who neither references a prior poet or poems nor dwells on a shared subject but who instead adopts mode or approach resembling how a metaphysical poet typically or famously proceeds. Are any shadows cast through such a modal resemblance, or is the sun now directly overhead?

My test case will be two poets as seemingly far apart in a formal sense as one might guess: Donne and American poet Ronald Johnson, whose predilection for experimentalism in his found, concrete, and projectivist poetry issued from different aesthetic.[1] Johnson's masterpiece *ARK*, which he began in 1970 and completed in 1990, has been described as a protean "American epic" in the tradition of Louis Zukofsky and Charles Olson, a postmodern pastiche, and notably as a "metaphysical poem," in the words of Guy Davenport.[2] That last term, "metaphysical," cannot help but stir our curiosity in the present context. In describing *ARK* as metaphysical, Davenport appears to have had in mind the same philosophical emphasis as the first critic to link Donne with metaphysics as a signature interest: John Dryden, who, in *The Discourse Concerning the Original and Progress of Satire* (1693), asserts that Donne "affects the metaphysics" unnaturally in his satires and love poetry.[3] By the time Johnson began writing *ARK*, as we have seen, "metaphysical poetry" had come to encompass a variety of characteristics and commitments beyond simply a subject matter (metaphysics). For Joseph E. Duncan, writing in 1959, its primary characteristics are a distinctive relationship between logic and metaphor; an investment in theories of correspondences; an emphasis on verbal wit; a preoccupation with the "problem of personal expression"; a close relationship between thought and feeling; a tolerance for various kinds of ambiguity borne from what seem conflicting attitudes (playfulness and seriousness, for example); and a commitment to integrate "life and learning."[4] Sona Raiziss, drawing heavily but not exclusively from Eliot, defines it in similar terms:

> Metaphysical poetry, then, is the attempt to reconcile the body of the world with the universal mind. Its poet strives to resolve the paradox inherent in any experience by evoking simultaneously its emotional and intellectual powers. His image or his poem is the passionate endeavor toward union between the conceptual and the sensuous.[5]

For Earl Miner, writing at the end of the 1960s, the "chief 'radical' of Metaphysical poetry" is what he calls its "private mode," its treatment of "time and space" in ways "describable" through dramatic narrative, argumentation, and definition yet distinctive from the "social and public modes of other poetry written in modern English before the late eighteenth century and the Romantic poets."[6] The remit of such definitions in the years before Johnson began writing *ARK* was wide enough to include poets as distinctive as Eliot and Stevens, Wylie and Sitwell, and Ransom and Empson.

Johnson, more obviously indebted to Charles Olsen and Louis Zukofsky, resembles none of these poets. Nevertheless, one can see why Davenport called *ARK* "metaphysical," given its preoccupation with considerations of being, causation, and perception. Then, too, the ambitiousness of Johnson's work calls to mind the seventeenth-century poets who conceived of poems within intricately wrought overarching structures. Johnson memorably fashioned his prior poem *RADI OS* directly from the first four books of *Paradise Lost*, crossing out all the words he didn't want so that what remained was unmistakably his. Originally, Johnson intended *RADI OS* to serve as the fourth part of *ARK* but then published it separately in 1977. While *RADI OS* is

Johnson's version of a rewriting of *Paradise Lost* in a manner similar to portions of Zukofsky's *A*, a recent collection of essays posits *ARK* as "Paradise Found."[7] Johnson describes *ARK* as an "architecture" "fitted together with shards of language, in a kind of cement of music" that is "[b]ased on trinities, its cornerstones the eye, the ear," and "the mind."[8]

Indeed, the overt structured-ness of *ARK*—its identity as a collection of parts, long in-the-making and fashioned to form a larger whole or unity—is reminiscent of Herbert's *The Temple* in architectural ambition. As with the three parts of *The Temple*—"The Church-porch," "The Church," and "The Church Militant"—Johnson analogously laid out his *ARK* in three books figured in architectural terms, thirty-three poems each: part one, *The Foundations*, consists of thirty-three "beams"; part two, *The Spires*, of thirty-three "spires"; and part three, *The Ramparts*, of thirty-three "arches." Rather than conceive of the poem as an "argument" or "diatribe," Johnson thought of it as a "structure" or "artifact," a "veritable shell of the chambered nautilus, sliced and polished, bound for Ararat unknown." As if the artifactual design of *ARK*, framed as it is according to a biblical conceit (an Ark bound for Ararat), were not enough to recall the seventeenth-century poets, *ARK* additionally follows a temporal progression worthy of them as well. As Johnson describes it, the beams are laid out from "sunrise to noon"; the spires finish "at sunset with only Mt. Ossa set on Pelion reflecting back light"; and the arches enact a "night of the soul."[9] Much here invites comparison, at least from a wide-angle perspective.

When we turn to the unfolding of individual poems within *ARK*, however—those beams, spires, and arches—"metaphysical" falters as a descriptor: the term emphasizes a presumed content, a set of questions or concerns, rather than a way or a set of ways of proceeding. Johnson's choice of subjects within individual poems most often differs greatly from those of the seventeenth-century metaphysical poets. Even so, one can detect a certain resemblance of approach. Mindful of the distinction between content and approach, as well as of the heavy influence of Donne and Herbert especially on Hopkins, Yeats, Eliot, Stevens, Pound, and those who followed them, Louis L. Martz in the 1950s and early 1960s proposed that the term "meditative" possessed more descriptive value than "metaphysical" for what happens in a metaphysical poem. Martz's argument proceeds from a detailed study of the impact of early modern formal meditative practices on religious poetry. The meditative poem, in his words, "records" the "creation" of a "self that is, ideally, one with itself, with other human beings, with created nature, and with the supernatural."[10] It encourages a certain range of interior movements:

> a meditative poem is a work that creates an interior drama of the mind; this dramatic action is usually (though not always) created by some form of

self-address, in which the mind grasps firmly a problem or situation deliberately evoked by the memory, brings it forward toward the full light of consciousness, and concludes with a moment of illumination, where the speaker's self has, for a time, found an answer to its conflicts.[11]

As a working through of one's intellectual, spiritual, and/or emotional urgencies, the poem, "wrought out as part of a search for the common basis of humanity," emerges typically in the language of the poet speaking to himself or herself.[12] It "must have common speech as a basis, yet being also part of a personal quest, the language must also express that one, essential personality that is every man's unique possession." So defined, Martz perceives a continuity between early modern meditative poems and those of his twentieth-century contemporaries. The roots of the modern meditative poem reach deep into the past.

In the late sixteenth and early seventeenth centuries, Martz demonstrates, the most influential English religious lyricists, following the lead of the Jesuit martyr Robert Southwell, SJ, transferred into their poems structures and techniques they learned from formal meditative practices. Among the most prominent of these was the Ignatian meditation from *The Spiritual Exercises* of St. Ignatius Loyola, especially the three-part sequence of the meditation proper. Such a meditation begins with a composition of place—"a practice of enormous importance for religious poetry"—in which the person meditating visualizes a place and event of deep spiritual significance—the Nativity, say, or the Passion—by imagining specific sensory details.[13] It then ventures into an analysis of points that addresses what the meditator desires from the meditation. While the composition of place relies on memory (memories of biblical stories as well as memories of everyday experience, the details of which bring remembered events to imaginative life), the analysis of points requires the application of understanding in an effort to reconcile what is learned and felt through visualization with divine principles. The analysis culminates in a colloquy with God. An action of the will, the colloquy is the "climax, the end and aim, of the whole exercise" during which the "soul thus reformed is lifted up to speak with God in colloquy and to hear God speak to man in turn."[14] Martz notes that St. Ignatius, Luis de la Puente, St. François de Sales, and others all acknowledged that colloquies could be addressed to a variety of persons apart from a member of the Trinity.[15] The important consideration is that the direct address as a last step offers a focal point for the actions of the will.

In the hands of poets, the art of meditation combined with other learned habits—logic and rhetoric, for example—in generative ways. For Donne, the Ignatian meditation held a special appeal. In his Holy Sonnets, Donne preferred the Italian sonnet form to the English sonnet, and as Martz explains, the "threefold structure" of the Ignatian meditation "easily accords with the traditional 4-4-6 division of the Petrarchan sonnet, and thus provides a particularly interesting illustration of the way in which poetic tradition may be fertilized and developed by the meditative tradition."[16] Holy Sonnet 7 from the Revised Sequence ("Spitt in my face yee Iewes") follows this threefold structure exactly. The first four lines powerfully locate the speaker at the scene of the Crucifixion:

Spitt in my face yee Iewes, and peirce my side,
  Buffett, and scoff, scourge, and crucifie mee,
For I haue sinn'd, and sinn'd, and only hee
  Who could doe none iniquitie hath dyed. (ll. 1-4)

The next four lines analyze the situation by venturing into theological considerations:

But by my Death cannot bee satisfied
  My sinnes which pass the Iewes impietie;
They kill'd once an inglorious man, but I
  Crucifie him daily, being nowe glorified. (ll. 5-8)

That last thought—the speaker's daily Crucifixion of Christ—then launches a colloquy, in which the speaker requests an affective change within and through which he expresses a more gainful understanding of the lessons learned:

Oh lett mee then his strange loue still admire,
  Kings pardon, but hee bore our punnishment;
And Iacob came cloathed in vile harsh attire,
  But to supplant, and with gainfull intent;
God cloath'd himself in vile mans fleash that soe
  Hee might bee weake enough to suffer woe. (ll. 9-14)

The three-fold structure directs the speaker to arrive at a different mindset. Holy Sonnet 4 of the Revised Sequence ("At the round Earths imagin'd corners") also issues from an apparent fusion of Petrarchan and Ignatian structures. This time, the first four lines project the meditation to the Apocalypse, and the next four, in imagining the array of souls returning to their bodies for final judgment, catalogues the many ways death can occur. Call it an analysis of mortal fragility during a period with a high mortality rate. Then, in the colloquy, mindful of his profound unreadiness, the speaker calls out to God to postpone this whole process:

But lett them sleepe Lord, and mee mourne a space
  For if aboue all these, my sinnes abound
'Tis late to aske aboundance of thy grace
  When wee are there; here on this lowly ground
Teach mee howe to repent, for thats as good
  As if thou'hadst seal'd my Pardon with thy bloud. (ll. 9-14)

Once again the Ignatian structure encourages a meditative process that leads to new or renewed insights for the meditator.

Martz treats Donne's "Good friday / Made as I was Rideing westward, that daye," Donne's enactment of a spiritual reorientation while traveling to Montgomery Castle on Good Friday, April 2, 1613, as a touchstone example of the poetic rendering of an Ignatian meditation.[17] Other scholars have likened its structure to a painted triptych;[18] a symmetrical nine-part arrangement of lines;[19] a "Protestant occasional meditation upon experience";[20] a "circle" containing "nine balanced parts" like the "nine ordered spheres" of the Ptolemaic system of the universe;[21] a "highly compressed sequence of three sonnets that leads, as most Petrarchan sonnet sequences do, only to ongoing desire and irresolution";[22] a four-part "dramatization";[23] and the traditional homiletic tripartite *division* of a sermon.[24] Regardless of how else we construe its structure, however, few would deny that its central movement involves an interrogation, perhaps even a refashioning, of the self in response to the pressures of an occasion. In addition, the poem accords perfectly with the Ignatian structure of composition of place, analysis, and colloquy.

Technically speaking, as Martz notes, the first twelve lines of the Good Friday poem enact a "composition by similitude," an acceptable variance of the composition of place. In another sense, however, the terms of his similitude locate Donne on a cosmic scale, one of the grandest scales an early modern poet could imagine:

Let Mans soule bee a Sphere, and then, in this
Th'Intelligence that moues, devotion is.
And as the other Spheres, by being growne
Subiect to forreine motions, loose their owne
And being by others hurried euery daye
Scarce in a yeare their naturall forme obey
Pleasure, or Buisiness, soe our soules admit,
For their first mover, and are whirl'd by it;
Hence is't that I am carried towards the west,
This day, when my soules forme, bends towards the East. (ll. 1-10)

Martz believes these lines "precisely set the problem" of the ensuing poem: "profane motives carry the soul away from God, while the soul's essence ('forme'), *devotion*, longs for another, greater object."[25] Donne composed the poem while he was intensely weighing the prospect of entering the English priesthood. This also was a period when the heliocentric theory of Copernicus was receiving substantial support from the theories and discoveries of Kepler and Galileo. I shall have more to say about these in a few pages. For now, however, it is enough to notice that Donne's astronomical analogy for his soul introduces both the tension between his physical movement westward and a spiritual pressure to look eastward as well as a tension between what should be the soul's constant devotional motion and the external obligations that alter or obstruct it.[26]

By traveling on a holy day, Donne, in theory, cannot undertake the proper devotion he should be doing. So his analysis of points cleverly recreates the Crucifixion through a series of questions and thereby engages the "traditional paradoxes of the scene":

Yet dare I almost bee glad I doe not see
That Spectacle, of too much weight for mee.
Whoe sees Gods face, that is self life, must dye;
What a death were it then to see God dye?
It made his own Lieutenant Nature shrinck;
It made his footstoole crack; And the Sun winke.
Could I behold those hands which span the Poles
And turne all Spheres at once pierc'd with those holes?
Could I behold that endless height, which is
Zenith to vs, and to our Antipodis
Humbled belowe vs? Or that bloud, which is
The seate of all our soules, if not of his
Make durt of Dust, or that flesh which was worne
By God for his apparell, ragg'd, and torne?
If on these things I durst not looke, durst I
Vppon his miserable Mother cast mine eye
Whoe was Gods partner heere, and furnish'd thus
Half of that Sacrifice which ransom'd vs? (ll. 15-32)

This passage, in effect, is a second composition of place even as Donne questions his worthiness to perform devotional work. In an intriguing reading of this section of the poem in particular, Piers Brown explains that the "speaker's mind moves through the stations of the cross, but does so backwards, processing the moment of Christ's death, through the agony on the cross, to the initial scourging," a reverse ordering that mimics the traveler's own "physically backward" movement from east to west.[27] The memorial reconstruction of the Crucifixion thus offers a "stable locus in which Christ can be seen" to counter the "eccentric movement of the imagination."[28] After his de facto account of Christ on the Cross, the ten lines of Donne's colloquy balance the ten lines of the poet's composition by similitude, thereby bringing the meditation to a close formally and devotionally:

Though these things as I ride bee from mine eye
They'are present yet vnto my Memorie
For that lookes towards them, and thou look'st towards mee
O Saviour, as thou hang'st vpon the tree;
I turne my back to thee, but to receiue
Corrections; till thy mercies bid thee leaue
O thinke mee worth thine Anger, Punnish mee
Burne off my Rusts, and my deformitye,
Restore thine Image soe much by thy grace
That thou maist knowe mee, and Ile turne my face. (ll. 33-42)

From the oddly calm and confident analogy of soul and Ptolemaic sphere in the opening lines, through the vexed, graphic portrayal of Christ on the Cross in the middle lines, to Donne's impassioned request to "Burne off" his "rusts" and "deformity" and "Restore" Christ's "Image" in his soul in the final lines, Donne dramatizes a progressively inward movement that seeks resolution and new understanding. The meditation is at once intensely intellectual and intensely introspective—intellectual, in drawing on cosmology, philosophy, and theology to such a degree as to invite a multitude of interpretations; introspective, in that the poet's horseback ride hardly registers as a sensory experience.[29] Martz again:

> Thus similitude, visualization, theological analysis, and the eloquent motions of the will have all fused into one perfectly executed design—a meditation expressing the state of devotion which results from the integration of the threefold Image of God: memory, understanding, will. And thus once again the process of meditation appears to have made possible a poem which displays this "articulated structure," this "peculiar blend of passion and thought": the perfect equipoise of a carefully regulated, arduously cultivated skill.[30]

As a product of a process of mind, the meditative poem need not issue from a single meditative tradition. Indeed, the genre of meditative poetry, as Martz defines it, includes a variety of poets (e.g., Dickinson, Yeats, and Stevens) significantly distant from early modern Catholic practices. Nevertheless, in

> certain eras, under certain conditions of distress and disorder, some poets will inevitably be led to cultivate a unity of interior life through processes of thought

that bear some degree of similarity to the meditative exercises of the seventeenth century.[31]

The Ignatian meditative structure in particular surfaces where one might least expect it. Yeats is a good example. Deeply spiritual yet disconnected from anything like the major Judeo-Christian traditions, Yeats essentially created his own theosophical religion, encapsulated in the two editions of *A Vision* (1925, 1937). Nevertheless, some of his most notable poems achieve completion through this threefold structure, as if its fulfillment were tantamount to completing them. For example, the earliest draft of what would become "The Stare's Nest by My Window," the fifth part of "Meditations in Time of Civil War," shows little indication of this structure:

>   Civil War
>   I
> The Bees build in crevices
>   loosened
>   ~~Of loosening masonry~~ & there
> The mother birds bring grub and flies
>   ~~Come to my window bees:~~ O honey bees
> ~~and Build And~~ build in the empty nest of the stare
>   Come.[32]

The beginnings of a description are here, along with a first take of what would be a chorus throughout the poem: "Come build in the empty nest of the stare." Yet the draft of this first stanza and those following it lack a firm meditative focus as well as sufficient development. Through ensuing drafts, however, Yeats deepened his meditative focus. The poem started as four numbered stanzas, but by the end of his compositional process, Yeats eliminated the stanza numbers in a final act of unification. In the final version, published in *The Tower* (1928), the first stanza composes a place—a description of where stares build a nest in the masonry of Thoor Ballylee:

> The bees build in the crevices
> Of loosening masonry, and there
> The mother birds bring grubs and flies.
> My wall is loosening; honey-bees,
> Come build in the empty house of the stare. (ll. 1-5)[33]

You can still go to Thoor Ballylee and see the spot where the stares built their nest.

The next two stanzas meditate on being closed in during the Irish Civil War. They showcase the uncertainty of non-combatants who have hunkered down: "somewhere / A man is killed, or a house burned, / Yet no clear fact to be discerned" (ll. 7-9). Each stanza ends with a refrain: "Come build in the empty house of the stare" (ll. 5, 10, 15, 20). In the last stanza, the analysis ends in a one-and-a-half-line colloquy to the honey bees:

We had fed the heart on fantasies,
The heart's grown brutal from the fare;
More substance in our enmities
Than in our love; O honey-bees,
Come build in the empty house of the stare. (ll. 16-20)

By grounding the poem—and meditation—with a focusing description at the start, Yeats authorizes his inclusion of general statements. His direct address to the honey bees sounds a sure concluding note. The cumulative effect is the articulation of a mind that has succeeded in integrating several emotions into a resonant, even uncanny commentary on a particular moment. By addressing the bees in this way, the poet pleads for a return to a lost normalcy and a lost connection to a more natural state of affairs.

The threefold structure is so reliable it recurs in some of Yeats's other notable poems. "The Wild Swans at Coole" begins with a description of the fifty-nine swans swimming on Lough Coole in the "October twilight" (l. 3). Then the description becomes a reflection on the poet's aging and the swans' symbolic significance before culminating in a question: "Among what rushes will they build, / By what lake's edge or pool / Delight men's eyes when I awake some day / To find they have flown away?" (ll. 27-30). It is not immediately clear whether the poet asks this of himself or of someone or something else. But the question operates like a colloquy to provide closure. Other poems similarly enacting this threefold structure—"The Second Coming," for example, and "Leda and the Swan"—also end with a question in this same way. Meanwhile, "Sailing to Byzantium" extends what would be the colloquy in an Ignatian meditation across half the length of the poem. Stanza one describes the poet's idealized vision of Byzantium, that country for the young, while stanza two defines the enervating effects of old age and the power of the soul to nonetheless still "clap its hands and sing" (l. 11). The last two stanzas begin as a colloquy to the sages to whom Yeats appeals for instruction: "O sages standing in God's holy fire / As in the gold mosaic of a wall, / Come from the holy fire, perne in a gyre, / And be the singing-masters of my soul" (ll. 17-20). The presence of the threefold structure in poems such as these is one but not the only reason why much of Yeats accords with Martz's definition of meditative poetry. It demonstrates how the meditative mode of Donne et al. can transcend religious commitments or affiliations as a resource for poetic making for any poet who chooses to use it.

Ronald Johnson would balk at the suggestion that his meditations in *ARK* derived from the meditative treatises informing Martz's account of the meditative poem. In the afterward of *ARK*, after citing Pound, Williams, Zukofsky, and Olson as influences, he recalls his conscious desire to chart a new poetic course: "If my confreres wanted to write a work with all history in its maw, I wished, from the beginning, to start all over again, attempting to know nothing but a will to create, and matter at hand," he writes. "William Blake would be a guiding spirit: his advice to pay attention to every moment: the very lightning, then thunder: a voice out of a cloud"[34] (311). Nevertheless, as with Yeats, several poems throughout *ARK* follow the familiar threefold structure. Take "ARK 53, STARSPIRE," for example, a poem dedicated to R. Buckminster Fuller. Like other poems, *ARK* is concrete: it assumes the shape of a suspended crystal. It begins with a pyramid of asterisks—typographical stars—one, then two, then three—that cap, like the tip of a crystal, twenty-eight tercets, each line of which almost never measures longer than two words. The first four tercets of the spire capture the following Fuller quote, which precipitates Johnson's own thoughts:

```
    *
   * *
  * * *
```
"The sight
of a great
suspended,

swinging
crystal,
huge, lucid,

lustrous,
a block
of light,

flashing
back every
impression."
(ll. 1-12)

What follows, then, might be described as a three-part meditation like Donne's or Yeats's but in the distinctive style of Johnson. Not surprisingly, the poet begins by composing a scene in the imperative mood—a quiet countryside.

>   Conjure lesson
>   from the
>   ground up,
>
>   mortal coil
>   lock horn
>   galactic swarm,
>
>   domed horizon
>   measureless
>   as Zion.
>
>   Plain feats
>   lept fact
>   incarnate day—
>
>   elephant delicate
>   trunk up
>   grassblade &
>
>   untold greenery
>   stood sawn
>   geometry
>
>   while cliffed
>   whole countryside
>   mount gust
>
>   an Acropolis
>   still told
> withholding reason. (ll. 13-36)

His deliberate omission of connectives is characteristic of the voice throughout *ARK*. Some passages sound like pidgin at times, as he drops articles, conjunctions, and transitions and leaps from one association to another. Donne, too, has his moments of compressed syntax, which can strain comprehension if not considered carefully: "Though parents grudge, and you, w'are met / And cloistered in these living walls of Jet," for instance.[35] But Johnson's lines more regularly tax readers in this way. They can take time to get used to. Even so, his diction in tercets five through twelve (just quoted) succeeds in conveying a sense of pleasure and/or wonder in the act of taking in a view of the enormous countryside beneath the "measureless" "domed horizon" of sky. His opening composes a place.

Johnson then shifts from imperative command—"Conjure lesson / from the / ground up"—to direct statement in the middle section of the poem. He analyzes what he has just perceived, just called forth, by referring to Greek and Egyptian mythology, zoology, husbandry, geology, and legal discourse:

> Any spade so
>   terms soil
>   in season:
>
> swans, worlds
>   withstood
>   Odysseus,
>
>   Osiris lift
>   limb by
> sparkling limb,
>
>   bold Helen
> died and gone,
>   again.
>
>   As mole toil
>   to loam
> Antarctic pole,
>
> least testament
>   expound
>   plowed clay
>
>   take place!
>   of more
>   than flesh.
>   (ll. 37-57)

His approach functions like a cryptic analysis of points in an Ignatian meditation, an attempt to understand the scene at hand, in this case through a tissue of allusions loading significance into the ordinary soil.

Finally, the poem concludes with another discursive shift to a series of imperative commands: "Sever the / ever veiled / however evolved . . . ," "be chariot / of Deity . . . ," "Remove above . . . ." No colloquy to any Divine, the way it would be in one of Donne's religious poems, the final section nevertheless draws its energy—as Donne's colloquies do—from the urgency of direct address, this time directed at a self that presumably can be transformed through future action. The poem concludes,

Remove above.
  Vault earth
    devised

   at once,
  announce full
    Arcady.
     * * *
      * *
       *
(ll. 79-84)

The last three lines of the poem form an upside-down tercet of asterisk-stars, the mirror image of the first three lines. As above, so below.

Johnson nowhere alludes to Donne or to Yeats in *ARK*, to say nothing of St. Ignatius Loyola. Nevertheless, the three-part structure of "ARK 53, STARSPIRE" belongs to that species of meditative poetry that works through such a structure to achieve a sense of unity or new understanding. The poem bears a family resemblance to the other similarly structured poems.

This structural similarity is not the only way in which the operations in some poems in *ARK* resemble those of Donne's poems, however. Johnson's mental action, like Donne's, often draws on an impressively diverse range of knowledge. His poems are loaded with references to astronomy, anatomy, biology, music, alchemy, mythology, history, philosophy, and the Bible. The meditative mode of both Johnson and Donne shares this commonality: both meditate through their learning, which furnishes each with the necessary imagery, metaphors, similes, and ideas to develop their lines of inquiry. Both are fascinated by scientific debates and discoveries, for example, and so both appropriate imagery from the sciences as part of their meditative efforts. The first ten lines of Donne's Good Friday poem, to return to that obvious example, concentrate several scientific and theological frames of reference in an introductory analogy that seems much more elaborate than Donne's situation otherwise calls for. Here are the lines again:

Let Mans soule bee a Sphere, and then, in this
Th'Intelligence that moues, devotion is.
And as the other Spheres, by being growne
Subiect to forreine motions, loose their owne
And being by others hurried euery daye
Scarce in a yeare their naturall forme obey
Pleasure, or Buisiness, soe our soules admit,
For their first mover, and are whirl'd by it;
Hence is't that I am carried towards the west,
This day, when my soules forme, bends towards the East. (ll. 1-10)

Donne's analogy concentrates on the centuries old conversation about the divergence between the annual motion of the fixed stars and the motions of the "wandering stars" or planets. By invoking "intelligences," the lowest form of angels, charged with keeping the inner spheres of the cosmos in motion, he relies on the Christianized version of the Aristotelian-Ptolemaic universe. But his emphasis on "forreine motions," to which he likens pleasure or business, draws attention to the problem of the retrograde motion of the planets, which preoccupied Copernicus and was a key element in the construction of his heliocentric system. Kepler's first two laws of planetary motion, which Donne was aware of, along with the telescopic revelations of Galileo's *Sidereus Nuncius*, further cast in jeopardy the Aristotelian-Ptolemaic system Donne's opening lines assume.[36] In 1612, Galileo's *Letters on Sunspots*, which was published in Rome in 1613, provided evidence that Venus had phases, like the moon, which delivered a further death blow to the Aristotelian-Ptolemaic system of Sacrobosco's *De Sphaera*, though it would be quite a few years yet until that death was formally recognized throughout Europe.[37] A sense of the same uncertainty that caused Donne to declare the previous year that the "new Philosophy cals all in doubt, / The Element of fire is quite put out"[38] creeps into his account of erratic celestial motions here. Indeed, the presence of this uncertainty might well have informed his choice to start his meditation in just this way. Here is a classic example of the way in which Donne's meditative mode required thinking through the urgencies of his learning.

Equally immersed in the scientific thought of *his* time, Johnson also thought with and through scientific ideas he learned, and this process recurs throughout *ARK*. "BEAM 11, FINIAL," for example, includes a meditation on the sun. Notice how, in the following passage, Johnson marshals several scientific ideas to define the wonder of the sun on both a macrocosmic and microcosmic scale:

> It is said the sun blinds us because it is a HOLE
>   in the three-dimensional scenery.
> —and light "diminishes in inverse proportion to the square
>   of the distance"
>   but the imaginary sphere
>   it illuminates, increases in the same
>   proportion—
>
> Its Zodiacal Light is in the form of a lens
>   the lash of which intersects earth.
>
> It is one-ten-thousandth the diameter of its "system"
>   as is ovum to human.
>   VISION is seeing as the sun sees.
>
>   "midway between the absolute
>   and man"
>
>   (Fludd said)
>
> The Mind & Eye, the solar system, galaxy
>   are spirals coiled from periphery
>   —i.e. Catherine wheels—
>   of their worlds.
>   Whorls.
>   (ll. 16-35)

Soon after describing the optical effects of looking at the sun (afterimage as a "HOLE"), Johnson quotes Newton's formulation of the inverse square law to define both the size of the "sphere" of the solar system as well as the degrees of solar illumination within it. By referencing the inverse square law *and* "imaginary sphere," he yokes ideas from either side of the early modern scientific revolution. He makes a similar move when juxtaposing a Robert Fludd quotation about the daimon with his own description of galactic spirals.[39] The quoted passage launches from mere description to poetic rendering when Johnson connects the sun with the human body through analogy and metaphor. He starts be likening "Zodiacal Light," or false dawn, to a lens, which prepares the way a few lines later for presenting "Mind & Eye" as part of a system of light and seeing that encompasses the solar system and the galaxy to which all belong. In between, he crafts a startling analogy: the relative size of the sun and the sphere of the solar system are analogous to the relative size of ovum to (presumably) fully developed human body. "VISION is seeing as the sun sees," he declares (l. 27),[40] and we have just glimpsed what such seeing entails: a capacity to see large and small at once as if on the same plane. The analogy has a Donnean feel to it. Or perhaps it is more accurate to say that the meditative mode of both poets, requiring as it does healthy doses of facts from diverse domains, can produce similar effects when enacted by poets sensitive to the resemblances between even apparently disparate things.

Though Donne was experimental in creating stanza forms, Johnson's poems encompass a wider territory of forms on the page. The beams, spires, and arches appear in prose, poetic lines, concrete shapes, diagrams, images, numbered lists, and other typographical confections. "BEAM 16, THE VOICES," for instance, includes a diagram of a plinth of Hermes with an erect phallus. "BEAM 5" ends with part of a staff of musical notation. "BEAM 25, A BICENTENNIAL" begins with the praise of a single cell and presents a step-by-step illustration of cell division. "BEAM 18" is merely a Xeroxed copy of a right-hand print. "ARK 55, THE ABC SPIRE" contains word clusters of the entire alphabet, culminating in a single word, "Zion," shaped as a box made from two lines, two letters in each line. Throughout the poem, in the selection of words, one can detect an effort to move forward in a meditative direction. Consider the second pair of strophes, built from the letter "B":

behind   beheld
beyond   belief
beings   belong

become   beacon
enable   belfry
baffle   bedlam

These twelve words trace a movement from shedding "belief" to a sense of belonging, assumed in luminous terms—"become beacon"—that promises to empower a resistance to the "bedlam" of the presumably modern world, as Johnson experienced it. Stylistically, a poem like this differs greatly from Donne's. Nevertheless, the trajectory of reasoning is similar to Donne's in some of that poet's moods.

A meditative mode presides throughout the "the chambered nautilus" that is *ARK*. Even in spatially or linguistically playful beams, spires, and arches, Johnson's thoughts move in a meditative direction toward a sense of integration or understanding as Martz defines it. Seen in this light, *ARK* comes across as the result of a sustained, decades-long effort of a poet working to define the cosmos and his place in it in ways we can recognize when reading the seventeenth-century metaphysical poets, especially Donne. Does this mean we can discern a Donnean shadow here? Perhaps not in the sense of direct poetic influence but perhaps so in the realm of poetic resemblance. Such is the nature of shadows at noon. At the very least, the term "meditative" merits inclusion in the lexicon of ways we are slowly coming to recognize Johnson's achievement as a notable American poet.

NOTES

1. My thanks to my colleagues poet Serena Chopra for bringing Johnson's poetry to my attention, and physicist David Boness, who, for years now, has been my sure sounding board on all matters related to science and the early modern scientific revolutions.

2. The first two are common descriptions. Eric Murphy Selinger describes *ARK* as "Garden of Revelation" (see his essay by the same name in *Ronald Johnson: Life and Works* [Orono, Maine: The National Poetry Foundation, 2008]), 323–342. Ross Hair describes it in terms of bricolage in *Ronald Johnson's Modernist Collage Poetry* (New York: Palgrave Macmillan, 2010). Davenport describes it as a "metaphysical poem" on the outside blurb of the Flood edition.

3. Dryden, *Of Dramatic Poesy and Other Critical Essays*, vol. 2, ed. George Watson (London: J. M. Dent & Sons Ltd, 1962), 76.

4. Duncan, *The Revival of Metaphysical Poetry: The History of a Style* (Minneapolis: University of Minnesota Press, 1959), 6–28. For more on the tradition of *serio ludere* ("playing seriously"), see Thomas Healy, "Playing Seriously in Renaissance Writing," in *Renaissance Transformations: The Making of English Writing (1550-1650)*, ed. Margaret Healy and Thomas Healy (Edinburgh: Edinburgh University Press, 2009), 15–31.

5. Raiziss, *The Metaphysical Passion: Seven Modern American Poets and the Seventeenth-Century Tradition* (Philadelphia: University of Pennsylvania Press, 1952), 10.

6. Miner, *The Metaphysical Mode from Donne to Cowley* (Princeton: Princeton University Press, 1969), x-xi.

7. Joel Bettridge and Eric Murphy Selinger, eds. *Ronald Johnson: Life and Works* (Orono, Maine: The National Poetry Foundation, 2008).

8. Johnson, *ARK* (Chicago: Flood Editions, 2013), 312. Unless otherwise noted, all quotations from Johnson (both poems and prose) come from this edition, cited parenthetically.

9. Johnson, *ARK*, 312–313.

10. Martz, *The Poetry of Meditation: A Study in English Religious Literature of the Seventeenth Century* (New Haven, CT and London: Yale University Press, 1954; rev. ed. 1962), 322.

11. Martz, *Poetry of Meditation*, 330.

12. Martz, *Poetry of Meditation*, 323.
13. Martz, *Poetry of Meditation*, 27.
14. Martz, *Poetry of Meditation*, 36.
15. Martz, *Poetry of Meditation*, 37.
16. Martz, *Poetry of Meditation*, 49.
17. See Martz, *Poetry of Meditation*, 54–56.
18. George Herman, "Donne's 'Goodfriday, 1613. Riding Westward,'" *Explicator* 14 (1956): 13.
19. Anthony F. Bellette, "'Little Worlds Made Cunningly': Significant Form in Donne's *Holy* Sonnets and 'Goodfriday, 1613. Riding Westward,'" *Studies in Philology* 72 (1975): 342–346.
20. Barbara K. Lewalski, *Protestant Poetics and the Seventeenth-Century Lyric* (Princeton: Princeton University Press, 1979), 278.
21. Sibyl Lutz Severance, "Soul, Sphere, and Structure in 'Goodfriday, 1613. Riding Westward,'" *Studies in Philology* 84, no. 1 (1987): 25–27.
22. Theresa M. DiPasquale, *Literature and Sacrament: The Sacred and Secular in John Donne*, Medieval & Renaissance Literary Studies, gen. ed. Albert C. Labriola (Pittsburgh, PA: Duquesne University Press, 1999), 105.
23. Philipp Wolf, "Early Modern to Romantic: The Secularization of Memory," in *Modernization and the Crisis of Memory: John Donne to Don DeLillo*, Costerus New Series, 139, ed. C. C. Barfoot, Theo D'haen, and Erik Kooper (Amsterdam and New York: Rodopi, 2002), 44.
24. Thomas Sloane, "The Poetry of Donne's Sermons," *Rhetorica* 29, no. 4 (2011): 425–427.
25. Martz, *Poetry of Meditation*, 54.
26. Quite a few scholars have offered readings of the poem predicated on deep dives into its theological, devotional, and liturgical contexts. See especially A. B. Chambers, "'Goodfriday, 1613. Riding Westward': The Poem and the Tradition," *English Literary History* 28 (1961): 31–58; "*La Corona*: Philosophic, Sacred, and Poetic Uses of Time" in *New Essays on Donne*, ed. Gary A. Stringer (Salzburg: Institut für englische Sprache und Literatur, Universitat Salzburg, 1977), 140–172; and "'Goodfriday, 1613. Riding Westward': Looking Back," *John Donne Journal* 6, no. 2 (1987): 185–201; Dominic Baker-Smith, "John Donne and the Mysterium Crucis," *English Miscellany* 19 (1968): 62–85; Jonathan S. Goldberg, "Donne's Journey East: Aspects of a Seventeenth-Century Trope," *Studies in Philology* 68 (1971): 470–483; Terry G. Sherwood, "Conversion Psychology in John Donne's Good Friday Poem," *Harvard Theological Review* 72 (1979): 101–122; J. A. W. Bennett, *Poetry of the Passion: Studies in Twelve Centuries of English Verse* (Oxford: Clarendon Press, 1982); Eleanor J. McNees, "John Donne and the Anglican Doctrine of the Eucharist," *Texas Studies in Language and Literature* 29, no. 1 (1987): 94–114; Ann Hollinshead Hurley, "Donne's 'Good Friday, Riding Westward, 1613' and the Illustrated Meditative Tradition," *John Donne Journal* 12 (1987): 67–77; R. V. Young, *Doctrine and Devotion in Seventeenth-Century Poetry: Studies in Donne, Herbert, Crashaw, and Vaughan* (Cambridge and Rochester, NY: Boydell and Brewer, 2000); and Kirsten Stirling, "Liturgical

Poetry," in *The Oxford Handbook of John Donne*, edited by Jeanne Shami, Dennis Flynn, and M. Thomas Hester, 233–241 (Oxford: Oxford University Press, 2011), 233–241.

27. Piers Brown, "Donne's Hawkings," *Studies in English Literature* 49, no. 1 (2009): 76.

28. Brown, "Donne's Hawkings," 77.

29. Brown takes Donne's ignoring the sensory experience of his horseback ride as indicative of the strength of his focus on the implications of his westward journey. See Brown, "Donne's Hawkings," 75–77.

30. Martz, *Poetry of Meditation*, 56. The first quote comes from *The English Works of George Herbert*, ed. George Herbert Palmer, vol. 1 (Boston, MA and New York: Houghton Mifflin, 1905), 140, and the second from Grierson, *Metaphysical Poems & Lyrics*, xxi.

31. Martz, *Poetry of Meditation*, 324.

32. Yeats, *The Tower (1928) Manuscript Materials*, ed. Richard J. Finneran with Jared Curtis and Ann Saddlemyer (Ithaca, NY and London: Cornell University Press, 2007), 157.

33. Yeats, *The Collected Works of W. B. Yeats*, vol. I: *The Poems*, ed. Richard J. Finneran, second ed. (New York: Scribner, 1997). All quotations of Yeats's finished poems come from this edition.

34. Johnson, *ARK*, 311.

35. "The Flea," ll. 14–15.

36. The most sustained account of Donne's interest in the new science is Charles M. Coffin's *John Donne and the New Philosophy* (New York: Columbia University Press, 1937). On Donne's reaction to Kepler, see Marjorie Nicholson, "Kepler, the *Somnium*, and John Donne," *Journal of the History of Ideas* 1 (1940): 259–280. For more recent accounts of Donne's reactions to the emerging scientific developments of the first two decades of the 1600s, see Philip Ball, *Curiosity: How Science Became Interested in Everything* (Chicago and London: The University of Chicago Press, 2012), 217–219, 230–231; David Wootton, *The Invention of Science: A New History of the Scientific Revolution* (New York: Harper Perennial, 2015), 6–10; and Massimo Bucciantini, Michele Camerota, and Franco Giudice, *Galileo's Telescope: A European Story*, trans. Catherine Bolton (Cambridge and London: Harvard University Press, 2015), 129–153.

37. Wootton, *The Invention of Science*, 226–231.

38. *The First Anniuersary*, ll. 205–206.

39. Ross Hair suggests the line from Fludd also applies to Johnson's treatment of history (*Robert Johnson's Modernist Collage*, 191–192).

40. Hair considers this idea one of the main themes in "The Foundations" section of *ARK* (*Ronald Johnson's Modernist*, 115 and 118).

Part II

LATE TWENTIETH- AND EARLY TWENTY-FIRST-CENTURY SHADOWS

Chapter 5

What Did Suffice

Scintillas of Vaughan in the Poetry of Anne Cluysenaar

In his poem "Of Modern Poetry," Wallace Stevens says that a modern poem, which he considers a "poem of the mind," cannot be trapped in the scripts of the past but must "find what will suffice" on the "new stage" of its own making (ll. 1-2, 11).[1] In this theatrical conceit, the poet-actor is a "metaphysician in the dark" who must follow the movements of the mind, attuned to their true sounds and to the emotions they express (l. 20). Welsh poet Anne Cluysenaar, herself a devotee of Stevens, believed Stevens was a "good place to begin" when reading the poetry of Henry Vaughan.[2] When she made this comment, she was thinking primarily of Stevens' essay "The Nobel Rider and Sound of Words," in which Stevens asserts the importance of the mutual interdependence of imagination and reality. Stevens believed the twentieth century had succumbed too much to the "pressure of reality" at the expense of the imagination, which is why the "idea of nobility exists in art today only in degenerate forms or in a much diminished state."[3]

For Cluysenaar, Vaughan's poetry embodied this interdependence and therefore succeeded in helping Vaughan find what did suffice when he grieved for the death of his younger brother, the loss of the royalists in the English Civil War, and the subsequent dismantling of his church. It provided necessary comfort when he sought to regain his health during what seems to have been a life-threatening illness. The healthy balance of imagination and realism, what Cluysenaar near the end of her life characterized as Vaughan's "questioning intelligence," in turn, enabled her to see flowing in Vaughan's poetry a quickness, a "deep tide of life little effected [*sic*] by culture or time."[4] Vaughan's reading of lived moments caused her to respond "more intensely" to him than to "Herbert because in our time, as in his, it is harder than in Herbert's to find stable 'confirmations' at any level."[5] In multiple senses, Stevens' remarks summarize Vaughan's value for Cluysenaar as well as the value of poetry for Vaughan: for Cluysenaar found in Vaughan what did suffice to inspire her poems and to enhance a profound sense of connection to Wales, her adopted home, against a larger world too easily prone to division, destruction, and violence.

Born in Brussels, educated in Ireland, and living in Wales after her retirement from teaching, the multilingual linguist and poet Cluysenaar found much in common with the multilingual Vaughan. For the last twenty-seven years of her life until her tragic murder on November 1, 2014, she and her husband Walt lived and worked a small holding—Little Wentwood Farm—that overlooked the Usk Valley, where Vaughan spent much of his life.[6] As he was wont to take long walks into the countryside (see, for instance, the pilcrow poem "I Walkt the other day"), she loved to go for long horseback rides through this same landscape and pay attention, as he did, to what she saw and encountered. Small noticings of interconnectedness grew into poems as it did for him. After her move to Wales, Vaughan's example occupied a central place in her work. Inspired by what began as impromptu conversations with her colleague Peter Thomas at Cardiff University, she and Thomas held the first Vaughan Colloquium in 1995 to commemorate the tercentenary of Vaughan's death. That first gathering became an annual affair that quickly led to the genesis of the Usk Valley Vaughan Association (now simply the Vaughan Association). She became the first general editor of *Scintilla*, a new annual journal of Vaughan scholarship and original poetry "in the metaphysical tradition" and served also as the poetry editor for volumes 1–15. In addition, she edited a volume of Vaughan's selected poems as part of The Golden Age of Spiritual Writing series.[7] All of this activity suggests a pervasive influence, a steeping of one poet in the life and work of another, what Cluysenaar herself acknowledges as an obsession.[8]

But the word "obsession" may well be misleading. Cluysenaar's poems are not imitations of Vaughan's even when they turn to Vaughan's as points of departure. According to Jeremy Hooker, Cluysenaar's relationship to Vaughan is a conversation. "Vaughan is a presence; he speaks through his poems, and he speaks to the poet in her own need," Hooker explains. "Clusenaar has faith in language's power to communicate between individuals and to transmit across time."[9] It was a relationship between friends on equal footing, though living centuries apart. The best metaphor for describing the literary interactions between them may well come from Vaughan himself. The title of Vaughan's breakthrough collection *Silex Scintillans: Or Sacred Poems and Private Ejaculations*, the "sparking" or "flashing flint," was depicted emblematically on the title page of the 1650 edition as a flinty heart being struck by a divine thunderbolt. Louis L. Martz notes that a human face peers out from within the heart through an opening in its wall. Each hammer blow of the thunderbolt yields both fire and tears.[10] The sparks or tears may well be the poems in the volume, the sum of which amount to the freeing of the poet from his interior stoniness. The metaphor of poems as sparks captures quite well the nature of Vaughan's practical influence on Cluysenaar's poetry, as in several notable cases, particularly the "Vaughan Variations," Vaughan's words ignite her own.

Cluysenaar and Thomas were mindful of the aptness of the sparks metaphor in a communal sense when they named the new journal *Scintilla*. The writings of Henry and Thomas Vaughan were to spark new work that nevertheless proceeded from perennial concerns. In her editorial preface in the first volume, Cluysenaar describes the intended relationship of old and new in what sounds like a mission statement. While she asserts that "contributors will direct *Scintilla*'s gaze in whatever directions seem most significant to them at the time," she also sees in this "first issue, several strands which seem likely to recur"

> the relationship of processes of writing and reading to psychological and bodily healing; the limitations and possibilities of historically-conditioned language as a means of addressing spiritual or "threshold" experience; poetic form as a significant contribution to the effectiveness of linguistic communication; humanity's relationship to nature, whether nature is envisaged as "poisoned" or pristine; and the vital interest, for many modern writers, of metaphysics and the fluctuations of scientific thought.[11]

She posits these concerns in opposition to the "fashionable trends" through which late twentieth-century "literary life" set "inexplicit but all the more effective limits to the scope of thought and of poetry" in contrast to "[r]eal experience." She considers such limits "dangerous" and reminds readers that "*Scintilla* means no more than 'a spark' . . . but no less either." The spark *Scintilla* intends to provide draws heavily on the ways in which Henry and Thomas Vaughan brought "together mathematical and mystical insights initiated by Pythagoras into meaningful relationship with humanity's ancient, honourable determination to understand reality through observation and experiment."[12] The twenty-first century, she believes, should do the same for "its own health."

Cluysenaar's spark logic grew from her personal encounters with Vaughan in the late 1980s and 1990s, after her move to Wales. Throughout most of her career, she was principally a poet who wrote for the occasions of the everyday as part of a daily practice rather than as a poet responding merely to extraordinary events. The sequence "Open Ways," for example, consists of nine poems written on different days in September 1981. In each one, she fixes on something she has noticed or remembered and follows the movements of her concentrated mind toward some new understanding or realization. "Poems on Visual Materials," also published in the 1997 collection *Timeslips: New and Selected Poems*,[13] proceeds in a similar meditative fashion, only this time focused on objects encountered in a museum. As object poems, they are reminiscent of some of the poems in Heaney's *North* (1975), particularly "Viking Dublin: Trial Pieces," "Bone Dreams," and "Strange Fruit." Her 2008 collection *Batu-Angas: Envisioning Nature with Alfred Russell Wallace* engages the travels and discoveries of the nineteenth-century British naturalist through a series of imaginative reconstructions and meditations, prompted by quotations from Wallace's writings. Her last collection *Touching Distances* consists of a series of diary poems proceeding from her everyday reflections.

In making her "Vaughan Variations," a third sequence in *Timeslips*, Cluysenaar folded her deep reading of Vaughan's poetry and prose into her habit of writing in response to the occasions of the moment.[14] It consists of twenty-three numbered poems, each one following an epigraph of lines from a Vaughan poem. At times, the relation between epigraph and ensuing poem accords with the musical analogy: the epigraph establishes a theme to which the poem enacts a variation. In a few cases, the epigraph functions less as a precipitating event than as a comment upon or response to a present urgency. But in all twenty-three, Vaughan's lines are scintillas that light Cluysenaar's poetic making in some fashion. Snippets from lines 10 and 11 of Vaughan's "Love-sick" serve as epigraph to the sequence as a whole: "make these mountains flow, / These mountains of cold Ice in me." Cluysenaar's implicit treatment of these lines is indicative of how she approaches the rest of these scintillas from Vaughan throughout the sequence. In "Love-sick," Vaughan prays to Jesus for the Holy Spirit to "strongly move" him (l. 2). He figures Christ as a "[r]efining fire" whose heat can "refine" his heart. The image of being internally glaciated, locked in mountains of ice, bespeaks Vaughan's lack of feeling, and yet the poem is full of exclamations, evidence that some emotional heat must emanate here.

Cluysenaar excerpts lines 10 and 11 in such a way that they refer not to Christ but to Vaughan. The poet is the "you" to whom she turns to make her own mountains flow. She approaches Vaughan not for spiritual guidance per se but for inspiration. There is a contextual irony here: in *Silex Scintillans* (II), where it first appeared, "Love-sick" immediately follows "The Garland," in which Vaughan criticizes the vanity of writing secular poems. Even so, Cluysenaar's epigraph appears to ask that Vaughan, with his keen awareness of the processes of natural flow, thaw her own blockages, perhaps even in ways she cannot foresee. She invokes Vaughan for present help.

That Cluysenaar turns to Vaughan as part of a concerted effort becomes clear in the first poem, for she has gone to St. Bridget's churchyard to visit the poet's grave. She describes Vaughan's gravestone and addresses him in a way suggestive of an affinity already established:

Broken across 'sepulchrum' and
'voluit', your stone is perhaps,
after all, as you would have wanted:
needing to be sought out, letters
(though legible) well greened over,
and the eye drawn away to where,
against the light, dispositions
dear to you are being restored,
things short-lived steeped in dusk, edge-lit—
a heap of eastward-facing ground,
and below (what's hardest to change)
falling water between mountains
whose high heads throw moving shadows
to tell time, emptying the fields. (ll. 1-14)

A pilgrimage, certainly, this graveside visit also seems to commence an unspecified process of growth and recovery. The poem's epigraph comes from lines 25 and 26 of "Affliction (I)": "that's best / Which is not fixt, but flies, and flowes." These lines occur during Vaughan's discussion of the importance of change in that poem. "Beauty consists in colours," he writes, by which he means contrasts as much as harmonies. This is why "that's best / Which is not fixt, but flies, and flowes." The reference to flowing connects with the lines previously quoted from "Love-sick," the suggestion of glacial runoff emblematic of the fulfilled desire to thaw and flow again.

Cluysenaar has studied Vaughan's life and writings in an effort to flow again herself. Mindful of the law of the conservation of mass, she wonders whether some matter that was once Vaughan's person "still / lives" near the churchyard but concedes it "never" could be Vaughan again (ll. 17-19). She stands by the grave as one still grieving. "At other times, I've looked for you / in your own language," she tells the poet, "shapes that you'd own / traced by words that change and die off" (ll. 20-22). Remembered imaginings creep in. She thinks of how place and circumstance, including their mother's native Welsh, would have shaped the Vaughan twins' path into language. These thoughts "near your grave," she says, have "made you too real, / like a parent after his death" (ll. 32-33). Hooker notes that "Cluysenaar's relationship to Vaughan has been described as a love affair" as well as that of daughter-father. "Both descriptions point to the emotional intensity of the relationship," he writes. "It is a love that recognizes difference, together with what cannot be known."[15] Here Vaughan's status as father figure is in the ascendant but also as something more. As she grieves for the long dead poet, the kinship she feels for him through his words blurs the boundaries between them: "My temples ache as if with tears," she writes in the final lines. "It's a betrayal to say 'you' / to the self your words breathe in me" (ll. 34-36).

We quickly discover that, in part, Cluysenaar is struggling with how to make sense of the violence in Sarajevo at the time of her writing. She wants Vaughan's words to "breathe" inside her because Vaughan, too, was a survivor in a turbulent world who wrote his way through personal calamities. Vaughan Variation 2 starts by imagining Vaughan writing the poem "The True Christmas," which furnishes the one-line epigraph: "Who empties thus, will bring more in" (l. 25). Cluysenaar thinks of how Vaughan would not have us hide in remembered green during the Christmas season but instead "face the cold" of winter. The winter she faces includes a horrific story from Sarajevo about how an artillery shell killed the sister of a young mother and left a hole the "size of a ten-pence piece" in her infant's forehead, and how the weeping official who imparted this news "knelt to pray" with the surviving mother (ll. 11, 24). "I have no prayers for the dead / or the living," Cluysenaar admits in response to this story. At best, she imagines what it must have been like for the shell to blow through that room.

But then she seems "to see" Vaughan writing "The True Christmas" by candlelight, his impatience with "unseasonal frippery" that detracts from the true meaning of Christmas, and the "page slowly filling with thoughts" (ll. 42, 44). By the time he wrote "The True Christmas," Vaughan likely had begun his career as a country doctor. So Cluysenaar imagines him riding his cob through the snow on valley paths "to the next bedside, death or birth" (ll. 48-49). She has no prayers for those in Sarajevo, her speaking self-frozen against the horrors. But her thoughts about Vaughan have thawed her enough to offer what seems like a prayer for the poet:

May he discover, as he rides,
the clean grey branches of the ash
preparing their black buds, and in
a sheltered covert those hanging
dashes of hazel, loosening,
as they do now. Something we can't
stop, or bring on. Not metaphors. (ll. 53-59)

Given the blurring of boundaries in the previous poem, might this prayer, of sorts, be for her as well? A reminder, perhaps, that despite winter (in multiple senses), renewal inevitably follows.

Vaughan's imagined presence serves as an inspirational lifeline in the third Vaughan Variation as well. This is a poem of shadows in multiple senses. The epigraph, a half-line from "Rules and Lessons"—"Give thy soul leave"—presides as advice for moving past a creative blockage. Meanwhile, Cluysenaar is haunted by the shadow of Vaughan's handwriting as visualized in the previous poem: "I invented it, so why / since then, do I see your hand / come of its own accord to the mind's eye?" (ll. 1-3). This time, the view widens somewhat. Vaughan is sitting near a window. A "short shadow" from the candle "nudges the page when the flame gutters" (ll. 6-7). The windowpanes are "pale squares," the dark beyond acquiring shapes near dawn. Later in the poem, we discover Vaughan's imagined situation parallels her own: she, too, is writing near dawn but by the light of an electric bulb, not a candle. Writing seems difficult for her. Reimagining Vaughan's hand leads not to some new place but returns her to her own, a space that "tastes of self" (l. 20). She tries to commit to words, and a "double shadow / patterns half-written thoughts, shed" onto the page (ll. 23-24). At this point, she returns to Vaughan, his love of the night and its illuminating capacity:

> It's at this hour
> your heart's events, genesis, restoration,
> come, though in new terms, nearer.
> How I need your frankness here!
> A stuttering permission
> (though all the *but's* crowd in) to praise.
> Standing at the window, I hear you say
> quietly, 'Mornings are mysteries.'
> Despite the disgraces that mark our century,
> still the page calls for difficult honesties.
> And would pass them on, from here to there. (ll. 25-36)

"Mornings are mysteries" comes form line 25 of "Rules and Lessons" after Vaughan's directive to go out and notice the morning hymns sung by all the plants and creatures. "How I need your frankness here!" Surely, the frankness she desires must have issued from Vaughan's following his own advice—to give his own soul leave to speak or sing what it must, a permission Cluysenaar has yet to grant herself.

Gradually, as the "Vaughan Variations" continue, Cluysenaar does not just *see* Vaughan through imaginative recreation but comes to *see like* Vaughan and thereby understand her environment in new ways. In Vaughan Variation 5, while she is on a horseback ride in the rain, she becomes immersed in the flow of water and light all around her:

> The hillside's a fall of water—
> loud, late-spring shower
> dropping warm light
> from leaf to leaf.
> Bright sprays of beech
> drop shadow, dots of it,
> onto the dry grit road.
> At the edge, there's a shine of ivy,

its pale downy new tips
feeling out for firm ground. (ll. 1-10)

This opening contrasts sharply with the epigraph, line 2 of "The Holy Communion": "Dead I was, and deep in trouble." In circumstances not unlike Vaughan's when he wrote "The Waterfall," she nonetheless has become "grit dry" after "months in the this and that" (ll. 14, 11). She thinks of Vaughan finding his way to God through love. Her sense of Christianity differed from his: while Vaughan lamented the loss of Established Church rituals at the time he wrote the poems of *Silex Scintillans*, Cluysenaar became a Quaker in her last years. Yet she admires and feels drawn to his habits of observation with an eye toward discerning insights: "Attention becoming prayer." After the rain stops, the image of steam rising from the path, her mare's neck, and her jersey "like breath" (l. 26) suggest she is on her way toward moistening the "dry grit" of herself. She acknowledges she has much to learn even as she leans into a commitment to keep paying attention:

What I don't know how to make words of
seems to be said all around me.
I copy what I can. Images.
Taking advantage. The rest
works on untainted. Still distant. (ll. 30-35)

What is utterly Cluysenaar and utterly refreshing about these lines is their honest admission that the poet is not some master but someone still learning how to be in the world and on the page.

Cluysenaar's exploration of the problem of poetic inspiration climaxes in a sequence of poems at the center of the "Vaughan Variations." Vaughan Variation 9, which she says is written in "the ninth year since my father's burial," confronts her difficulties in writing about that experience: "I wanted words (needed and lacked them) / then and, for this, ever since he died" (ll. 1-2). In spite of this admission, she embarks on describing the burial, as if emboldened by the habits of writing and observation responsible for the previous poems. The memory of her father's casket lowering into the ground leads to a visualization of her father's paintings and then to memories of her childhood in England, after her parents emigrated from Belgium in an effort to avoid the conflict of World War II. As with Vaughan Variation 5, the epigraph of this poem comes from "The Holy Communion," this time lines focused not on being dead but alive: "Nothing that is, or lives, / But hath his Quicknings, and reprieves" (ll. 11-12). Perhaps this reminder of quickenings, of the ebb and flow of life, nudges her to focus on her father living, not dead. By the end of the poem (with Vaughan's help?), she imagines him as a young man before the family emigration:

It's not the father that comes to mind but the youth
Crouching in Brussels, as he told me, with a shark's tooth.
Out of his depth in a more-than-social turmoil. (ll. 48-50).

Having broken though what had been an impasse in writing about her father, the next poem engages the subject of inspiration more directly. Its setup resembles a typical meditative setup in Vaughan: full descriptive immersion at a specific time and in a specific location transitions into a reflection on what she perceives. As described in chapter 4, in an Ignatian meditation, a composition of place entrancing the senses transitions to an analysis of points, which culminates in a colloquy with the divine. Vaughan Variation 10 follows this structure, roughly speaking, but without any religious reference. Lines from Vaughan's "Midnight" ("What emanations / Quick vibrations / And bright stars are here," ll. 11-13) segue into a description of sheep on the hillside. The title of Vaughan's poem—"Midnight"—sonically triggers Cluysenaar's first word:

Midday.

The sheep lie
on the ground.

This is their habit,
to seek a vantage
before they sleep.

The hills from this height,
and the valley, look shadowless,
as if light from within
had replaced the sun (ll. 1-10)

She immerses herself in this scene, at one point appearing to lie on the ground, where she observes the trembling of a single blade of grass. The smell of a "warm / ewe's wool as a lamb / butts and suckles" precipitates a thought about the afterlife: "For me too / a place waits / in which love can be / natural as death" (ll. 30-38). That place largely escapes definition.

Bumping once again against the limits of expression before a backdrop sheep on the hillside, Cluysenaar recalls what has to be one of Vaughan's most often quoted but puzzling accounts of poetic inspiration, his October 9, 1694, letter to his cousin John Aubrey. Aubrey had asked Vaughan for information on the ancient Welsh bards. By his own admission and that of his brother Thomas, Vaughan's beloved childhood tutor Matthew Herbert, whom Vaughan calls "old Amphion" in *Daphnis. An Elegaic Eclogue* (l. 55), had taught him at least some of the poetry of the old Welsh bards. So Aubrey must have presumed at least some degree of prior expertise. In his response, Vaughan notes that neither he nor anyone else he knows has detailed knowledge of the most ancient Welsh bards, whose lore, like that of the druids, had escaped the written word. But he can speak more authoritatively of the more recent bards, based on his reading and on personal acquaintance. He refers Aubrey to a book by John David Rhees before offering his own account of the Welsh bardic understanding of inspiration:

> [Their] vein of poetrie they called Awen, which in their language signifies as much as Raptus, or a poetic furor; & (in truth) as many of them as I have conversed with are (as I may say) gifted or inspired with it. I was told by a very sober & knowing person (now dead) that in his time, there was a young lad father & motherless, & soe very poor that he was forced to beg; butt att last was taken vp by a rich man, that kept a great stock of sheep vpon the mountains not far from the place where I now dwell. who cloathed him & sent him into the mountains to keep his sheep. There in Summer time following the sheep & looking to their lambs, he fell into a deep sleep; In wch. he dreamt, that he saw a beautifull young man with a garland of green leafs vpon his head, & an hawk vpon his fist: with a quiver full of Arrows att his back, coming towards him (whistling several measures or tunes all the way) & att last let the hawk fly att him, w^{ch}. (he dreamt) got into his mouth & inward parts, & suddenly awaked in a great fear & consternation: butt possessed with such a vein, or gift of poetrie, that he left the sheep & went about the Countrey, making Songs vpon all occasions, and came to be the most famous Bard in all the Countrey in his time.[16]

Cluysenaar prints this passage by itself as Vaughan Variation 12. For the moment, though, in Vaughan Variation 10, as she contemplates the lounging sheep and remembers this letter, she cannot understand how the scientifically minded doctor Vaughan could give credence to the shepherd story:

How could Henry believe
that an orphan lad
shepherding on the mountain
saw a youth garlanded
in green? Who loosed
a hawk (as he slept)
which flew through his mouth
to his inward parts,
so he woke gifted
with fear and poetry. (ll. 46-55)

The terminal punctuation is interesting. By ending the poem with a period, not a question mark, is Cluysenaar accepting Vaughan's story? Is poetic inspiration, expressed here through myth or folklore, a mystery that can be experienced but never fully rationalized? Vaughan Variation 11 implicitly sets out to answer these questions through another creative imagining of Vaughan writing.

This time, Cluysenaar imagines him at his writing desk as he ponders how to answer Aubrey's query about the Welsh bards. The third stanza of Vaughan's "The Queer" or "The Quere" or "The Query"[17] furnishes the epigraph:

> who did thee bring
> And here, without my knowledge, plac'd,
> Till thou didst grow and get a wing,
> A wing with eyes, and eyes that taste? (ll. 9-12)

Vaughan's lyrical poem inquires about the joy resulting from a felt connection with the divine. Here, through selective quotation, Cluysenaar describes the feeling of being inspired creatively: a sudden acquisition of wings and presumably of heightened perception. The first lines of her poem amplify the acceptance implied by the terminal period in the previous poem:

> He didn't deny them, the contradictions,
> the twists of mind and mood, the boring
> *et ceteras*, the grit between visions,
> and the visions themselves, unaccountable,
> unearned, hard to own up to.
> Because of war, imperfection, change. (ll. 1-6)

She seems to accept these contradictions herself. She certainly understands the aims of Vaughan's labors: "To heal himself / and others, with words or herbs" (ll. 7-8). She sympathizes as well with his situation: an "old fogy" being asked to supply material for a "footnote on ancient things" (ll. 20-21). Her Vaughan is mindful of the vast difference in context between himself, ensconced in the Brecon countryside, with a view of the hills in the distance and a swan who has taken to approaching the door for scraps from time to time, and his cousin living in noisy, polluted London. How to explain the close connection between Welsh poetry and nature to a man living in world Vaughan cast off decades before? Cluysenaar's Vaughan is amused by the situation. She lets him answer for himself in Vaughan Variation 12. In this moment, she has Vaughan remembering Matthew Herbert and the way Herbert's recitations of the old bardic poems inspired him:

> Something about his body shape
> as he leans to dip the quill
> brings their schooldays back, the voice

of old Matthew (learned and loving—
father, in the spirit, of his spirit)
telling by heart the visions of 'our'
Bard, 'the black, but brightest', while Tom's
hard-pressed nib is scratching
in his corner, such scatterings
of excited science! and himself,
'a wing with eyes', truant,
beyond the window, on the rippling hill.

Whatever he writes now will be,
he knows, both legacy and avowal. (ll. 25-38)

A "wing with eyes," an image from "The Query" describing the feeling of being touched by the Holy Spirit, here captures the feeling of being inspired by a poetic vocation connected to the land. While Herbert's teaching propels his twin brother Thomas eventually into a career as a hermeticist and natural philosopher, it confirms in Henry a desire to become a poet. A "wing with eyes" also connects to the shepherd's story, the way poetic vocation and inspiration are figured as a hawk swooping through the mouth and into the body and living inside the shepherd-bard presumably for the rest of his days.

Hooker, too, considers the inclusion of the excerpt from the Aubrey letter the "centre-piece" of the "Vaughan Variations" and emphasizes how it demonstrates Cluysenaar's "sense of Vaughan as a 'green' poet and a poet with, at least, a bardic strain."[18] After quoting the story from Vaughan's letter, Cluysenaar offers no comment on it in the rest of the sequence. Elsewhere, however, she stresses its importance. Aside from the preface to the second edition of *Silex Scintillans*, it is the only other selection of Vaughan's prose in her edition of the *Selected Poems*. There she acknowledges the vital importance of the Welsh bardic tradition to Vaughan through "its unique insistence on the communal role of the poet."[19] In her essay on Vaughan's poem "Distraction," she similarly accords the letter a place of prime importance:

> I have a fancy, though, that this passage may echo a tale told to the young Henry by Matthew Herbert, not merely to encourage him in his poetic vocation but also to confirm him in his sense of a spirit in nature and of the community as central to poetic vocation: two key aspects of Vaughan's nature work.[20]

She considered this Welsh poetic inheritance, fused with other English and European traditions, as Vaughan's distinct way into his art. The sequence on poetic inspiration within the "Vaughan Variations" culminating in this letter suggests Cluysenaar's own acceptance of the story as an affirmation of the mystery of inspiration in the creative process and of Vaughan's shaman-like role in mediating between the empirical observation of nature and its spiritual significance. This role is one she also seems to have aspired to in her own numinous poems right up until her untimely death.

Quoting Vaughan's "The World," Susan Bassnett writes,

> When I think of Anne now, I like to think of her as one of those singers who soared up into the great Ring of Eternity, whose wide-open eyes can never be dazzled by the calm of that endless light.[21]

For fellow poet Fiona Owen, this mediation between the everyday and the spiritual was a continual presence in Cluysenaar poems:

> While her poems display a keen sense of *journeying*, her focus tends to be not so much a literal traveling over surfaces but, rather, a more inward journeying through past, present and imagined future experiences, probing boundaries and wondering at the permeability of selves, so crucially a part of the mystery of being.[22]

The example of Cluysenaar shows us how relevant a metaphysical poet can be in our present. Hooker believes, I think rightly, that Cluysenaar's openness to Vaughan during the last phase of her career and her life proved essential in defining her art as a way of being during her years in Wales. Vaughan's poems

> so alive to the place she came to know and love—the natural, cultural, sacred Welsh landscape—enabled her to belong to that world, and that world to belong to her. Her belonging made no claim to possession or mastery. It was a way of being. The conversation with Vaughan helped her to know herself as a woman and a poet, and as 'a part of reality.'[23]

Seen in this light, Cluysenaar seems to have fashioned for herself a bardic relationship with Vaughan, lines from his poems sparking in hers like figments of a tradition passed down from one bard to another. In her role as a founding editor of *Scintilla*, as a poetry editor from 1997 to 2011, as a judge of annual poetry competitions, and as an editor of Vaughan's poems, she worked tirelessly to transmit this rich inheritance to others as best she could.

NOTES

1. Stevens, *Collected Poetry & Prose*, ed. Frank Kermode and Joan Richardson (New York: Library of America, 1997). All quotations of Stevens come from this edition.
2. Cluysenaar, "Rereading Henry Vaughan's 'Distraction,'" *Scintilla* 1 (1997): 93.
3. Stevens, *Collected Poetry & Prose*, 649–650.
4. Cluysenaar, "ABSENCE, PRESENCE: Recalling Peter Thomas," *Scintilla* 18 (2015): 172.
5. Cluysenaar, "Rereading," 107.
6. For a general outline of her life and career, see Meic Stephens's obituary "Anne Cluysenaar: Writer and academic whose numinous poetry drew on her fascination with science as well as her spirituality," *The Independent* (Friday, 14 November 2014): https://www.independent.co.uk/news/obituaries/anne-cluysenaar-writer-and-academic-whose-numinous-poetry-drew-her-fascination-science-well-her-spirituality-9862395.html.
7. *Henry Vaughan: Selected Poems*, ed. Anne Cluysenaar, The Golden Age of Spiritual Writing (London: Society for Promoting Christian Knowledge, 2004).
8. Cluysenaar, "ABSENCE, PRESENCE," 171.
9. Hooker, "'Vaughan Variations': Anne Cluysenaar in Conversation with Henry Vaughan," *Scintilla* 19 (2016): 97.
10. Martz, *The Paradise Within: Studies in Vaughan, Traherne, and Milton* (New Haven, CT and London: Yale University Press, 1964), 5.
11. Cluysenaar, "Preface," *Scintilla* 1 (1997): 5.
12. Cluysenaar, "Preface," 6.
13. *Timeslips: New and Selected Poems*, Manchester: Carcanet, 1997.
14. I say "deep" because the epigraphs of each of her Vaughan Variations draw not just from the two editions of *Silex Scintillans* (1650 and 1655), the collections most well-known, but also from lesser-known poems from *Poems, With the Tenth Satyre of Iuvenal Englished* (1646), *Olor Iscanus* (1651), and *Thalia Rediviva* (1678).
15. Hooker, "Vaughan Variations," 96.
16. *The Works of Henry Vaughan*, vol. 2, 810–811.
17. The editors of the Oxford edition of *The Works of Henry Vaughan* print the title as "The Queer," an arcane spelling. Cluysenaar modernizes it to "The Query" in the "Vaughan Variations" but prints it as "The Quere" in her edition of Vaughan's *Selected Poems*.
18. Hooker, "Vaughan Variations," 104.
19. Vaughan, *Selected Poems*, 2.
20. Cluysenaar, "Distraction," 2.
21. Bassnett, "In Memoriam: Anne Cluysenaar 1936-2014," *Scintilla* 18 (2015): 184.
22. Owen, "'Into all this': A Tribute to Anne Cluysenaar," *Scintilla* 18 (2015): 177.
23. Hooker, "Vaughan Variations," 108.

Chapter 6

Donne, Heaney, and the Boldness of Love

As the publication of Dennis O'Driscoll's *Stepping Stones: Interviews with Seamus Heaney* (2008) provided nearly unprecedented access to a major modern poet's experience of his career, it also underscored the degree to which Heaney depended on the specific insights of other poets to guide his way in his poetic making and in his life as a poet.[1] Just as a physicist or a philosopher will refer to ideas or theories in a shorthand of individual phrases—Hobbes's pure state of nature, say, or the Big Bang—Heaney treated the words of fellow poets with a similar authority in conveying the true nature of art and experience. He retained from poems touchstones for how to learn, how to remember, how to pay attention, and how to live. For example, when speaking of his many literary pilgrimages, he turns naturally to Yeats: "I'd have thought the urge to go these places was common enough. A matter of dedicating, as Yeats says in one of his Coole Park poems, 'a moment's memory to [a] laurelled head.'"[2] When asked to explain the apparent disjunction between the poems on sectarian violence in *Field Work* (1979) and his earlier description of that collection as a "door into the light," he offers a list of similar touchstones: "Synge's remark about style being the shock of new subject matter comes to mind. And Lowell's line, 'Why not say what happened?' And Milosz's respect for 'one clear stanza.'"[3] He speaks as if these precedents, taken together, helped shaped his artistic conception.

Heaney also speaks of the work of others in the same fashion. In *Spelling It Out*, the 2009 publication of a speech made to honor Brian Friel on the occasion of Friel's eightieth birthday, he encapsulates the playwright's work through a small collection of literary descriptors culled from diverse sources:

> No contemporary playwright has a greater lexical range or relish than Friel, no cast of characters is more endowed with original speech. There is fecundity

and felicity and at the same time a forensic vigilance in everything he writes, a Shakespearean rough magic which does not preclude Beckettian fine-tuning. There is what Robert Frost calls "the wonder of supply," the more-than-enoughness which distinguishes the great ones, a scale that runs from the demotic to the rhapsodic, as capable of mocking wit as elegiac wisdom or lyric fantasy. He is a type of Keatsian "chameleon poet" as well as a Joycean forger of conscience.[4]

Each of these descriptors captures a single, precise distinction, so that the accumulation creates a particularity of reference that is especially communicative. Heaney thought about literature in no small part through the insights of other writers, which became for him a series of truths accurately describing real-life phenomena. What he observes about Ted Hughes applied equally well to him: his "conversation was full of poets from every time and place, all very real to him, and whoever he talked about would attain a terrific new solidity."[5] This habit of thinking in terms of other writers, of treating literature as a source of wisdom for explaining the large and the small, placed him in excellent company.

W. B. Yeats, another poet who often thought in terms of literary touchstones, was especially fascinated by the artistry and individual contributions of Early Modern English poets. For him, Spenser, Jonson, and Donne not only furnished sturdy examples of artistic integrity for which he felt an intimate kinship but also shared a "tradition that drew uncommon strength and substance—i.e., *images*—from the well of the *Anima Mundi*."[6] Spenser provided a host of symbols and images to which Yeats returned throughout his writing life, right up until the time of "The Municipal Gallery Re-visited." Jonson, in addition to informing the development of his plays, also suggested to Yeats the compositional habit of starting the process of writing poems with prose sketches, which he then shaped into finished poems, sometimes over a period of years. Yeats knew whole passages of Donne by heart, was friends with Herbert Grierson during the period when Grierson was editing his landmark 1912 edition of Donne, and undertook what Wayne K. Chapman describes as a "series of imitative exercises after his marriage in 1917."[7] From the 1890s onward, Yeats repeatedly turned to the style and major images of specific poems and passages to create new work. Indeed, so heavy and noticeable was the Early Modern influence during his middle period that by the time of the composition of *Responsibilities* (1914), "Elizabethan" became a pejorative term that Ezra Pound occasionally used to deride ornamental excesses during the winters of 1913–1916, when he and Yeats lived and worked together at Stone Cottage on the edge of Ashdown Forest in Sussex, as if the influence of the earlier poets had to be kept at bay with a charm.[8]

Heaney's engagements with the work of the seventeenth-century metaphysical poets are also well-attested, both by his own report and to a lesser extent by critics. In the early 1960s, as he began writing poetry in earnest and embarked on his teaching career, he more seriously studied the work of several influential canonical writers than during his own student days. In 1975, when he taught as a lecturer in English at Carysfort College of Education in Dublin, he lectured on the metaphysical poets and credited especially Andrew Marvell with showing him the power of the "plain style" of traditional meter: he began "discovering that element of 'tough reasonableness' that Eliot spoke of in Marvell," and "had this sudden powerful admiration for Marvell's 'Horatian Ode' and his very strange piece 'The Nymph Complaining for the Death of her Fawn.'"[9] On several notable occasions in his critical writings, he touts George Herbert as the true poet of integrity, wholly committed to the demands of his art and therefore capable of withstanding the distorting influences (political, social, or otherwise) that might compromise artistic vision. For Heaney,

> Herbert surrendered himself to a framework of belief and an instituted religion; but in his case, it happened that his personality was structured in such a way that he could dwell in amity with doctrine, writing poetry which was intellectually pure, emotionally robust, and entirely authentic.[10]

Herbert's example offers a "redress of poetry" to those who would argue that poetry is insufficient to make a difference in our politically charged world:

> Even the most imposed-upon colonial would discern in the clear element of Herbert's poetry a true paradigm of the shape of things, psychologically, politically, metaphorically and, if one wants to proceed that far, metaphysically.[11]

Herbert's work "is an example of that fully realized poetry I have attempted to define, a poetry where the coordinates of the imagined thing correspond to and allow us to contemplate the complex burden of our own experience." So consistent and assiduous is Heaney's endorsement of Herbert that one fully expects to be able to root out the tall tops of the Herbertian phrase in Heaney's own poems, a task for someone else, perhaps, at another time.

And what of Donne, that figurehead of the so-called metaphysical mode? Touchstones from Donne's writings do not appear in Heaney's interviews and essays with the same frequency as those of Marvell or Herbert, or of the more recent poets Wordsworth, Yeats, and Czeslaw Milosz. Yet some Donne references appear at various junctures throughout his career, and in these instances we see that Donne offered Heaney important insights into the condition of loving. As discussed in chapter 1, the tenth "Glanmore Sonnet" from *Field Work* (1979) recalls the physical disposition of lovers in "The Extasie"

("We were laid out / Laid breathing effigies on a raised ground," ll. 6–7). In "Chanson d'Aventure," more than thirty years later, Heaney returned to "The Extasie" this time to speak of "love on hold, body and soul apart" (l. 12) as he lay in a speeding ambulance and held his wife's hand during the immediate aftermath of the stroke he suffered in 2006. That Heaney was mindful of Donne's singular contributions as a love poet is attested in the choices made in the assembly of the poetry anthologies he edited with Hughes: he and Hughes eschewed Donne's religious verse but did include "The Baite" in *The Rattle Bag* (1982) and "A Valediction forbidding mourning" in its sequel, *The School Bag* (1997).[12]

Heaney did not answer, rewrite, or substantially appropriate Donne's poems in the manner of, say, Paul Muldoon or Geoffrey Hill. But in a few cases the presence of certain Donne poems can be felt more in the approach to a specific experience within the domain of love than in direct reference. And when this occurs, one cannot say that Heaney imitates Donne or is even influenced by Donne's point of view. Instead, the Donne poem acts as a fixed, assumed feature on the landscape that shapes Heaney's path, in much the same way that a natural barrier—a river, say, or a canyon or a mountain—influences the way a road might be built over, around, or through it. Donne's status as landmark is suggested on those few occasions in the essays when Heaney invokes his name, along with those of other canonical writers, as an indexing reference point for major literary developments. Thus, when speaking of J. M. Synge's *The Aran Islands*, Donne becomes a landmark in the history of English style: Synge's development of a local idiom may have looked like

> an attempt to refresh the language of English literature, one of those periodic returns to the spoken idiom which Donne and Dryden and Wordsworth had initiated in their times, and which T.S. Eliot would set in motion shortly after Synge's own death.[13]

When speaking of Thomas Kinsella's "Interlude," the Donnean landmark, along with a few others, lies in the territory of the epigrammatic: "The formal ancestry of 'Interlude' may include the Auden of 'Death of a Tyrant' and the epigrammatic side of Pope and Donne and Jonson."[14] Such references clearly posit Donne as a landscape feature to be reckoned with, here from the safe distance of a literary horizon, but Heaney negotiates Donne from much closer distances as well.

A case in point, "Valediction," from *Death of a Naturalist* (1966), draws significant energy from its title, which implicitly hearkens to "A Valediction forbidding mourning," one of the Donne poems Heaney and Hughes later anthologized. While Donne certainly did not invent the valediction as poetic kind (four examples is hardly enough to corner a poetic market), any English speaker educated in the canon as it was understood in the 1950s and 1960s would have been hard-pressed *not* to think of Donne's legendary poem when confronted with "Valediction" as a title, especially when Heaney does not modify it like the Donne headings do (i.e., "A Valediction forbidding mourning," "of weeping," "of the booke," and "of my name in a window").[15] The single word "Valediction" is left to ping the reader's memory entirely on its own.

The poetic situation of this poem also resonates: not the farewell of two lovers all-too-easily parted by the coming of day or the end of some social occasion, these two share a house, and their parting is significant enough, in both time and distance, for the "Lady's" absence to create an "emptiness" that "has hurt / All thought" (ll. 3–5). As with "A Valediction forbidding mourning," this parting comes across as a dire event in need of being addressed. Yet the lines just quoted signal the first of several key departures from Donne. In this case, the Lady, not the male speaker, has left home. She is the traveler away on some unspecified business, a shift in the gendering of agency. Furthermore, there is some slippage between the title and the ensuing poem. The implied gesture of a *valediction* poem is to bid farewell at the time of parting, the poem itself often some attempt to resolve or control the usually unpleasant effects of the impending absence. Yet this parting already has transpired. The speaker now attempts to explain his turbulent state, presumably to demonstrate his affection for his love or perhaps even implicitly argue for her swift return. The ensuing description of interior tumult depends on a prior assumption of harmony, an assumption consistent with Donne's poem, which figures harmony first as the mild passing from life to death of "virtuous men" (ll. 1–4), then in the serene "trepidation" of the Ptolemaic spheres (ll. 11–12), and culminating in the compass conceit and the perfect circle (itself the perfect shape in Renaissance thought) made whole through the firmness of Donne's lady's love (ll. 25–36). All these images depend on notions of balance, the basis of mutual, soulful love. Heaney, too, assumes balance to be the necessary condition of love, the means by which time normally passes easily:

> In your presence
> Time rode easy, anchored
> On a smile; but absence
> Rocked love's balance, unmoored
> The days. They buck and bound
> Across the calendar,
> Pitched from the quiet sound
> Of your flower-tender
> Voice. (ll. 5–13)

The Donnean grounds for consolation—that soulful bond attenuated but not broken like "gold to ayery thinnesse beat" (l. 24)—fails to accord with the pain of the present circumstances. Elsewhere, in a later poem, as noted previously, Heaney depends on another of Donne's articulations of soulful connection in his recall of "The Extasie" during the ambulance ride in "Chanson d'Aventure." But not here. Here, need dictates the expression of rootlessness in the face of absence. As is common with Heaney, experience is grounded in precise physical detail. Time rides "easy" because of the reassurance of his love's anchoring "smile." Without her "flower-tender / Voice," the days "buck and bound / Across the calendar" presumably without stopping. The loss of her physical presence induces this chaos.

In these lines, there might seem an answer contradicting Donne's poem, for, in two of its most famous stanzas, Donne sharply contrasts the soulful lovers (the speaker and his love) with genital lovers wholly invested in the physical:

Dull sublunary lovers love
  (Whose soule is sense) cannot admit
Absence, because it doth remove
  Those things which elemented it.

But we by'a love, so much refin'd,
  That our selves know not what it is,
Inter-assured of the mind,
  Care lesse, eyes, lips, and hands to misse. (ll. 13–20)

Is Heaney implicitly pressuring Donne's distinction here? Perhaps. But his dependence on the physical presence of his beloved also accords with Donne's refusal elsewhere in the "*Songs and Sonets*" (and also implicitly in the ensuing compass metaphor) to define soulful love as divorced from sex. What would Donne have said if he had been the one left behind? Regardless, Heaney, having invoked Donnean notions of harmony (through "Valediction" and "balance"), refashions an earlier Petrarchan idiom of loss at sea as more fit to convey the truth of the speaker's perceptions.

Rather than figure *himself* as a tossed ship *à la* Petrarch and later Wyatt, however, Heaney describes his *days* as "unmoored." It is in this sense that he is "at sea" (l. 14), trapped in a self-mutiny, until she returns and in so doing "resume[s] command" of his time (l. 15). This Lady is not the cruel mistress withholding the guiding stars of her eyes; rather, she is simply away, and without her, profound disharmony has ensued. Neither Donne nor Petrarch, Heaney nonetheless finds his way through this poem via some guiding landmarks from each, thereby establishing his own course the way any poet should.

Such direct engagements with specific Donne poems are rare, however. One cannot rightly call Heaney the love poet an imitator of Donne, nor can we call him an imitator of anyone else. Throughout his oeuvre, he remains very much his own person with a distinctive angle of vision and an individual voice. Furthermore, if we understand the Donnean voiceprint strictly in terms of allusion, echo, or other intertextual engagement, or more broadly as "trying on [Donne's] language and looking inside his imagination," in the words of Judith Scherer Herz, we would have to concede that Donne's voiceprint registers only quietly in the Heaney corpus overall.[16] "Valediction," the Glanmore Sonnets, and "Chanson d'Aventure" represent a small percentage of his love poetry. Most of the time, Heaney's love poems do not make overt or implied references to Donne. Finally, the scope of each poet's exploration of love differs markedly. Donne's love poems together offer a sustained meditation on the many facets of desire and loving, both in the particular case and in a general sense; Heaney's were written over a much longer timespan (almost fifty years) but center principally on one relationship. In the *Elegies* and *Songs and Sonets*, Donne covers a wide range of experiences and situations within the overarching conditions of lust and love. He explores them sometimes through various personae (e.g., the rake, the unrequited lover, the other woman, Sappho) and sometimes tantalizingly in his own person. By contrast, while Heaney occasionally employs amorous love as a metaphor—for instance, to describe the way sea and land try to "possess" each other in the early poem, "Lovers on Aran" in *Death of a Naturalist*—most often his love poems concern his courtship and marriage to Marie Heaney (née Devlin). They issue from and appeal to specific biographical circumstances, the kind we might crave to know in Donne's case but probably never will.

Nevertheless, despite these qualifiers and beyond the touchstone appearances of Donne so far referenced, we can discern less poem-specific grounds for resemblances between the two poets—not a later poet intertextually dialoguing with a notable precursor, but two poets using language in similar ways when working within a similar subject matter. When writing about love, the two poets employ some of the same techniques. One therefore can detect in some Heaney poems what seems a Donnean boldness, rendered through similarities of approach. The remainder of this chapter will coax Heaney's Donnean boldness into the light by exploring three of these techniques: a tendency to begin love poems in an abrupt, surprising fashion; a tendency to construct metaphysical conceits and striking, unforeseen comparisons; and a tendency to dramatically shift directions within a poem toward the conveyance of a precise, often unexpected insight about love. These three techniques, I submit, contribute to the Donnean feel of some of Heaney's love poems. Whether Heaney consciously learned them from Donne is anyone's guess. But reading Heaney's love poems alongside Donne's *Songs and*

Sonets reveals an unanticipated and intriguing similarity in how the two poets present the honest boldness of love.

Boldness, as a concept, mattered greatly to the courtier and coterie poets in the English Renaissance because it was one way in which a poet could generate *energia* that literary quality suggestive of the energy or urgency of life. The presence of *energia* gradually became seen as fundamental in the success of a poem. Its absence could be a contributing factor to a poem's collapse into doggerel. Long an important principle in classical rhetoric, *energia* received important emphasis in the example and critical thought of Sir Philip Sidney. In the famous reference to *energia* in his *An Apology for Poetry* (c. 1579), Sidney implicitly links it to his definition of "songs and sonnets" as a poetic kind and denounces those poets who have forgotten or insufficiently understood the importance of appealing to the passions of readers:

> Other sorts of poetry almost have we none, but that lyrical kind of songs and sonnets: which, Lord, if He gave us so good minds, how well it might be employed, and with how heavenly fruit, both private and public, in singing the praises of the immortal beauty, the immortal goodness of that God who giveth us hands to write and wits to conceive; of which we might well want words, but never matter; of which we could turn our eyes to nothing but we should ever have new budding occasions. But truly many of such writings as come under the banner of unresistable love, if I were a mistress, would never persuade me they were in love; so coldly they apply fiery speeches, as men that had rather read lovers' writings, and so caught up certain swelling phrases, which hang together, like a man which once told me the wind was at north-west and by south, because he would be sure to name winds enough, than that in truth they feel these passions, which easily (as I think) may be bewrayed by that same forcibleness or *energia* (as the Greeks call it) of the writer. But let this be a sufficient though short note, that we miss the right use of the material point of poesy.[17]

For a poem to succeed, it must capture and convey the passion(s) motivating its content. Love poems, for example, fail when their "fiery speeches" are applied "coldly." Any poems fail when the poet's relishing of his own words and knowledge severs the necessary connection with the underlying emotion that should be an integral part of the poem's invention. Passion, in this understanding, the fuel for *energia*, must come from the poet, who uses it for inspiration as well as for representation. *Energia*, then, is both a matter of underlying idea *and* of style. It cannot be relegated to one or the other but belongs to both.[18] It must be part of the poet's conception and compositional process.

Elizabethans found Sidney's example so compelling because the *energia* in his writings greatly enhanced the verisimilitude of his rendering of psychological states. For example, John Hoskyns, himself a wit of note, created an instruction manual, *Directions for Speech and Style*, for an unnamed young gentleman using almost exclusively quotations from Sidney's prose and poetry as his examples of literary excellence.[19] Donne, a friend of Hoskyns as a fellow Inns of Court man, shared this admiration and as Roger Kuin has recently shown, succeeded in capturing a Sidnean *energia* in his own poems.[20] The passionate character of Donne's verse is hardly a new subject. But most relevant here is how in his love poems especially he frequently sought to create *energia* from his opening lines. More often than not in the *Songs and Sonets*, his beginnings contain a "forcibleness" that demands our attention and concentration right from the first words. Here are a few representative examples:

He is starke mad, who ever sayes,
  That he hath been in love an houre,
Yet not that love so soone decayes,
  But that it can tenne in lesse space devour;
            ("The broken heart," ll. 1–4)

When I dyed last, and, Deare, I dye
  As often as from thee I goe,
  Though it be but an houre agoe,
And Lovers houres be full eternity,
            ("The Legacie," ll. 1–4)

When by thy scorne, O murdresse, I am dead,
      And that thou thinkst thee free
From all solicitation from mee,
Then shall my ghost come to thy bed,
            ("The Apparition," ll. 1–4)

Now thou hast lov'd me one whole day,
To morrow when thou leav'st, what wilt thou say?
Wilt thou then Antedate some new made vow?
      Or say that now
We are not just those persons, which we were?
            ("Woman's constancy," ll. 1–5)

      Busie old foole, unruly Sunne,
        Why dost thou thus,
Through windowes, and through curtaines call on us?
Must to thy motions lovers seasons run?
            ("The Sunne Rising," ll. 1–4)

If yet I have not all thy love,
Deare, I shall never have it all,
I cannot breath one other sigh, to move;
Nor can intreat one other tear to fall.
                    ("Loves infiniteness," ll. 1–4)

Aside from "The Apparition" and "The Sunne Rising," two of Donne's most frequently taught poems, I have steered clear of the usual suspects to make the simple point that Donne's energetic openings are everywhere in these love poems. Held in the suspense of the speaker's immediately identifiable emotional state, many readers of poetry would be hard-pressed *not* to keep reading after encountering these openings. But passion is not the only factor here: these openings additionally plunge us into an already fully developed situation, often but not always a conversation (or at least one side of one), that we then experience first-hand. The plunge becomes an essential means by which we come to know the speaker's passion.

A similar kind of boldness, predicated on the immediacy of a situation rapidly conjured, attends Heaney's love poems as well. Heaney was well aware of English Renaissance critical discussions about *energia*, including Sidney's *Apology*. In the early essay, "Feeling into Words," one of the best accounts of the development of a poet's voice that I know of, Heaney quotes Sidney's description of the ancient Roman definition of the poet as *Vates*.[21] In *Stepping Stones*, O'Driscoll asks about Sidnean *energia* directly during a discussion of the Scottish poet Hugh MacDiarmid:

> *"Forcibleness" is a quality you have attributed to Hugh MacDiarmid and also to Christopher Marlowe. Do you see "forcibleness"—Sir Philip Sidney's translation of the Greek* Energeia—*as a litmus test of true poetry?*
>
> It's certainly what sets the seal of inevitability on much of the best writing. It's "the force that through the green fuse drives the flower". The attribute that makes you feel the lines have been decreed, that there has been no fussy picking and choosing of words but instead a surge of utterance.[22]

Like Donne, Heaney the love poet often creates this "surge of utterance" with his first words, setting in motion an energy capable of snaring and keeping a reader's attention:

Love, I shall perfect for you the child
Who diligently potters in my brain
Digging with heavy spade till sods were piled

Or puddling through muck in a deep drain.
>("Poem," ll. 1–4)

Her scarf *á la* Bardot,
In suede flats for the walk,
She came with me one evening
For air and friendly talk.
>("Twice Shy," ll. 1–4)

I am afraid.
Sound has stopped in the day
And the images reel over
And over. Why all those tears,

The wild grief on his face
Outside the taxi?
>("Wedding Day," ll. 1–6)

Was it wind off the dumps
or something in the heat

dogging us, the summer gone sour,
a fouled nest incubating somewhere?

Whose fault, I wondered, inquisitor
of the possessed air.
>("Summer Home," ll. 1–6)

After the sudden outburst and the squalls
I hooped you with my arms

and remembered that what could be contained
inside this caliper embrace

the Dutch called *bosom*;
>("Polder," ll. 1–5)

The white toweling bathrobe
ungirdled, the hair still wet,
first coldness of the underbreast
like a ciborium in the palm.
>("La Toilette," ll. 1–4)

There we were in the vaulted tunnel running,
You in your going-away coat speeding ahead
And me, me then like a fleet god gaining
Upon you before you turned to a reed

Or some new white flower japped with crimson.
                    ("The Underground," ll. 1–5)[23]

In each case, the opening lines establish the emotional territory of the ensuing poem as well as its immediate situation, either directly (e.g., "There we were in the vaulted tunnel running," a literal description of "The Underground") or metaphorically (e.g., "After the sudden outburst and the squalls," suggestions of argument). Because they perform their work swiftly and forcefully, the lines carry that sense of inevitability to which Heaney alludes, that sense of being "decreed." While Heaney might be right in suggesting that "forcibleness" attends "much of the best writing," at least since the Early Modern poets, the high premium both Donne and Heaney placed on locating it from the start of their love poems lends their work a strength not always present in the work of their contemporaries.

One also can discern similarities in their approach to the architecture of individual love poems. Donne's metaphysical conceits are surely the one hallmark no undergraduate facing him in a British survey course can escape, just as Samuel Johnson's famous description of "metaphysical wit" ("The most heterogeneous ideas are yoked by violence together") may well be the *only* Johnsonian excerpt many an undergraduate will encounter.[24] "The Baite," "The Flea," "The Canonization," "A Valediction forbidding mourning"—all seize on the opportunities new and startling comparisons create for description and explication, as Donne seeks to put his immediate addressee (usually his mistress) and his implied readers (members of his various coteries) into a new relationship with the subject at hand (sex, love, grief at parting). Entire poems depend on such opportunities for definition.

Heaney's love poems also hinge on extended comparisons for definition. "The Underground," for example, the beginning of which was just quoted, conveys the remembered exhilaration of a moment during the Heaneys' honeymoon through three comparisons. In the first, Heaney likens his pursuit of his new bride through the vaulted tunnel to a classical deity's chase of some gorgeous, virtuous nymph. He is like Pan after Syrinx before the water nymphs turn her into a reed to keep her out of his hands. Perhaps fearful that his luck cannot hold, that she will be turned into "some new white flower japped with crimson" (l. 5), he nevertheless feels powerful and potent in this extraordinary rush for the train, so much so, in fact, that the memory of this moment lingers. Here a second comparison enters the poem, the fairytale *Hansel and Gretel*, as we discover the earlier description was simply the speaker's memory. Once again in the same London underground years later, he remembers how the buttons flew off Marie's coat. Now he collects them in his memory, like Hansel, "[r]etracing the path back" but in a place that seems colder and with a mindset more seemingly fragile:

       a draughty lamplit station
After the trains have gone, the wet track
Bared and tensed as I am, all attention
For your step following and damned if I look back. (ll. 13–16)

The last line returns to classical myth, but one myth with much different implications, Orpheus's rescue of Eurydice from the underworld. No longer potent like a god, the speaker now remembers the very human poet-singer whose mistake ends up costing him the company of his beloved.

While none of these comparisons is especially "metaphysical" in the sense normally associated with Donne (though the likening of spilled buttons to fairytale breadcrumbs is novel enough), some of Heaney's other extended conceits are much closer to the mark. That Heaney realized what this mark was is attested in his own description of the treatment of sexuality in "Undine," from *Door Into the Dark* (1969): "I'd still stand by 'Undine,'" he explains, "farm drainage and burgeoning sexuality yoked by violence—literary violence, that is—together."[25] Mindful of the Johnsonian description as well as the Donnean example, Heaney constructs his own metaphysical conceits with like skill. In "Scaffolding," from *Death of a Naturalist*, his meditations on his hopes and perceptions of his then-new marriage lead him to figure himself and his wife as masons embarked on the construction of a new stone building. As masons verify the solidity of their scaffolding before they can attend to the serious work (they must "Make sure that planks won't slip at busy points, / Secure all ladders, tighten bolted joints," 3–4), so the Heaneys have taken like care in constructing their marriage. This comparison enables Heaney to offer reassurance about the inevitable changes inherent in any well-founded, long-term relationship:

So if, my dear, there sometimes seem to be
Old bridges breaking between you and me,

Never fear. We may let the scaffolds fall,
Confident that we have built our wall. (ll. 7–10)

The comparison structures the entire poem. "Scaffolding" is reminiscent of an older aesthetic in another sense, too: unlike much of Heaney's other work, which is rooted in the visceral details of everyday life, such details emerge here firmly within the boundaries of analogy, as they would in a Donne or Herbert poem—an analogy not predicated on a particular time and place but somehow universally true.

Two of Heaney's most famous love poems, "The Otter" and "The Skunk," also rely on metaphysical conceits, this time involving animals as a way into sensuality.[26] Neither animal, by itself, conjures associations with amorousness for most people. But in Heaney's hands, each comparison renders something exquisite about the nature of everyday desires. In "The Otter," the beloved's dive and swim in the wavering light of Tuscany arrest the speaker's attention:

I loved your wet head and smashing crawl,
Your fine swimmer's back and shoulders
Surfacing and surfacing again
This year and every year since.

I sat dry-throated on the warm stones. (ll. 4–9)

This description is brilliant because it applies equally well to both a human swimmer and an otter, the latter introduced by the poem's title. In fact, if it were not for the direct address ("When you plunged," l. 1, and "your head," l. 4), a reader might think the swimmer actually is an otter, and even in this case the poet could be addressing an animal. The relationship between tenor and vehicle is not clarified until the fourth stanza, specifically lines 14 and the following: "When I hold you now / We are close and deep / As the atmosphere on water" (ll. 14–16). The average person would not be holding an otter.

And yet the comparison unlocks a surprising sensuality, as the poet's conceit turns his hands into the water that loves to cover the otter's "lithe" body:

My two hands are plumbed water.
You are my palpable, lithe
Otter of memory
In the pool of the moment,

Turning to swim on your back,
Each silent, thigh shaking kick
Re-tilting the light,
Heaving the cool at your neck. (ll. 17–24)

Suddenly, woman-as-otter captures, with a Donne-like precision, the poet's admiration for his beloved's body as well as the intensity of his desire for her. We see a beloved's beauty through her lover's eyes.

In "The Skunk," a recollection of an evening when Heaney was house-sitting for Mark and Ruth Schorer in North Berkeley while teaching at the University of California, Berkeley, the actual nonhuman animal appears right from the start:

Up, black, striped and damasked like the chasuble
At a funeral mass, the skunk's tail
Paraded the skunk. Night after night
I expected her like a visitor. (ll. 1–4)

The ensuing poem is one new whole made from a collision of associations, as the skunk's nightly visitation connects in the poet's mind with the ordinary action of his wife rooting through a bottom drawer for a nightgown. During the skunk's remembered visitations, Heaney had been writing "Love-letters again, broaching the word 'wife' / Like a stored cask, as if its slender vowel / Had mutated into the night earth and air / Of California" (ll. 10–13). Whether it was the love letter writing or the "intent and glamorous, / Ordinary, mysterious" skunk's proud parading (ll. 18–19) or both together, Heaney recalls the innate sensuality of that episode as he watches his wife ready herself for bed:

It all came back to me last night, stirred
By the sootfall of your things at bedtime,
Your head-down, tail-up hunt in the bottom drawer
For the black plunge-line nightdress. (ll. 21–24)

And so skunk finds connection with the "black plunge-line nightdress" by the end. Helen Vendler cites this poem, along with others in *Field Work*, as examples of Heaney's "capacity for detachment" in the service of capturing accurately the everyday:

> The deadpan observation—skunk's tail; damasked striped chasuble; wife's head-down, tail-up stance; black nightdress—mixes levels and usages with an outsider's indifference to the decorum that a culture imposes on its members.[27]

Yet such apparent indifference might well be a prerequisite for a metaphysical conceit, in that it is the operative force in the "violence" of yoking together ideas hitherto considered unlike. Here the association memorably captures the latent eroticism of an ordinary moment. It is a Donne-like gesture delivered through a distinctly Heaney vocabulary.

The last technique I perceive as shared by Donne's and Heaney's love poems pertains to how both poets occasionally end poems: by abruptly changing directions to record some precise insight about the nature of love, desire, or relationships. The best example in Donne occurs in "The Indifferent" that outrageous defense of the rake's indiscriminate and insatiable pursuit of just about any woman. After cataloguing the many kinds of women he can love and challenging the resistance of those who would insist on constancy (ll. 1–18), the rakish speaker ends with Venus' reported verdict on faithful women, the speaker's assumed interlocutors:

Venus heard me sigh this song,
And by Loves sweetest Part, Variety, she swore,
She heard not this till now; and that it should be so no more.
She went, examin'd, and return'd ere long,
And said, alas, Some two or three
Poore Heretiques in love there bee,
Which thinke to stablish dangerous constancie.
But I have told them, since you will be true,
You shall be true to them, who'are false to you. (ll. 19–27)

Unlike many other Early Modern English poets, Donne delivers his comparatively few classical references almost always in a tongue-in-cheek fashion. Here, Venus, who likes to swear, "Variety!", seems much in keeping with Donne's norm. And her appearance also accords with the tenor of the rest of the poem, this "song" the outrageous speaker "sigh[s]." But the last two lines stage a surprising turn. When Venus sentences the faithful lovers to a special kind of misery ("Since you will be true, / You shall be true to them, who'are false to you"), Donne draws attention to a recurring real-life scenario within the arena of human desire: Why is it that those who are the most invested in monogamy fall so hard and so easily for the most unfaithful, those who would be the worst possible fits for them? When undergraduates encounter this poem, most credit it with an uncanny contemporary currency. Most recognize immediately the character types and the situation as familiar in the current dating scene. Through an unexpected change in direction, Donne surprises us with a serious truth.

A similar phenomenon sometimes occurs when Heaney meditates on areas of love or desire not exclusively tied to his relationship with his wife. In "Mother of the Groom,"[28] for example, one of several poems assaying the whirl of emotions associated with his wedding and its immediate aftermath, Heaney imagines how the proceedings must appear to his mother. The poem begins with the memory of her son as an infant taking a bath, then shifts to the welcoming of a new daughter through marriage and how her son's change in status is akin to his slipping "her soapy hold" (l. 8). But then, in the final stanza, Heaney shifts the focus away from the son's loss:

Once soap would ease off
The wedding ring
That's bedded forever now
In her clapping hand. (ll. 9–12)

This sudden turn to the embedded ring transitions the poem from a concentration on loss to an epigrammatic commentary on the durability of marriage over time, an inevitability within the life of the traditional family, as if to say, "This loss, too, shall pass."

In another example, "The Guttural Muse," from *Field Work*, Heaney's observations of a "young crowd" (ll. 5) leaving a discotheque give rise to an unforeseen conclusion about growing older. The speaker, presumably in his hotel room for the night, observes this crowd from his window. He enjoys listening to their voices, which "rose up thick and comforting / As oily bubbles the feeding tench sent up / That evening at dusk" (ll. 6–8). But then, when he watches the ensuing courtship of a girl in the parking lot, a new thought occurs:

A girl in a white dress
Was being courted out among the cars:
As her voice swarmed and puddled into laughs
I felt like some old pike all badged with sores
Wanting to swim in touch with soft-mouthed life. (ll. 11–15)

The poem ends with this sharp, uncomfortable contrast between the young people and the older speaker, which draws our attention to his nostalgic desire for the simpler, seemingly irrecoverable pleasures of youth, an unlooked for truth about the ramifications of aging. The epigrammatic turn in this poem, like that of Donne's "The Indifferent," provides a ready way for Heaney to record a small resonant truth in a short space without the need for excessive elaboration.

For Donne and for Heaney, poetry existed within its own order, an order of language that also functioned as a way of knowing and a way of becoming known. Poets are mindful of this order to a degree and in some ways scholars sometimes are not. They often think of predecessors not just as precursors ensconced in time but also as contemporaries sharing an investment in capturing the essence of experience in words. While the examples I have quoted illustrate that Donne and Heaney possessed highly distinctive voices, a kinship nonetheless exists in how they used their voices to speak about love. As a way of conveying the urgencies of love, both created a "forcibleness" deriving, at least in part, from the skillful use of some of the same literary tools.

NOTES

1. O'Driscoll, *Stepping Stones* (London: Faber and Faber, 2008).
2. O'Driscoll, *Stepping Stones*, 251–252.
3. O'Driscoll, *Stepping Stones*, 210.
4. Heaney, *Spelling It Out* (Loughcrew, County Meath, Ireland: Gallery Books, 2009), 12.
5. O'Driscoll, *Stepping Stones*, 298. Heaney again invokes Donne when describing how Hughes "also had what John Donne called an hydroptical immoderate desire for learning."
6. Wayne K. Chapman, *Yeats and English Renaissance Literature* (New York: Macmillan, 1991), 69.
7. Chapman, *Yeats and English Renaissance Literature*, 143.
8. For an account of their time together, see James Longenbach, *Stone Cottage* (Oxford: Oxford University Press, 1988).
9. O'Driscoll, *Stepping Stones*, 448, 193.
10. Heaney, *The Government of the Tongue* (New York: The Noonday Press, Farrar, Straus, and Giroux, 1988), 97. This quotation comes from the title essay, "The Government of the Tongue," first delivered as the first of the T.S. Eliot Memorial Lectures in October 1986 at Eliot College, University of Kent, UK.
11. Heaney, *The Redress of Poetry* (New York: Farrar, Straus and Giroux, 1995), 9–10. This remark came from the title essay, first delivered as one of his lectures as Oxford Professor of Poetry in 1989, then printed as a pamphlet by Oxford University Press in 1990, before being gathered into the aforementioned book.
12. Ted Hughes and Seamus Heaney (eds.), *The Rattle Bag* (London: Faber and Faber, 1982) and *The School Bag* (London: Faber and Faber, 1997).
13. Heaney, "Earning a Rhyme," *Finders Keepers: Selected Prose, 1971–2001* (London: Faber & Faber, 2002), 59–60.
14. Heaney, "The Place of Writing," *Finders Keepers: Selected Prose, 1971–2001* (London: Faber & Faber, 2002), 241.
15. As with most of Donne's other poems, the authorial authenticity of the titles of the four valedictions cannot be certain. In the case of "Valediction of the booke," the title could well be authorial, in that it appears in the Group 1, Group 2, and Group 3 manuscripts, as well as in several of the manuscripts traditionally associated with Group 3. It seems to have been associated with the poem from the beginning of its circulation—or at least the evidence does not argue the contrary. In the case of "A Valediction of weeping," however, the case is less clear. The Group 1 manuscripts print simply "A Valediction" without modification; the Group 2 manuscripts print "Valediction of weeping" without the initial article; the Group 3 manuscripts replace weeping with "teares"; and the manuscripts associated with Group 3 print "weeping" or "tears," depending on which word they received. This variety of titling, located in

several distinct transmission streams, argues against Donne's direct authorship of the title. A similar situation attends "A Valediction forbidding mourning": the Group 1 manuscripts simply call it "A Valediction"; several of the Group 2 manuscripts (the associated pairs, CT1-B7 and DT1-H4, along with WN1) print "Valediction forbidding mourning," while two others (TT1 and TT2) print "Elegie"; the Group 3 manuscripts print "Vpon the parting from his Mistresse"; and the manuscripts associated with Group 3 sample freely from these options, while one, VA2, calls the poem, "To his Loue upon his departare fro hir." Regardless of who titled these poems originally, however, the majority of the earliest manuscript witnesses modify "Valediction" in some way to distinguish the ensuing poem from others of this kind.

16. Herz, "Under the Sign of Donne," *Criticism* 43, no. 1 (2001): 31.

17. *An Apology for Poetry*, Forrest G. Robinson (ed.) (Indianapolis: Bobbs-Merrill Educational Publishing, 1970), 80–81.

18. Older Sidney scholarship, in my view, at times tries too hard to relegate *energia* to one or the other of the parts of rhetoric. Forrest G. Robinson, for example, resists Neil L. Rudenstine's insistence in *Sidney's Poetic Development* (Cambridge: Harvard University Press, 1967) that *energia* depends on the poet's success in his

> effort to discover forms at every level of language—rhythm, sound, syntax, rhetoric, stanza, genre—forms which draw their energies from a writer's strong feelings and release them with such force as to move, convince, and teach (in the broadest sense) an audience (Rudenstine, 159–160) on the grounds that this conception casts "a romantic coloring over Sidney's more or less neoclassical aesthetic" (Robinson, 131).

Robinson would treat *energia* as more purely conceptual and suggests that it "should not be so closely associated with the verbal and technical aspects of poetry" (132). See Robinson, *The Shape of Things Known: Sidney's* Apology *in Its Philosophical Tradition* (Cambridge: Harvard University Press, 1972), for his full discussion. Yet such a separation between idea and elocution seems to run against Sidney's thought in this passage and elsewhere in the *Apology*.

19. See John Hoskyns, *Directions for Speech and Style*, ed. Hoyt H. Hudson (Princeton: Princeton University Press, 1935).

20. See Kuin, "Sustainable Energy: Philip Sidney and John Donne," *John Donne Journal* 33 (2014): 63–93.

21. Heaney, *Preoccupations: Selected Prose, 1968–1978* (New York: Farrar, Straus and Giroux, 1980), 48.

22. O'Driscoll, *Stepping Stones*, 365–366.

23. "Poem" and "Twice Shy" appeared in *Death of a Naturalist* (London: Faber and Faber, 1966); "Wedding Day" and "Summer Home" in *Wintering Out* (London: Faber and Faber, 1972); "Polder" in *Field Work* (London: Faber and Faber, 1979); and "La Toilette" and "The Underground" in *Station Island* (London: Faber and Faber, 1984).

24. A. J. Smith, ed., *John Donne: The Critical Heritage* (London and Boston: Routledge & Kegan Paul, 1975), 218.

25. O'Driscoll, *Stepping Stones*, 312.

26. Both poems appear together in *Field Work*.
27. Vendler, *Seamus Heaney* (Cambridge: Harvard University Press, 1998), 70.
28. *Wintering Out* (London: Faber and Faber, 1972).

Chapter 7

The Depth of Herbert's Voiceprint in the Poetry of Alfred Corn

As Judith Scherer Herz explains, the "voiceprint" of one poet in the work of a subsequent poet is the product not so much of the latter's occasional imitation of the former but of a more profound, more substantial engagement of one poet with the "psychology" and "linguistic system" of another.[1] A voiceprint registers when a "later writer greets" an early modern writer, "trying on his language and looking inside his imagination." It is fundamentally an act of sympathetic investment, a willingness to experience through another's language and perceptions, an enlargement of one's own word hoard by going to school off of that which genuinely speaks to one in the work of someone else. The ensuing "encounter," Herz explains, "happens less in the manner of a Bloomean agon or an overreaching than simply as a willingness to listen, to reimagine, to make over as one's own." Often enough, it results from the kind of preoccupation non-poets might consider obsession: Edgell Rickword carries his two-volume Muse's Library Donne to the Front in 1917; Rupert Brooke tours Germany with Baedecker and Donne (the latter as much of a guide as the former?); Joseph Brodsky learns English for the express purpose of translating Donne; Tennessee Williams asks a friend to read him Donne poems for several hours as consolation on the night his first play *Battle of Angels* bombed during its first performance; and Paul Muldoon "swallows Donne whole" to elegize Warren Zevon.[2] In each case, one poet finds in another poet's imagination a spur for moving his or her own. The voiceprint is the verbal residue of this activity. Like a fingerprint, which captures in finely oiled lines a unique material trace of the original, it is composed of all the verbal traces that show through in the subsequent new work—allusions, echoes, stanza forms, logical or grammatical structures, phrasings, and of course, repeated words, all refracted through the imagination of another and in response to the demands of the new poetic context.

Donne's voiceprint often enough issues from a fascination with his personality and with his fascinations—with death, say, or love, or what Raymond-Jean Frontain aptly calls, the "need to make disparate parts or experiences cohere."[3] To return to Herz, "It is Donne *in* his texts" the later poet "greets," Donne who fascinates through a "language" and a "vision" "oddly transportable over the centuries."[4] For the character of the Herbertian voiceprint, we would do well to start with a distinction Seamus Heaney makes in contrasting a "political activist" view of poetry with what he terms a "visionary" view of poetry, the latter emerging from the "self-delighting inventiveness" at the heart of poetic craft.[5] In contrast to the "heckler" for whom poetry must be harnessed to social movements to be useful, Heaney believes we must not slight the "imperative" to "redress poetry *as* poetry, to set it up as its own category, an eminence established and a pressure exercised by distinctly linguistic means."[6] During the writing process, the visionary poet's "movement is from delight to wisdom and not vice versa," Heaney writes. "The felicity of a cadence, the chain reaction of a rhyme, the pleasuring of an etymology, such things can proceed happily and as it were autistically, in an area of mental operations cordoned off by and from the critical sense." The poet must dive into the pleasures of wordsmithing to render a compelling vision, a "counter-reality" capable of balancing his/her "historical situation."[7]

Not surprisingly, Heaney finds in Herbert's "self-delighting" verbal "inventiveness" an example of a "fully realized poetry," where the "co-ordinates of the imagined thing correspond to and allow us to contemplate the complex burden of our own experience."[8] That Herbert's poetry is more readily approachable "*as* poetry" than that of the majority of his contemporaries is a central condition of the nature of his influence for many practicing poets today. For, more often than not, it is less the specific claims Herbert makes about his particularly Protestant point of view that show through in the work of subsequent poets than it is a habit of language use that enables other poets to grasp, however momentarily, the insights available in their own experiences. In much the same way, Herbert grasped the mini-movements of his own spiritual life. Herbert's verse invites poets more insistently than that of many other poets to engage in the delights of wordplay in the pursuit of recording the nuances of felt experience, regardless of whether that experience accords with the particulars of Herbert's own.

Plenty of poets corroborate the appeal of Herbert's poetry *as* poetry. But rather than concentrate on the usual suspects (Eliot, Bishop, Larkin, Glück, or even Heaney himself)[9] and risk repeating what already has been noted, I will enhance the resolution of the Herbertian voiceprint by attending to its manifestation in the poetry of Alfred Corn, the author of twelve well-received collections of poems and one of the strongest and most wide-ranging American practitioners of formalist verse today.[10] Corn's example becomes intriguing in the present discussion not only because of his finely tuned skill but also because he offers a wonderful occasion for us to assess the distinction between the *conscious invocation* and *unconscious intrusion* of a predecessor's work, both equally important dimensions of the voiceprint. A full account of any poet's voiceprint, whether Herbert's, Donne's, or anyone else's, must encompass more than just the intended traces, those allusions, echoes, phrases, or structures consciously invoked; it also must assess the seepage or run-off of the poet's absorption in the voiceprint's original, those words or constructions that creep in beyond the poet's conscious awareness. The unconscious, the unintended, when noticed and not simply imposed, enriches the meaning of a poetic utterance the way the recognition of any additional semantic layer would.[11]

A recipient of the Levinson Prize from *Poetry* magazine and of Fulbright, Guggenheim, and National Endowment for the Arts fellowships, Corn is a master both of poetic technique and of acute observation. Yet despite his accomplishments and the richness and distinctiveness of his voice, he is not as widely studied within the academy as he should be. The reason may be, as Thomas M. Disch has remarked, that Corn's "is not the mode among poetry academics at the moment, but since at least the time of Byron and Wordsworth it has been the kind of poetry that most commends itself to *readers*."[12] Within the world of contemporary American poetry, however, Corn is a significant figure whose work, according to Harold Bloom, should be canonized.[13]

Corn's interest in Herbert has been nearly lifelong and occasionally on prominent display. In 1993, for example, Poets House and New York University asked him to plan and emcee a 400th birthday celebration in honor of Herbert, during which he, Amy Clampitt, Henri Cole, Jane Cooper, and Stanley Kunitz read and commented upon favorite Herbert poems to give a "hint of the richness of the work in its entirety."[14] Throughout his introductory remarks for the evening, one senses Corn's admiration for Herbert's abilities to craft "consummately achieved poems" and for Herbert's courage in facing and recording so precisely the "fierceness of the struggle" to "replace pride with humility" in his life as a country parson.[15] Herbert, he notes elsewhere, is "one of those authors we value for the literary corpus he left behind and for our sense of the life he led."[16]

Beyond the admiration of one poetic master for another, however, lies a deeper interaction. For, Herbert's sensibility, by which I mean not only his temperament and spiritual outlook but also more broadly his treatment of language as a resource for memory, experience, and understanding, intrudes in Corn's verse and at times provides the kind of personal aid only the most heart-read poetry can offer.

Compelling evidence for Corn's engagement with Herbert's sensibility and for the ensuing voiceprint appears in the poem "Resources" published in

Tables (2013). Corn shared this poem with me in the Fall of 2007 as part of a correspondence on the nature of Herbert's influence:

Late May remakes the park, even
the part laid out behind wrought iron
fence railings, one pigeon on promenade,
crisp feathers a not so common
cocoa and dishrag-gray, the compact head
ticking along fast forward,
a changing silk rainbow as its collar.
Heavy leafage, pollen and nectar poured
from the locust flowers' galactic cloud ...
Breathe in the fragrant troposphere, then pause:
and let today recover its first cause.
*

I've been paging through compendia and sources
to find that timeless tale, the one in which
a peasant princess wearing star-bright pearls
(the dowry offered by a guardian witch)
drops her gaze and lets a sneering rival
snatch away the favor. Who, when she forces
its clasp shut, shrieks to see her pillage shrivel
into a snarl, a torque of snakes and lizards—
the same for all wearers but the fair and gentle.
*

A fifties living room. "Consider the *source*."
For emphasis, her last word's octave leap
struck a dulcimer that rang out silver
as wires glinting in permanent elderly
waves, waves a tearful grandson shouldn't muss.

Consolation was built on fortitude.
Dunces spat venom, ragged us with their cheap
jokes, but disgrace was theirs alone, the fruit
of a defective character bedeviled
by our brain's reptilian taproot. "It's misplaced

response to hurts they've undergone themselves.
Treat them as *you* should treat them, not as they
do you. Wherever we are known as ourselves,
there's love enough. Say, curly head, who made us?
Then raise your eyes, lamb, and consider the Source."

*

Pre-summer anti-twilight lingers late,
the last knife, plate and cup not put away
till well beyond eleven. What's made me
burn insomnia's glaring kilowatt,

stacking chips on the actuarial table?
A decade's grace; then sky-high interest on the Debt . . . .
Life-lender, you've let it stay outstanding yet
collection agencies all know my name.

Lamplight. A cloudburst of bygones. One free
hand sprawled on facing pages of a book.
"Call in they death's head there; tie up they fears."
Smithy of resource, the ringing anvil shapes
what sleep's lithe silver ouroboros took
from one day's solo round, till the prologue clears:

Late May remakes the park, even
the part laid out behind wrought iron
fence railings, one pigeon on promenade.

The poem is a meditation on how one forgets and then remembers who one is. The arrangement of the movements within it differs from the order of the experience described. The poem begins with the perception of a "pigeon on promenade" (section one), then shifts to a past search through books for a remembered tale (section two), then ventures further back—to the 1950s—to a memory about the speaker's grandmother offering him consolation in the face of bullying (section three), and concludes at a time after the park with a vision of reading Herbert while "burn[ing] insomnia's glaring kilowatt," an action that returns to the beginning (section four). The poem moves full-circle in two senses: through the repeated lines (*Late May remakes the park, . . .*) and through the repeated image of the collar, in the pigeon's plumage and in Herbert's poem. The reader cannot say for sure which came first, the specific notice of the pigeon or the speaker's immediate connection with Herbert's poem, whether the poem encouraged a way of seeing or whether the noticing triggered associations by itself. In any case, the opening image—the "pigeon on promenade"—establishes the central issue of the meditation while the quoted line ("Call in thy death's head there; tie up thy fears") highlights the process of remembrance.

Corn's choice of the pigeon as a symbol for pride contrasts sharply with the experience of humiliation the grandmother counters through her reassurance. In a New York City park in May, what could be more common than a pigeon? Yet this pigeon's distinctiveness attracts notice, its "crisp feathers a not so common / cocoa and dishrag-gray," a "shimmering rainbow as its collar" (ll. 4–7). Like much of Corn's work, "Resources" addresses the issue of standing out against the expectations of the crowd. In "A Goya Reproduction," his essay on his initial exposure to art generally and to Goya in particular, Corn recalls having to pass regularly through a gauntlet of bullies to enter the local library, the refuge that clearly marked him as different from his peers:

> A dreaded obstacle was the phalanx of bullies often waiting on the lawn outside to pounce on the skinny weirdo who didn't like to trade punches with them, which would have been the only path to equality and friendship. My humiliating response to being pushed to the ground and pummeled was merely to lie still until the attackers got bored and left. After which I'd get up, adjust myself, and trudge onward.[17]

This account usefully sketches the background behind the grandmother's remark, "It's misplaced / response to hurts they've undergone themselves" (ll. 30-1) and enriches the symbolic value of the pigeon. Confident in its individuality, the pigeon struts "on promenade," unlike the "skinny weirdo" who lay on the ground.

Such contrasts between the individual and external expectations inform much of Herbert's verse as well, including "The Collar." Does the same contrast with the pigeon "on promenade" apply to the adult speaker of Corn's poem? I am less certain. He has been searching for a cautionary tale about the cost of stealing the "peasant" princess's "pearls" (l. 14). Is he supposed to identify with the rightful owner, the witch who originally bestowed the pearls, or the thief? What is certain, however, is that he turns to Herbert for aid in figuring out his situation. The open book upon which one "free" hand is "sprawled" must be an edition of Herbert (or one including Herbert's poems) because it is opened to "The Collar," hence the quoted lines (ll. 41–3).[18] Herbert's poem operates as a "[s]mithy of resource," a way into other resources (pigeon, fable book, memory), so that the speaker can recall, and in recollection, find comfort in his identity in a created universe full of pressures to forget. The repetition of lines one through three at the end emphasizes the cyclical nature of the experience, how consolation in the face of discrimination comes in the remembrance of one's identity, a temporary recognition. In Herbert's "The Collar," regular meter reasserts itself as the speaker remembers his collar is not that of a *doulos*, or a slave, but of a *pais*, a favored servant, a member of God's clergy.[19] Calm ensues, as it does here. Yet it is a temporary calm, the cycle perhaps a day or less away from repeating.

Certainly the allusion to Herbert and the process of the poem—both conscious artistic choices in Corn's design—are Herbertian enough. So, too, is the humility with which he treats his role as poet: "Like Herbert I'd like to be a harmonious blacksmith, turning the anvil into a dulcimer, as I forge my day," he writes. "I want to be worthy of my Source, of sources like Herbert; and become a resource to others coming after me."[20] And so is the conclusion: consolation and desolation both are temporary states.

Corn's engagement is deeper still, however, the Herbertian voiceprint more complex. For in the third section of the poem, arguably its emotional core, the memory of the grandmother's words of consolation to the speaker's childhood self is laced with the presence of "Love (III)." Compare Herbert's second stanza:

A guest, I answer'd, worthy to be here:
        Love said, You shall be he.
I the unkinde, ungratefull? Ah my deare,
        I cannot look on thee.
Love took my hand, and smiling did reply,
        Who made the eyes but I?

with:

"Treat them as *you* should treat them, not as they
do you. Where we are known as ourselves,
there's love enough. Say, curly head, who made us?
Then raise your eyes, lamb, and consider the Source."

Herbert's "Love" and Corn's "Source" both are capitalized to underscore their metonymic reference to the divine. Both poems place the notion of divine making into a question addressed to a speaker in need of reminding: "Who made the eyes but I?" and "Say, curly head, who made us?"[21] Finally, and most importantly, both poets use the same three freighted words—love, made, and eyes—in the same order within a span of two lines.[22] The presence of the earlier poem in the later one seems unmistakable.

Yet—and here is the important point—it is an *unintended* presence. When I noted it in my correspondence with Corn, he acknowledged he hadn't noticed it before, but that it didn't surprise him: "I have read Herbert so many times," he writes, "that I suppose he must now be part of the fabric of consciousness, the text of the composing self. So I wouldn't be surprised to discover many echoes of his poems in mine."[23] Corn's remarks at the 1993 Herbert gathering lend credence to his reaction here. The unintended presence of "Love (III)," a product of Corn's unconscious "self-delighting inventiveness," is a seepage of Herbert's language into Corn's in exactly the right place to drive home the venerability of the advice. It produces a resonance heard most strongly by those who know the precursor poem, and subsequently this resonance enriches Corn's poem.

In the case of "Resources," I had the luxury of asking the poet whether the echoes I heard were intentional. But how do we detect the unintended traces of a voiceprint in the work of those long-dead or otherwise unavailable? The present example suggests a method: close attention to the grammar, the proximity, and the order of repeated significant words. If a voiceprint consists of the inclusion of multiple significant words from the source text, then the proximity of those words in what may be a different semantic context suggests a lack of conscious reference. The repeated words in "Resources" are not arranged to comment or respond explicitly to "Love (III)" in a recognizable fashion; rather, they address the immediate expressive context of the speaker's meditation. When placed together, though, they tickle the associative capacities of readers who share a reading background with the poet. Just so must the unintended traces of a voiceprint appear more generally in the work of any poet who has digested the work of a beloved predecessor thoroughly enough for it to become an implement for his or her imagination.

In conjunction with the verbal traces of specific Herbert poems, we also can detect in Corn's work Herbertian habits of rhetorical patterning. Herbert frequently relies on rhetorical figures of repetition to heighten an awareness of affective and/or spiritual processes and conditions and to reinforce his poetic structures. In "The Thanksgiving," for instance, a poem about a process (giving thanks) expressing a condition (gratitude), Herbert's speaker uses verbal repetitions within and across his rhyming pentameter/tetrameter couplets (highlighted below by my italics) to emphasize the intensity of his desire both to thank Christ for His sacrifice and to follow Christ's example:

Oh King of wounds! how shall I *grieve* for thee,
    Who in all *grief* preventest me?
Shall I *weep* bloud? why, thou hast *wept* such store
    That all thy body was one doore. (ll. 3-6, my emphasis)

Shall thy *strokes* be my *stroking*? thorns, my flower?
    Thy rod, my posie? crosse, my bower? (ll. 13-14)

If thou dost give my *honour*, men shall see,
    The *honour* doth belong to thee. (ll. 21-22)

I'le build a spittle, or *mend* common wayes,
    But *mend* mine own without delayes.

Then I will *use* the works of they creation,
    As if I *us'd* them but for fashion. (ll. 33-36)

My musick *shall* finde thee, and ev'ry string
    Shall have his attribute to sing;
That all together may accord in thee,
    And prove *one* God, *one* harmonie. (ll. 39-42)

Nay, I will reade thy book, and never move
    Till I have found therein thy *love*,
Thy art of *love*, which I'le turn back on thee:
    O my deare Saviour, Victorie! (ll. 45-48)

Each repeated pair suggests the reciprocity the speaker desires to share with Christ. Together, they add to the music of the couplets and prepare the reader to hear the jangling contrast of the final lines: "Then for thy passion—I will do for that—/ Alas, my God, I know not what" (ll. 49-50). The near rhyme here, an off-note, and the absence of a repeated pair emphasize the contrast between human and divine and the impossibility of repaying Christ for the Passion.

If the use of ploce, anaphora, epizeuxis, and the like in this manner is truly Herbertian, then Corn shares it, too. As part of his conversion to Christianity, which he recounts in *Incarnation: Contemporary Writers on the New Testament*, a collection of essays he edited in 1990, Corn has approached religious themes in verse as highly aware of the chiming effects of repeated words as Herbert's.[24] In "Easter Eucharist," a villanelle, he relies on verbal pairs in a way reminiscent of Herbert's "The Thanksgiving":

To witness resurrection of the Christ,
Light's freshest morning dawns—and is outpoured.
What rose again again is sacrificed.

A cyclic, quickening narrative is spliced
To ours, that flesh approximate the Word
And witness resurrection of the Christ.

Some media event of the Zeitgeist?
No, and no bland diversion for the bored:
What rises rises to be sacrificed.

"Thanksgiving" roughly translates eucharist,
Which martyrs bodied forth through fire and sword
To witness resurrection of the Christ.

Seamless garment Roman soldiers diced
For, you gave all that we could not afford:
Your loss our gain, and again sacrificed.

What space- or time-bound gift would have sufficed?
Beholden guests approach the groaning board
To witness resurrection of a Christ
Who couldn't rise if never sacrificed.[25]

Within his re-creation of the Crucifixion (or his re-creation of the re-creation of the Crucifixion), Corn employs figures of repetition to emphasize the cyclical nature of sacrifice and of resurrection, the lesson we are meant to learn from Christ's Passion. The epizeuxis in line three—"What rose *again again* is sacrificed"—beautifully holds these two phases of rebirth in balance, and when Corn adjusts this refrain through ploce and diacope in line fifteen ("Your loss our *gain*, and *again* sacrificed"), he introduces the new signification of "gain" to the cycle: we gain through another's sacrifice, we gain through our own. In between, near the halfway point of the poem, two other verbal pairs (a ploce/diacope combination and epizeuxis)—"*No*, and *no* bland diversion for the bored:/What *rises rises* to be sacrificed" (ll. 8-9)—defend the cycle from a charge of superficiality. The first refuses to consider it a mere "media event" and denies its relegation to mere "diversion for the bored"; the second emphatically recognizes that rising, that life itself, prefigures as well as follows sacrifice. Resurrection requires sacrifice, which both follows and precedes rebirth, as in the feast of the Eucharist. The lyric is especially rich, form reinforcing content, in a way that many Herbert poems are rich. As with Herbert's poem, formal and verbal pairings reinforce the depiction of a spiritual phenomenon as a cyclical process. Although the reference to "Thanksgiving" (l. 10) may not signal Herbert's poem of the same name, Corn's use of repeated pairs in such close proximity recalls a Herbertian relationship between figures of repetition and thematic significance.

We now are at the extreme edges of the voiceprint. Are these similarities in technique products of influence at the non-intentional level, or are they products of the phenomenology of reading more generally, evidence of how "one's prior experience of reading shapes one's present responses to a particular text or a series of texts"?[26] Can they be traced definitively to Herbert as a sole tutor, or are they aspects of an approach to poetic development that Herbert followed but did not define, one that others along the way adopted? Answers to these questions may be too subjective to be of much value. They arise naturally, however, from considerations of Herbert's voiceprint. For Herbert's delight in "poetry *as* poetry," a primary reason why he has become a poet's poet in modern times also means his influence cannot be measured strictly by the number of allusions or direct responses one finds. It intrudes more subtly. In the poems of a significant poet like Corn, the subtlety of its intrusions becomes part of the pleasure of the reading experience. A sense of the Herbertian voiceprint triggers associations in much the same way as Corn's poems on European art do for those familiar with the works described. Because of the colloquial simplicity of Herbert's language, his tendency to use high numbers of monosyllabic words, the echoes sound all the more striking when heard in the work of strong poets like Corn, whose voices also are unmistakable.

NOTES

1. Herz, "Under the Sign of Donne," *Criticism* 43, no. 1 (Winter 2001), 31.

2. See Herz, "Under the Sign of Donne," for discussions of Rickword, Brooke, and Brodsky; Frontain, "Registering Donne's Voiceprint," for Williams; and Herz, "Tracking the Voiceprint of Donne," for Muldoon.

3. Frontain, "Registering Donne's Voiceprint," 196.

4. Herz, "Under the Sign of Donne," 31.

5. Heaney, *The Redress of Poetry* (New York: Farrar, Straus, and Giroux, 1995), 3–5.

6. Heaney, *The Redress of Poetry*, 5–6.

7. Heaney, *The Redress of Poetry*, 4.

8. Heaney, *The Redress of Poetry*, 10.

9. On Bishop's fascination with Herbert, see Joseph H. Summers, "George Herbert and Elizabeth Bishop," *George Herbert Journal* 18, no. 1–2 (Fall 1994/ Spring 1995): 48–58; Jeffrey Powers-Beck, "'Time to Plant Tears': Elizabeth Bishop's Seminary of Tears," *South Atlantic Review* 60, no. 4 (Nov. 1995): 69–87; and Stephen Yenser, "'Spontaneity': Herbert's Irruption in the Poetry of Elizabeth Bishop and James Merrill," in *George Herbert's Travels: International Print and Cultural Legacies*, ed. Christopher Hodgkins (Newark, DE: University of Delaware Press, 2011), 191–205. On Larkin's, see Christopher Hodgkins, "In a Serious House: Church-Going with George Herbert and Philip Larkin," in *George Herbert's Travels: International Print and Cultural Legacies*, 207–223; David Yezzi, "'Power of Some Sort or Other': On Poems & Prayers," *The New Criterion* 30, no. 8 (2012): 29–33; and Eric Meljac, "Windows in George Herbert and Philip Larkin: A Study of Poetic Metaphor," *Journal of Language, Literature, and Culture* 65, no. 3 (2018): 187–199. On stylistic similarities between Herbert and Glück, see Ann Townsend, "The Problem of Sincerity: The Lyric Plain Style of George Herbert and Louise Glück," *Shenandoah* 46, no. 4 (Winter 1996): 43–61.

10. Corn's collections of poetry are as follows: *All Roads at Once* (Viking, 1976); *A Call in the Midst of the Crowd* (Viking, 1978); *The Various Light* (Viking, 1980); *Notes from a Child of Paradise* (Viking, 1984); *The West Door* (Viking, 1988); *Autobiographies* (Viking, 1992); *Present* (Counterpoint, 1997); *Stake: Selected*

Poems, 1972-1992 (Counterpoint, 1999); *Contradictions* (Copper Canyon, 2002); *Tables* (Press 53, 2013); *Unions* (Barrow Street Press, 2014); and with Joanne Wang, *The Bamboo Pavilion* (Four Seasons Press, 2019). As a testament to Corn's range, Richard Abowitz relates the following anecdote:

> I invented a game with friends one afternoon. One of us would name a poet, and another would come up with an unlikely form for that poet. We then had to concoct the resulting poem. Examples ranged from Anthony Hecht as a language poet, to Philip Levine rendered in poulter's measure. When Alfred Corn's name came up, despite a familiarity with all of his then five books, I proved unable to come up with an uncharacteristic form. (204)

See "The Traveller: On the Poetry of Alfred Corn," *The Kenyon Review* 15, no. 4 (Fall 1993): 201–16.

11. Here I am mindful of John T. Shawcross's careful distinctions between author's text and reader's texts in the introductory chapter of *Intentionality and the New Traditionalism: Some Liminal Means to Literary Revisionism* (University Park: The Pennsylvania State University Press, 1991).

12. Corn has been favorably compared to Hart Crane, W. H. Auden, and James Merrill, three poets with whom he shares some similar interests, including a fascination with history, with place, and with the arts. See Thomas M. Disch, review of *Present, Boston Review* (December 1997/January 1998) and Christopher Matthew Hennessy, "Corn, Alfred (b. 1943)," *glbtq* (http://www.glbtq.com/literature/corn_a.html, 10 September 2008).

13. *The Western Canon: The Books and School of the Ages* (New York: Harcourt Brace & Co, 1994), 567. As further evidence of Corn's standing in contemporary literature, he was one only twenty-six writers interviewed by *American Literary History* to comment on the "Situation of American Writing" in 1999, especially the relationships between contemporary writing and literary studies (see Gordon Hutner and Madison Smartt Bell, et al., *American Literary History* 11, no. 2 [Summer 1999]: 215–353). The interviews together demonstrate persuasively the truth of editor Gordon Hutner's claim that "scholar-teachers have unwittingly abjured an animating connection to the literary culture of their day," and that as a result, "literary criticism is just not taken as seriously in the mainstream as it once was" (215). With very few exceptions (say, Bloom and Helen Vendler), scholar-critics have mostly lost the authority to shape the reading tastes and critical understanding of the reading public. Hutner's claims are difficult to refute.

14. I am grateful to Corn for permission to quote the text of his unpublished remarks as well as that of the poems and correspondence below.

15. The notion of balance, particularly of form with experience, is an important part of Corn's aesthetic. In "Stepson Elegy," the poem he wrote to his deceased stepmother Virginia Whitaker MacMillan Corn, he writes, "Though your own 'poetry' was never written down, / You'd seen how private, even trivial events, / Put in a form that balanced feeling with fact, / Might compose a record worth hearing more than once" (*Present*, 5). Herbert also valued such a balance, perhaps one reason for Corn's affinity for his work

16. Private correspondence, November 28, 2007.

17. Corn, *Present*, 12

18. Elsewhere in Corn's *oeuvre*, the work of others functions as resources for insight. See, for example, "Dreambooks" in *Stake*, 4–6.

19. See John R. Roberts, "'Me Thoughts I Heard One Calling, Child!': Herbert's 'The Collar,'" *Renascence: Essays on Values in Literature* 45, no. 3 (Spring 1993): 197–204.

20. Private correspondence, October 16, 2008.

21. The grandmother also echoes William Blake's "The Lamb," as Mark Strand noted during the session in which this paper was presented at the George Herbert's Living Legacies Conference (October 2008) and as Corn himself acknowledged in a private correspondence, October 16, 2008.

22. In his discussion of "Phonic Echo" (65–77) in *The Poem's Heartbeat* (3rd printing, Ashland, Oregon: Story Line Press, 2001), one of the finest treatments of prosody in English, Corn emphasizes that the best rhyming words possess not only a commonality of sounds but also be chosen so that they acquire an extra semantic weight when paired. The weight of individual words in combination is significant, another concern Corn shares with Herbert. *The Poem's Heartbeat* recently has been republished again by Copper Canyon Press.

23. Private correspondence, November 19, 2007.

24. Corn, *Incarnation: Contemporary Writers on the New Testament* (New York: Viking Penguin, 1990). The relevant section appears in "The Second Epistle of Paul the Apostle to the Corinthians," 142.

25. Though so far uncollected, an earlier version of this poem appeared in *The Sewanee Review*.

26. James Boyd White, "Reading One Poet in Light of Another: Herbert and Frost," *George Herbert Journal* 18, no. 1 & 2 (Fall 1994/Spring 1995): 59. White describes the reader's associative sifting of texts in a way that harmonizes with my account of one poet *writing* in light of another:

> For we cannot help placing what we read in contexts of our own making, defined by our educations; these contexts in turn give meaning to what we read, as certain features are highlighted or obscured by the expectations we have formed. The connections so established can be chronological, as one brings one's reading of Donne, say, to Yeats; or antichronological, as in my own reading of Frost and Herbert, for I was familiar with Frost, who was to me very much the ideal poet, long before I read Herbert with any care. (59)

Poets and readers, I would add, *cannot help but* write and read in light of others, at least some of the time.

Chapter 8

Verbal Relish in the Poetry of Donne and Kimberly Johnson

Kimberly Johnson,[1] one of the finest American poets writing today, is another poet whose imagination routinely draws inspiration from the metaphysical poets in powerful ways. Her second collection *A Metaphorical God* (2008) announces its indebtedness to Donne in both title and epigraph.[2] Its title borrows a phrase from the nineteenth expostulation of Donne's *Devotions upon Emergent Occasions*, Donne's moving, poignant account of his life-threatening battle with typhus, or "spotted fever," in December 1623/1624. Composed of twenty-three devotions in all, each corresponds to one day of his illness and enacts a movement in his reaction to his unfolding experience. At the beginning of the nineteenth expostulation, Donne marvels at the signifying powers of God. In the passage Johnson quotes, he emphasizes God's metaphorical prowess:

> My *God*, my *God*, Thou art a *direct God*, may I not say, a *literall God*, a *God* that wouldest bee understood *literally*, and according to the *plaine sense* of all that thou saiest? But thou art also (*Lord* I intend it to thy *glory*, and let no *prophane mis-interpreter* abuse it to thy *diminution*) thou art a *figurative*, a *metaphoricall God* too: A *God* in whose words there is such a height of *figures*, such *voyages*, such *peregrinations* to fetch remote and precious *metaphors*, such *extentions*, such *spreadings*, such *Curtaines* of *Allegories*, such *third Heavens* of *Hyperboles*, so *harmonious eloquutions*, so *retired* and so *reserved expressions*, so *commanding perswasions*, so *perswading commandements*, such *sinewes* even in thy *milke*, and such *things* in thy *words*, as all *prophane Authors*, seeme of the seed of the *Serpent*, that *creepes*; thou art the *dove*, that flies.[3]

As an epigraph, this passage segues beautifully into the ensuing collection of poems. In poem after poem, Johnson meditates on the many significations of the material world around her and of her own body. What emerges is a rich account of how a mind fully alive in the intersections between object and language makes sense of experience. The poet, in her individual way, works toward coming to terms with a "metaphorical god" so adept at loading into everyday encounters deep potentials for discovering connections and significance.

The natural question arising from such an epigraph and such a title is *what is Donnean about Johnson's book?* To say that Johnson follows Donne's manner in seeing metaphors wherever she looks is to state what would be obvious to anyone reading even the first few poems. As God is a *metaphoricall God*, Donne is a *metaphoricall* poet famously capable of startling and delighting readers through unexpected comparisons: the flea as marriage bed, soul as besieged town, tear as globe, face as hemisphere, shadow as love affair. So, too, is Johnson, ready to see a "bloody butterfly" in thyroid cancer, a "temptress" in an adder, or the heart as a "secret junco" in her "breast."[4] As she admits in "Easter, Looking Westward" (another echo and sly reversal of Donne), "I'm all exotic / metaphor, inkhorn snarls, never content / with the unelaborated *thing*" (ll. 4-6). One easily imagines Donne thinking the same of himself, albeit in his own vernacular.

While our modern predilections cause "metaphor" and "metaphorical" to ignite like flares in the dark, the rest of Donne's expostulation is more revealing for Donne, for Johnson, and for the similarities between their poems. Donne frames his thoughts about metaphor within the broader category of "figurative"—"thou art a *figurative*, a *metaphoricall God*," he says, reminding us centuries later that not even metaphor was an island entire of itself but was instead, for Donne and for his contemporaries, a part of the figurative mainland of discourse. John Hoskyns, a fellow Inns of Court man whose poems occasionally traveled with Donne's in miscellany manuscripts, considered metaphor the first of fifteen "Figures for Varying" one's speech to enliven it.[5] For Hoskyns, a metaphor is the "friendly and neighborly borrowing of one word to express a thing with more light and a better note, though not so directly and properly as the natural name of the thing meant would signify."[6] While enlivening our speech, metaphor also "enricheth our knowledge with two things at once, with the truth and with similitude."

This sense of metaphor-as-figure alerts us to the wider range of discursive moments animating Donne's account of the figurative, metaphorical God. God's words contain a "height of *figures*," and Donne marvels at the "*voyages*," "*peregrinations*," "*extentions*," and "*spreadings*"—all suggestive of the energy of creative effort necessary to bring forth such exemplary allegories, hyperboles, elocutions, persuasions, and commandments that allow God, like a dove, to fly above all "*prophane Authors*" creeping across the ground. There are "*sinewes* even in thy *milke*," Donne explains, a muscular vigor in God's style. And Donne's description flexes these same sinews through a similarly figurative, similarly vigorous style. The momentum of his words depends on anaphora ("such . . . such . . . such . . ." and "so . . . so . . ."), chiasmus ("so *commanding perswasions*, so *perswading commandments*"), and symploce ("Serpent, that *creepes* . . . dove, that *flies*"). He relishes the sounds of words in concert with one another and the forward momentum that gives God as dove lift. Later in the same passage, he extends his description of the figurative, metaphorical God beyond the Scriptures to the world as a whole: "Neither art thou a *figurative*, a *Metaphoricall God*, in thy *word* only, but in thy *workes* too. The *stile* of thy *works*, the *phrase* of thine *Actions*, is *Metaphoricall*."[7] The world embodies the same sinewy figurative vigor. Donne is attracted to it. So is Johnson.

This Donnean epigraph, then, signals much more than an avowal of metaphor; it pledges a commitment to verbal relish and stylistic vigor as means of apprehension and explanation that Johnson, like Donne before her, makes good on in the ensuing poems. Style becomes a way into the world, provided it enacts the vigor and immediacy of experience. It also becomes a pleasure for the poet and the reader who loves words.

"Easter, Looking Westward," that witty play on Donne's "Goodfriday, 1613. Riding Westward," honestly reflects on the *"extentions"* and *"spreadings"* of Johnson's style in her own words.[8] After confessing her discomfort with the "unelaborated *thing*," she elaborates

always the forced apotheosis,
every least sparrow a visible sign,
strong-arming water to wine. So tenderly

I love this world's profane loveliness,
its small, scarce loveliness, like a puritan
I batter magnitude out of homespun. (ll. 7-12)

The pleasure here is obvious. To "batter magnitude out of homespun" is not to fail at description but to perceive actively through a process that relishes words. Rather than focus on subjective inadequacies, as in Donne's Good Friday poem, this poem vents the poet's marveling at the disappearance of stars behind clouds and the star-like light of the sea. "The stars! The stars have fled the sky!—," Johnson begins. "Scratch that—the stars have *skyed the flood*, the sea / glimmering in pale beneath a starless black" (ll. 1-3). The rest of the poem, after Johnson's interlude on her love of the "world's profane loveliness," offers a demonstration of verbal relish in the service of capturing in words the perception of vanished stars. Her last attempt to describe them shifts the macrocosm to microcosm in a manner not unlike the Donne of the *Songs and Sonnets*:

> Start again: The stars are black with storms
> blown shoreward; the dinoflagellates
>
> smacked on the shoals leak light from shattered cells;
> they phosphoresce the breakers in their roister.
> Let me sing, then, the beauty of creatures
>
> microscopic, who make the vastness gleam
> in smithereens. (ll. 17-23)

The rich imagery of this celebration of the small is sonically rich as well, as the poet clearly relishes the sounds of her words and their cadences. A sense of wonder blooms largely from these sounds and the ways in which they chime with each other through consonance and assonance. This soundscape helps convey her love of "this world's profaneness."

Verbal richness additionally characterizes "Goodfriday," another poem glancing at Donne's Good Friday poem (note Johnson's spelling of "Goodfriday" as one word, not two, as in most modern editions of Donne's poem) and also, as it happens, another mini *ars poetica* on Johnson's style. "Goodfriday" connects directly with Donne's poem through three obvious echoes: its title, its description of the "waver[ing]" "hightop two-lane" road as "Westbound" (l. 4), and its declaration that the "magnitude" of a "moment's span" of thunder is "of too much weight for me" (ll. 17-19). Still, for all these nods to Donne, Johnson's "Goodfriday" corrects Donne's Good Friday meditation in one specific way: its embeddedness in locale. Donne's poem proffers a memorable sketch of the Aristotelian account of the spheres as a metaphor for the soul's devotional motion and a visceral recreation of the Crucifixion from the standpoint of a bystander. But as a journey poem—indeed, a poem purportedly written *while* journeying—it is notoriously non-localized, as John Carey has pointed out. Though composed "in transit like Wordsworth's *Tintern Abbey*," Carey notes, Donne's poem

> could not be less like *Tintern Abbey* in every other respect. Montgomery lies about sixty-five miles due west of Polesworth, and riding to it Donne traversed what has become one of the most poetically removed landscapes in the British Isles—the landscape of Housman's *Shropshire Lad*. Wenlock Edge, where Housman saw the wood in trouble, stretches southwards roughly halfway along Donne's route. But when we read Donne's poem we find that, for all he noticed of the countryside he rode across, he might have been traveling on the surface of the moon.[9]

By contrast, Johnson's poem centers on the poet in nature, a specific occasion—the arrival of a thunderhead "hoist[ing] its wet anvil aloft," about to erupt—and the poet pulling her truck over to the side of the road to watch the impending spectacle and wait out the inevitable downpour. How to render this scene in words? This question animates the poem. The emerging storm is a "viper fanged" "horror," a "verb / that forward thrusts the moment eternal, nails / each thing to its present" (ll. 9-11). Having lit on this metaphor—storm as verb—Johnson meditates how she might write the storm truly:

I should write *the thunderhead converges, lifts, rides*

the steep low, butts the front range, bunches like shoved
fabric, blisters, throws up lightning thirteen miles,
lets down rain in ribs, bubbles under the afternoon . . . (ll. 12-15)

The ellipsis would yawn into a seemingly endless continuance, an "endless poem of thunder" (l. 16) if the poet persisted.

But the thunderhead's unfolding, its "moment's span," would "whelm the longest page" (l. 18). Its size and scope, like the enormity of the Crucifixion for Donne, overwhelms Johnson's descriptive powers—"too much weight for me," she says. Nevertheless, she cannot stop herself from trying again, this time parenthetically in a description of lightning:

(*The leader forks, drops,*
attracts the charge from earthward, the molten air
expands, chills, slams shut, a riot of electrons . . .) (ll. 19-21)

And this attempt, also promising to be endless, results in a recognition that could apply to Johnson's poems generally, a paean to the power of verbs:

But God, I love the verb. I verb impenitent,
luxuriant, altaring up truth for immortality, for
the pleasure of unlikeness, the prick

of unlikeness! O happy deformation,
spunky verb, I embrace you in my
degradation, my shoddy embodiment

making thunder endless: impossible: sublime. (ll. 22-28)

As electricity powers the storm, verbs power Johnson's lines. The distance between heightened experience and heightened language lessens through the capacity of "luxuriant" verbs to immortalize truth in an act of memorable alteration. As before, the sounds of words in combination contributes a charge to the predicate work; consider the hissing "s" sounds in the description of lightning: *The leader forks, drops, / attracts the charge from earthward, the molten air / expands, chills, slams shut, a riot of electrons . . .*, for example. Sounds stitch the verbs together to chart the lightning's path. The poem ends not with a colloquy to God but to the "spunky" verb, the presiding deity of Johnson's style. The poet embraces the power of the verb to lend agency to her creative efforts.

In her prefatory discussion of the devotional lyric in *Before the Door of God: An Anthology of Devotional Poetry*, which she edited with Jay Hopler, Johnson reminds us that the "utterance of a lyric poem presents itself as arising in response to a particular occasion—not necessarily a specific event, but rather a sense of some conceptual predicament, impediment, a problem which generates the response of speech."[10] This description explains quite well the emphasis on occasion in both Donne's and Johnson's poems and their resulting immediacy. The Good Friday poems as well, both Johnson's and Donne's, emphasize another "generic trait" Johnson considers central in the lyric: the way in which "lyric poems enact the drama of a mind *figuring something out.*"[11] In Johnson's case, this drama often entails a quest for precision. When the traditional inventory of English verbs fails inspection, she turns to other figural resources for exactitude. She frequently employs anthimeria—using nouns as verbs, as in "altaring up truth for immortality"[12]—to ensure the right word fits the action and to maintain the visceral vigor of her speech:

O God my God, would you were an Abelard
bowing each long midnight in your close cell
over paper, quilling so fervent strokes
to tear the page, *My sister, my spouse.*
                          ("The Story of My Calamities," ll. 1-4)

Or

Thirty-three west basin days, and I
am sick to death of this campshack,
its ceilinged sleep coins me
claustrophobe. ("Aubade," ll. 4-7)

Or twice when describing how the cartographer who inscribed a rose into the directional compass diagram of a U.S. Geological Survey map:

What awful love worked this superfluity?
My U. S. Geological Survey map
grids the haphazard landscape into restrained

geometries, bulges and sandstone hoodoos
smoothed by the benign cursive of contour lines.
But look! — At the chart's least clustered corner,

the cartographer abandoned
his strict piety to boutonnière
the desert: . . . ("Three Bouquets," ll. 1.1-9)

Each sentence concretizes the action with a kind of cinematic joy. Note the Donnean echo in the first line of "The Story of My Calamities": "O God my God," the same exclamation embedded in the title of "Hymn to God my God. In my Sicknesse." "*O God, My God*" or "*My God, My God*" begins Expostulations five through twenty-three of *Devotions Upon Emergent Occasions*. But the larger point is that turning "grid" and "boutonnière" into verbs invigorates the description of the cartographical flower with economical precision. Such strong verbs and nouns often enough appeal to the auditory imagination as much as the visual imagination.

As the passages quoted thus far suggest, Johnson deploys an earthy high style across her lyric plain of rugged Utah, a style powered by her rigorously precise diction and the punch and sounds of her verbs. Together these elements contribute to an effect that X. J. Kennedy some years ago noticed as characteristic of Donne's style: loading the rift of every line with an ore of stressed syllables in excess of the prescriptions of one's chosen meter. Great poets, Kennedy maintained, often place more stresses in their lines than their chosen meters require.[13] This stressing of the line induces a vehemence and affords the poet a larger affective palette. Numerous examples come to mind in Donne's poetry. He often begins poems with surplus stresses or stresses shifted out of the straightforward iambic:

For Godsake hold your tongue, and let me love,
    ("The Canonization," l. 1)

   I am two fooles, I know,
For loving, and for saying so
   In whining Poëtry;
        ("The triple Foole," ll. 1-3)

'Tis true, 'tis day, what though it be?
O wilt thou therefore rise from me?
        ("Breake of day," ll. 1-2)

>   Take heed of loving mee,
> At least remember, I forbade it thee;
>   ("The Prohibition," ll. 1-2)

>   All Kings, and all their favorites
>   All glory'of honors, beauties, wits
> The Sun it selfe, which makes times, as they passe,
>   ("The Anniversarie," ll. 1-3)

> *Love*, any devill else but you,
> Would for a given Soule give something too.
>   ("Loves exchange," ll. 1-2)

>   Let me powre forth
> My teares before thy face, whil'st I stay here,
>   ("A Valediction of weeping," ll. 1-2)

> Marke but this flea, and marke in this,
> How little that which thou deny'st me is;
>   ("The Flea," ll. 1-2)

>   Here is no more newes then Vertu:'I may as well
> Tell you Calis, or St. Michels tale for newes, as tell
> That Vice doth here habitually dwell.
>   ("To Mr. Henry Wotton, 2 Iuly. 1598. At Court." ll. 1-3)

>   This is my Playes last Scene, Here heau'ns appointe
>   My Pilgrimages last Mile, and my race
>   Idly, yet quickly run, hath this last pace,
>   My spanns last inch; my minutes last point.
>   (Holy Sonnet 3, ll 1-4)[14]

> Batter my heart, three-person'd God; for, you
>   As yet, but knock, breathe, shine, and seeke to mend,
> That I may rise and stand, oerthrowe mee, and bend
>   Your force, to break, blowe, burne, and make mee newe.
>   (Holy Sonnet 10, ll. 1-4)[15]

The speaker's vehemence draws in readers. The same overstressing of lines appears elsewhere in poems when the speaker's emotion rises to the surface or breaks forth in exclamation—"O my America, my newfound land," to cite the famous example from Elegy 8: "To his Mistress going to bed," or when he pleads for God to break his marriage to the devil in "Batter my heart" (Holy Sonnet 10):

Divorce mee, vntye, or breake that knott againe;
  Take mee to you, imprison mee, for I
Except you inthrall mee, neuer shalbe free
  Nor euer chast except you ravish mee. (ll. 11-14)

The speaker's desperation is apparent in *how* he voices his thoughts.

Johnson's voice differs from Donne's. Yet she shares his instinct for the value of exceeding the stress counts of lines in the service of affective realism. Consider the unrhymed sonnet "Exercises in Translation," for example:

For me the broad wallop of swans just airborne
means your exorbitance, forlorn as I was
by both beside the lake: wings above me
too far to reach, and you beyond belief,
idiotically aloof. (ll. 1-5)

Pairs or trios of stressed or semi-stressed syllables—"broad wallop," "swans just airborne," "too far to reach"—add punch to her lines and emphasize her frustration at being forlorn. Our sentences become more stressed when we are under stress or when we are caught up in strong emotions that erupt into words. Quite a few of Donne's initial lines assume this truth. So do Johnson's:

Stay, adder, startled from the spikenard
by my step, Adder, stay—, lissome syrinx
temptress of my underbrush. Slither not ...
          ("Love Song," ll. 1-3)

or

Rank and damp vapors, backstaggering
out the greenhouse door for stricter soils
I set out, to instruct my looser soul.
          ("A Psalm of Ascents," 1, ll. 1-3)

or

Forget pearls, lace-edged kerchiefs, roomy pleats,—
this is my most matronly adornment:

stitches purling up the middle of me
to shut my seam, the one that jagged gaped
upon my fecund, unspeakable dark,
> ("Ode on My Episiotomy," ll. 1-5)

   The last example, from "Ode on My Episiotomy," highlights another Donnean dimension in *A Metaphorical God*: many of Johnson's rich, relished lines appear in poems minutely focused on the body, the poet's body often enough, anatomized in a fashion reminiscent of Donne's *Devotions*, hymns, and several of the Holy Sonnets. "The Melancholy of Anatomy," a poem about an anatomist's lab, calls attention to this interest. But so does the sequence of odes immediately preceding it: "Ode on Lanugo," "Ode on My Belly Button," "Ode on my Episiotomy," "Ode on My Appendix," and "Ode on My Cancer." These odes, whose focus on the body resembles Donne's in the *Devotions*, unfold much like several of Donne's Holy Sonnets in the ways they anatomize their startling subjects.

   In "Ode on My Appendix," for example, Johnson moves quickly to metaphorize, to see resemblance in apparently unlike things:

My old frivolity. How I admired
your gentle defiance in my side, your
droll x-ray like a stuck out tongue showed
sinews fooled to welcome . . . what? a tag-end,
embroidery, a thing indifferent. (ll. 1-5)

Flaring up, her appendix in full appendicitis becomes a "puckered heretic," the "searing / center of my frail cosmology," her "dearest intimate" fully capable of providing a definitive lesson on the medieval/Early Modern theological distinction between essential doctrine and lesser important issues, or "things indifferent": "In the body, / in the body's hot memory, in sickness / and in health, there are no adiaphora" (ll. 12-14). The easy traffic between thing observed, metaphor, and theological recall happens with the same swiftness of Donne's "This is my Playes last Scene" and in several of Donne's *Devotions* in which mortal occasion demands a heightened effort to make sense.

   "Ode on My Cancer" begins with the same driving pace as "Batter my heart," "At the round Earths imagin'd corners," and "Spitt in my face." Compare how Donne opens the last two with how Johnson introduces her readers to the sight of her thyroid cancer on a sonogram. Here is Donne:

At the round Earths imagin'd corners blowe
  Your Trumpetts, Angells: and arise arise

> From Death, you nomberles infinities
> Of Soules, and to your scattred Bodies go, . . .
> (Holy Sonnet 4, ll. 1-4)[16]

> Spitt in my face yee Iewes, and peirce my side,
> Buffet, and scoff, scourge, and crucifie mee,
> For I haue sinn'd, and sinn'd, and only hee,
> Who could doe none iniquitie hath dyed.
> (Holy Sonnet 7, ll. 1-4)

Now listen to Johnson:

> Rampant, bloody butterfly, my wayward
> thyroid flecked its winglike lobes with tumors,
> its antic throb across the sonogram
> all loveliness—: a vivid, sylvan show
> more terrible than the imagined black
> blotch, black canker corroding my tissues,
> black crab furtive with scuttering claws.
> ("Ode on My Cancer," ll. 1-7)

All three poems pull readers in through a tight focus on immediate situations and a fireworks display of verbal sounds and vivid images. Once underway, all three poems move through a mostly metaphorical logic to unforeseen conclusions, as startling in their separate ways as their subjects. While cancer of any kind naturally elicits fear and anxiety, Johnson's crab metaphor causes her to look again and see also an emergent beauty on the screen.

> Not crabbed at all, this lift of wings expanding
> to fill the screen, their cathode glow
> fills the clinical dark, flutters my skin
> in green. My heart flutters in my throat
> at this strange creature taking wing
> in whose cells I am magnified, lush in heyday. (ll. 8-13)

The "bloody butterfly" inspires a fluttering fear but cannot cancel the realization that, while lethal, cancer is also a manifestation of growth or magnification. This turn of thought affords more hope than the turns Donne typically makes in his Holy Sonnets; but it nonetheless belongs in the same rhetorical family.

"Ode on My Belly Button" similarly enacts a Donnean turn, not once but twice. This poem meditates on what happens to one's belly button during pregnancy. It begins by noting the profound loss of connection in the aftermath of birth: "My original wound was my deepest: / half-inch divot where the cord shriveled off / and a plunging ache that never scabbed / where my umbilical name sloughed away,—" (ll. 1-4). Pregnancy, however, pushes out the belly button, filling the divot. At nine months, Johnson's belly is "skin taut" (l. 6). In this first turn, the original wound heals through a recovered sense of belonging. But in the last movement of the poem, Johnson's "familiar agony" returns as she realizes how short-lived this intimate connection will be. The "mutual attachment" is "already / obsolescing" as the baby nears full-term, and Johnson concludes, with a palpable sadness, "you inherit your original wound. / —Your original loneliness" (ll. 12-14). The experience of loneliness, of isolation, receives ample treatment in Donne's religious writings. Both poets tend to assay this subject in similarly inventive and memorable ways. Yet each poet remains true to her or his experience.

The similarity-in-difference, or difference-in-similarity, of Donne's and Johnson's poems is amply apparent in another of Johnson's poems about the body, "On Divination by Filaments," a poem about biting one's fingernails. The habit of biting her nails quickly broadens into a meditation on the piecemeal nature of the person. "So easy-pieced, this thin humanity?" she asks. "So *insignificant*?" (ll. 4-5). Her "[t]en cuticles / fretted into orts" lead to a "confusion / of cut hairs on the salon linoleum," the emergent list then widening again to include "all unregarded" the "cells I dust behind me as I walk" (ll. 5-9). The angle of vision shifts to see us shedding ourselves unceasingly every day. And this movement, in turn, occasions a meditation worthy of Donne:

If I were holy,

I could believe my body accidental,
a mere adjective of soul, and trouble not
for its disintegration. But removed

so far from holy I take my sloughings hard,
as if each dropped particle were shot
with all my substance, a patchwork sacrifice,

an offering to plead me: *I die daily.* (ll. 9-16)

Plenty here and elsewhere in *A Metaphorical God* is Donnean. Johnson's stance—her suspicion that she is not "holy"—colors her understanding of the significance of this sloughing off of dead or discarded cells. The doubt of one's election sounds much like Donne's in the *Holy Sonnets*, especially "As due by many titles." Then, too, the natural desquamation the flesh is heir to appears here as a "disintegration," a move Donne similarly makes especially when writing about his own illnesses. And finally the ready shift between embodiment and linguistic metaphor marks this poem as very much within Donne's territory. We see here a temperamental affinity between Johnson and Donne but without a loss of Johnson's voice. It wouldn't be fair or accurate to call this poem an imitation of Donne, even as it is difficult to imagine it unfolding in just this way without the example of Donne in the ether of Anglophone poetry. Once again, a seventeenth-century metaphysical poet authorizes and inspires a later poet in an act of present creation that in turn, over time, may well come to inspire subsequent poets entirely on its own as the unceasing oratorio of world poetry continues for the collective good of all who read it and write it as a way of life.

NOTES

1. A scholar of early modern literature, as well as a poet, Johnson openly dialogues with early modern writers in each of her three collections of poems so far. Her three collections of original poetry are *Leviathan with a Hook* (Persea Books, 2002), *A Metaphorical God* (Persea Books, 2008), and *Uncommon Prayer* (Persea Books, 2014). In addition to these works, Johnson is the author of *Made Flesh: Sacrament and Flesh in Post-Reformation England* (Philadelphia: University of Pennsylvania Press, 2014); a notable translator of Hesiod's *Theogony* and *Works and Days: A Bilingual Edition* (Northwestern World Classics, Evanston: Northwestern University Press, 2017) and Virgil's *The Georgics: A Poem of the Land* (London: Penguin Books, 2009); and the editor, with Jay Hopler, of *Before the Door of God: An Anthology of Devotional Poetry* (New Haven, CT and London: Yale University Press, 2013).

2. Johnson, *A Metaphorical God* (Persea Books, 2008).

3. Donne, *Devotions Upon Emergent Occasions*, ed. Anthony Raspa, reissued edition (Oxford and New York: Oxford University Press, 1987), p. 97.

4. "Ode on My Cancer," l. 1; "Love Song," l. 3; "Love Letter," l. 8.

5. Hoskyns, *Directions for Speech and Style*, ed. Hoyt H. Hudson (Princeton: Princeton University Press, 1935), 8 and 51.

6. Hoskyns, *Directions*, 8.

7. Donne, *Devotions*, 100.

8. Johnson's fascination with Donne's titles as a way into poems extends to other collections as well. For instance, *Uncommon Prayer*, her third collection, includes "A Nocturnall Upon Saint Chuck Yeager's Day," an allusion to "*A nocturnall upon S. Lucies Day, Being the shortest day.*" At the 2020 MLA Convention in Seattle, Washington, Theresa M. DiPasquale gave a fascinating paper ("Compared with Me: Four Nocturnals") on what Johnson's nocturnal, along with other nocturnals by Australian poet Stephen Edgar and Scottish poet Liz Lochhead, reveal about why Donne's poem continues to move readers today.

9. Carey, *John Donne: Life, Mind, & Art*, 120–121.

10. Hopler and Johnson, *Before the Door of God: An Anthology of Devotional Poetry*, xxvi.

11. Hopler and Johnson, *Before the Door of God*, xxix.

12. The altar/alter pun in this instance of anthimeria is worthy not only of Donne but of Herbert as well.

13. Kennedy made these remarks during his address, "'Wit's Forge and Fireblast': Trying to Learn from Donne's Poetry," delivered at the Twenty-Fourth Annual John Donne Conference in Baton Rouge, Louisiana, on Friday, February 20, 2009.

14. This numbering reflects the poem's position in what the Donne Variorum editors have determined is the Revised Sequence of the Holy Sonnets. My text comes from this version as well. This sonnet appears as Sonnet 6 in the Original and Westmoreland sequences.

15. Revised Sequence. Donne likely wrote this sonnet after the Original Sequence started circulating. It appears as Sonnet 16 in the Westmoreland Sequence.

16. The number and text come from Revised Sequence. This poem is the eighth sonnet in the Original and Westmoreland sequences.

Chapter 9

The Tradition and the Individual Talent

Jericho Brown and the Donnean Note

On May 4, 2020, the Pulitzer Prize committee announced that Jericho Brown's third collection of poems *The Tradition* (2019) won the Pulitzer Prize for poetry. Brown became the only seventh African American to win the poetry prize since its creation in 1922.[1] In retrospect, the choice of Brown's book appears prescient, politically and culturally. Three weeks later, police in Minneapolis killed George Floyd, yet another unarmed African American man, without provocation. This horrific murder was captured on video and went viral. The ensuing outrage ignited protests, marches, and vigils in more than seventy-five cities across the United States and abroad during a summer of rioting and unrest as white supremacists attempted to sabotage Black Lives Matter marches, and the Trump administration stumbled toward an authoritative response. As if anticipating the upsurge in calls to defund the police, Brown's poem titled "The Tradition," which celebrates the names of flowers African American men lovingly cultivate (Caster, Nasturtium, Delphinian, Stargazer, Cosmos, Foxglove, Cosmos, Baby's Breath) in gardens they can call their own, ends by naming John Crawford, Eric Garner, and Mike Brown, all prior victims of the "tradition" of police killings of unarmed persons of color.[2]

Gardening and racist police killings are only two of the traditions highlighted in *The Tradition*. Brown also exposes the elements of rape culture in Greek mythology. He interrogates the tradition of white supremacy in the United States. He delves into the deleterious effects of systemic racism on the oppressed as well as on those who oppress them. As he had in his previous collections *Please* (2008) and *The New Testament* (2014), he bears witness to the personal traditions of domestic abuse, child beatings, and the sexual exploitation of gay men.[3]

Yet for all the ways *The Tradition* speaks powerfully to the concerns of our current historical moment, the collection grounds itself in the traditions of the poetic past. Brown's poems are in dialogue with this past as the poet adapts and remakes forms and appropriates diverse ways of proceeding to accommodate his distinctive angle of vision. "The Tradition," the poem, is a sonnet, the last two lines rhyming "everything cut down" with "*Eric Garner. Mike Brown*" (ll. 13-14). In other poems, Brown tends to favor the four-beat line, much as Yeats had done throughout his long career. Additionally, the collection includes five "duplex" poems, a form Brown created, which combines features of the sonnet, the ghazal, and the blues. In Brown's hands, the duplex becomes a hauntingly resonant example of how established art forms can energize present poetic occasions. While the content of *The Tradition* could not be more current in American conversations of race in 2020s, the *craft* of the poems therein is equally suggestive for conversations about the literary curriculum in the college classroom. We can learn from the juxtaposition of Brown's individual talent and the literary traditions informing his imagination how contemporary poets can learn from their predecessors. And this way of learning is not entirely consonant with how literature is taught much of the time. As in previous chapters of this book, the writings of Donne play a part in this story.

In the third "Duplex" (of five), Brown weighs the impact of sickness, presumably his HIV, on love. The poem ends with an image of isolation that cannot help but carry a Donnean resonance:

Here is one symptom of my sickness:
Men who love me are men who miss me.

    Men who leave me are men who miss me
    In the dream where I am an island.

In the dream where I am an island,
I grow green with hope. I'd like to end there. (ll. 9-14)

The duplex: fourteen lines like a sonnet, independent yet chained couplets like a ghazal, paired repetitions and rhythms like the blues. And here, in what might be called the sestet of this duplex, a corrective echo of the seventeenth meditation of Donne's *Devotions upon Emergent Occasions*. In contrast to Donne, for whom the tolling bell signals that "no man is an island," Brown's own involvement "in mankind" (in Donne's phrase) through his past and present loves persuades him he is very much an island, alone and missed by those who leave. But in his island dream, he would grow "green with hope," a place where he (and his poem) would end. Brown comes away from his exploration of sickness—not the transient sickness of typhus but the chronic condition of HIV—convinced of its isolating power yet with an intimation of hope.

Donne's seventeenth meditation, with its sweeping vision of interconnectedness of all humanity, also is implicitly hopeful, if not entirely in this life then in the Christian afterlife. No signposts shout the momentary presence of Donne in Brown's closing insight. Indeed, this island reference may be the only allusion to Donne in the entire volume. Earlier in his career, however, Brown affirmed his interest in Donne as someone from whom to learn. In an interview in January, 2016, Brown was asked about the degree to which his poems "work to incorporate English devotional poetic tradition with the tradition of black Christianity."[4] Specifically, does he "feel both John Donne and a New Orleans preacher behind these poems?" In answering, Brown admits the difficulties of "pars[ing]" this question and the ways in which it touches on the related question of how one navigates between whiteness and blackness generally. He concludes, though, by admitting Donne's importance in his writing: "I really do think about him [Donne] a great deal. Certainly, I would not have been able to write my poems if Donne had not existed." Brown leaves this tantalizing remark unexplained. Yet when I read his poems, I can hear, in his early books and in this latest one, something of the effect of Donne's example—not a texture of allusions or echoes, not even a distinct voiceprint but more a series of Donnean notes, borne from methodological resemblances (like the one explored in chapter 4) and similarities in approach or disposition (like those explored in chapter 6).

In both of Brown's first two collections, Christianity figures prominently but more in the turbulent, unsettled manner of Donne's Holy Sonnets than in the more acquiescent lyrics of Herbert's "The Church." "Prayer of the Backhanded," for example, a poem from *Please*, recalls the tortured thought process of a child trying to reconcile the Christian message of love with the physical abuse he suffered at the hands of his father.[5] Brown begins the poem, startlingly enough, by asking God to bless the back of his father's hand as it bruises his cheek. He asks forgiveness for "forgetting / The love of a hand / Hungry for reflex" (ll. 12-14). The last half of the poem toggles between father and son as Brown seeks blessing and healing for both:

    Father, I bear the bridge
Of what might have been
A broken nose. I lift to you
What was a busted lip. Bless
The boy who believes
His best beatings lack
Intention, the mark of the beast.

Bring back to life the son
Who glories in the sin
Of immediacy, calling it love.
God, save the man whose arm
Like an angel's invisible wing
May fly backward in fury
Whether or not his son stands near.
Help me hold in place my blazing jaw
As I think to say, *excuse me*. (ll. 18-33)

The violence of some of the imagery is reminiscent of Donne. So is the brutally honest vehemence (e.g., "Help me hold in place my blazing jaw"). Likening his father's backward flying arm to an angel's invisible wing delivers the same shock as Donne figuring God as an adulterous lover at the end of "Batter my heart." At most here Brown as an adult remembers the child praying simply to hold still his "blazing jaw" while accepting blame that is not truly his. The turn to religion in such raw circumstances unsettles the consolation most expect from Christian devotion.

A similar unsettling occurs in another moment of prayer a few poems later. In "Scarecrow," a five-part poem, the scarecrow represents the speaker at various stages of his life. The fifth part "In the Pulpit" intercuts a prayer against violence with two-line editorial comments about each line of the prayer. The "mouthless man of straw" seems overcome by the burden of carrying on: "*Oh, my God, there is so much to sing,*" "*Hear us, Lord. There is too much to pray*" (5.3, 6). Brown describes the children who harvest the scarecrow's field as murderers, for whom the scarecrow seeks forgiveness:

Sweet Jesus, how long before you come?

I am a mouthless man of straw.
I hang to keep your children fed.

The fruits they pick. The murders they make.
Forgive us, Father, the use of our hands. (ll. 13-17).

The hand, once again, becomes a symbol of violence because of what it can do. Donne, too, ends some of his religious sonnets by stressing the speaker's unworthiness: "*Moyst with one drop of thy blood, my dry Soule*"; "Satan hates mee, yet is loath to loose mee"; "That thou remember them, some clayme as debt, / I think it mercy, if thou wilt forgett"; "for I / Except you inthrall mee, neuer shalbee free, / Nor euer chast except you ravish mee"; and "Those are my best dayes, when I shake with feare."[6] Such expressions betray a sense of hopelessness in the face of conditions that show no signs of ending soon. Throughout his poetry, Brown only rarely imagines an end to the violence we commit against each other. On this point, his work is darker than Donne's as a whole.

While Brown at prayer can remind one of Donne, despite his vastly different historical position, other Donnean notes, small instances in which some startling image or phrase resonates with Donne's writings, sound in other poems from these early collections. Occasionally, Brown "affects the metaphysics," in John Dryden's phrase, as when in "Morning" from *Please* he imagines that the rain he slept through the night before must have reversed direction: "The entire planet must have cried / Upward—tears beneath a man / Always a silent thing" (ll. 7-9). The clouds parting to let the sun shine are like men who "would say goodbye before leaving" (l. 11). The physical world becomes malleable to bend toward the demands of the poet's need to bear witness to a moment. Think of how Donne treats the sun in "The Sunne Rising." The difference here is that Brown's subject accords more with a blues song than with the long Western tradition of love poetry. Yet the kind of imaginative movement is similar.

So is death's cameo in "Another Elegy" from *The New Testament*. This collection contains three poems called "Another Elegy," one in each of its three sections. In the first, an unarmed woman calls the second-person speaker to tell him she will murder his physically abusive brother if the violence doesn't stop. The poem begins with death personified as a home intruder: "Expect death. In every line, / Death is a metaphor that stands /For nothing, represents itself," (ll. 1-3). Brown's personification of death is not the proud, arrogant figure of Donne's "Death bee not proude" but a thief, an invader who can come at any time. But as with Donne's poem, the personification betrays the poetic speaker's frame of mind—in Donne's case, either a swelling confidence or an anxious self-deception, depending on whether you read the poem in the Original or Revised sequences of the Holy Sonnets; in Brown's case, a sense of helplessness in response to inevitable loss. Death, the intruder, takes what it wants, when it wants. Fearful because his brother is bigger and more violent than he is, the speaker takes his time reaching the scene. When he finally arrives, the poem suggests, he is too late: his brother is dead. He spies the corpse. Brown's use of imperatives in this poem cements a connection between death and the speaker. As death "stands for nothing," by the end the speaker does too. *The New Testament* contains quite a few poems that amplify or rewrite biblical stories and passages. This poem directly faces "Cain" in the Copper Canyon Press edition. "Another Elegy" is resonant in another sense as well: the imprecision of this title suggests such elegies must be written all the time in twenty-first-century America. The presence of two other poems with this same title confirms this impression.

In his previous and in his most recent work, Brown seems most like Donne in his treatment of sickness. He wrestles with some of the same vexing truths as Donne does in *Devotions upon Emergent Occasions*: the inevitable corruption of the body, uncertainty about the future, and the loss of agency in the presence of illness and of physicians. In "To Be Seen" from *The New Testament*, Brown recalls one of his frequent visits to his doctor. He is a "dying man" who is not dying "exactly" because his HIV can be treated (ll. 2-4). Nevertheless, his doctor "cannot be trusted" because no one who "promises you life for looking his way" can be trusted (ll. 6-8). Only the chosen ones can make promises, and Brown does not feel chosen (ll. 9, 12). Like Donne in the *Devotions*, Brown speaks of God and metaphor but in a vastly different way, implicitly questioning the existence of any transcendent reality. For Donne, God is a *"Metaphoricall God"* who communicates through the vehicles of the material world and whose signifying power astounds. Brown attributes metaphor-making to his doctor alone who is stuck on the metaphor of war. The body is the terrain, a passive space, in a way not unlike Donne figuring his body as a map in *Devotions* and in "Hymne to God, My God. In my sickness." Illness is a siege of this terrain. As with Donne being anatomized by his figuratively dissecting physician cosmographers, Brown's emphasis falls on the doctor's desire "to be seen" as an authority, almost as if the patient merely served some other self-serving end. Brown likens his doctor to the Old Testament God, figured as an angry father who wants to grab a recalcitrant child by the chin. As with other poems so far discussed, the parallels with Donne entail both similarity and difference. Both Donne and Brown speak to some of the same dimensions of sickness from the patient's point of view. Both connect God, metaphors, and physicians within a short discursive space. And both describe the physician's scrutiny of the ailing body in metaphorical terms. Yet Brown's perspective differs markedly from Donne's, and his description of the doctor is distinctly his own.

Brown's poems about HIV and the body in *The Tradition* sound similar Donnean notes. And they, too, present compelling displays of similarity and difference. In "Cakewalk," for example, Brown figures HIV in different bodies as different kinds of metals, a metaphysical conceit he uses to speak of desire and personal attractiveness:

My man swears his HIV is better than mine, that his has in it a little
gold, something he can spend if he ever gets old, claims mine is full
of lead: slows you down, he tells me, looking over his shoulder. But
I keep my eyes on his behind, say my HIV is just fine. Practical. Like
pennies. Like copper. It can conduct electricity. Keep the heat on or
shock you. It works hard, earns as much as my smile.

In this poem, the presence of the virus doesn't sap the speaker's desire. But he must transmute lead to copper for it to become apparent. Somehow I suspect Donne would have approved of this alchemical metaphor, given his own turns to alchemy in several of the *Songs and Sonets*. Metaphor becomes a way for both poets to mitigate the psychological impact of illness on their sense of self-worth.

Yet the confidence Brown voices in "Cakewalk" is transitory. In "The Virus," Brown describes the way knowledge of the omnipresence of the virus negatively colors everyday perceptions, even dampens what seem the smallest ordinary pleasures. Told from the point of view of the virus, it describes how knowledge of permanent sickness intrudes on even the simple pleasure of looking out a window to enjoy the pansies planted outside. While the virus cannot kill these flowers or even "blur" Brown's view of them, it nonetheless barges in on the poet's perceptions and insistently reminds him of its presence:

> I want you
> To heed that I'm still here
> Just beneath your skin and in
> Each organ
> The way anger dwells in a man
> Who studies the history of his nation.
> If I can't leave you
> Dead, I'll have you
> Vexed. Look. Look
> Again: show me the color
> Of your flowers now. (ll. 8-18)

"Oh to vex me, contraryes meete in one," Donne begins one Holy Sonnet. Contraries seem to vex Brown all the time. The creative presentation of being vexed is one of Donne's strengths as a poet. The same can be said of Brown. Through the startling personification of the virus, Brown conveys what it feels like to be reminded of one's precarious mortality.

Brown's language, of course, is distinctive, as is his insistence on reminding his readers of the incendiary, enraging history of race relations in the United States. But what else can we call poems like "Cakewalk" and "Virus" but metaphysical in a Donnean vein? And yet unlike others discussed in this book—Maureen Boyle or Kimberly Johnson, say—Brown exhibits very little, if any, evidence of swallowing Donne whole, in Herz's perennially apt phrase. He never quotes Donne extensively or responds to specific poems. He has not edited Donne's poems like Paul Muldoon or written about them like Johnson. He does not appear to think about them *in extremis*, like Heaney during that poet's ambulance ride. Most likely Brown encountered Donne while studying with Kay Murphy and John Gery at the University of New Orleans.[7] If not then, he must have turned to Donne subsequently. Regardless of when, Donne's example must have been powerful enough to exert a lingering influence on his understanding of what is possible in a poem, or else he would not have said he would "not have been able to write" his poems "if Donne had not existed."

Any talk of the individual talent against the backdrop of literary tradition cannot help but invoke T. S. Eliot's essay "Tradition and the Individual Talent," first published in 1919, one hundred years before Brown's *The Tradition*, and republished it in 1920 in *The Sacred Wood: Essays on Poetry and Criticism* (1920). In this oft-quoted, oft-reprinted essay, Eliot takes aim at the idea that the poet strives to be wholly original, and that critical evaluation should concentrate on the poet's supposed originality. Eliot counters these notions by stressing the complex engagements any writer negotiates with literary traditions. For Eliot, tradition

> is a matter of much wider significance. It cannot be inherited, and if you want it you must obtain it by great labour. It involves, in the first place, the historical sense, which we may call nearly indispensable to anyone who would continue to be a poet beyond his twenty-fifth year; and the historical sense involves a perception, not only of the pastness of the past, but of its presence; the historical sense compels a man to write not merely with his own generation in his bones, but with a feeling that the whole of literature of Europe from Homer and within it the whole of the literature of his own country has a simultaneous existence and composes a simultaneous order. This historical sense, which is a sense of the timeless as well as of the temporal and of the timeless and of the temporal together, is what makes a writer traditional. And it is at the same time what makes a writer more acutely conscious of his place in time, of his own contemporaneity.[8]

Eliot assumes that the then canonical European tradition was the primary one worth knowing but also stresses the importance of knowing thoroughly and deeply the literature of one's own country. One wonders what Eliot would make of our more globalized 2021, in which a variety of world literatures are much more widely available in their original languages and in translation.

Still, most important in this essay is the degree to which no mature poet emerges *ex nihilo*. Only through deep study can a poet offer a "truly new" work of art to the existing order of literature (37). If "we approach a poet without his prejudice we shall find that not only the best, but the most individual parts of his work may be those in which the dead poets, his ancestors, assert their immortality most vigorously."[9] Though I am convinced I hear the aforementioned Donnean notes when I read Brown's poems, it would be absurd of me to say that Donne—or indeed any other past poet—"assert[s]" his poetic "immortality" through Brown. A similar objection arises from the application of Eliot's comments on the process of artistic "depersonalization," or the "extinction of personality," to Brown's *The Tradition*.[10] Caught up in a chemistry analogy, Eliot considers the creation of a new poem a process of fusing emotions, images, and ideas into new combinations. Contra the preface to *Lyrical Ballads*, such a process entails "not a turning loose of emotion, but an escape from emotion; it is not the expression of personality, but an escape from personality."[11] I cannot imagine how Eliot's description of depersonalization could be reconciled with the poetry of witness or with the work of those poets for whom poetry is a means of acknowledging, drawing attention to, or even coping with traumatic events, social injustices, or personal injuries or tragedies.[12] Brown's collection offers no evidence of an extinction of personality, regardless of whether he writes in his own person or through an adopted persona.

Nevertheless, what Eliot says about the necessity for the poet to develop a "historical sense" applies quite well to Brown: "What is to be insisted upon is that the poet must develop or procure the consciousness of the past and that he should continue to develop this consciousness throughout his career."[13] Brown's poetic consciousness extends to multiple pasts, multiple traditions. Steeped in the poetry of the Harlem Renaissance, he also, in a recent interview with Michael Dumanis, enthused about Milton, whose depiction of the "irony of good and evil" entrances him and whose approach to rhyme has proven a resource.[14] In addition, he reports finding a personal connection with Milton through that poet's ability to write about and through his blindness:

> I don't know why I'm enchanted, I mean *enchanted*, but the fact that Milton was writing, was going blind and writing about going blind—there's something about the moment of knowing what's going on with someone and knowing that it's real for that person.[15]

This sense of identification attests to the way past poets can live in the contemporary present, as Eliot believes they should.

Brown's comments about Milton implicitly run counter to Harold Bloom's theory of the "anxiety of influence"; though Milton and Brown both would qualify as "strong poets" in Bloom's sense, the latter shows no signs of desiring to overcome the former. There would be no need, in part because of the globalization of contemporary poetry. As Brown explains, "Ultimately, I don't have tools that are different from Milton's tools, though I might know more about poetry, quite honestly" because Milton "didn't have access to the poetry of the East," for example.[16] Neither Eliot nor Bloom assume the extent to which the Western literary tradition (itself a compendium of multiple local and national literatures and traditions) might be only one inheritance informing a contemporary poet's development and imaginative engagement. Any poet writing today likely roams farther afield in searching for techniques, forms, subjects, and sources of inspiration than simply Europe or America alone.

Indeed, the East to which Milton lacked sufficient access provides another helpful way to conceptualize the twenty-first-century poet's relationship with the global poetic past. The *Shi jing*, the classic Confucian Book of Odes that has been foundational in Chinese literary education for more than 2,600 years, contains a song that has resonated strongly with *Western* poets who have found in Chinese poetry a powerful resource for their own work. This song likens matchmaking to fashioning an axe handle. Having a matchmaker to assist in arranging a marriage, this ancient song suggests, is as necessary as having an axe with which to cut a new axe handle: "How does one cut an axe-handle?" the poem asks (l. 1). The answer is simple: "The pattern is not far to seek" (l. 5).[17] The handle of the existing axe offers a template for the new one. Over time in Chinese literature, this analogy became an aphorism for describing the proper disposition of new poets learning from their predecessors. In the fourth-century CE, Lu Ji's *Wen Fu* ("The Poetic Exposition of Literature") assumes it is common knowledge among poets:

> When it comes to taking an ax in hand to chop an ax-handle, the model is not far from you; however, it is hard indeed for language (*tz'u*) to follow the movements (*pien*, "mutations") of the hand. What can be put into words is all here.[18]

More than a millennium later, the axe handle analogy impressed Ezra Pound, who translated the poem in his version of the Confucian Book of Odes *The Classical Anthology* (1954).[19] The examples of both the Chinese poets and Pound, whose *Cathay* did wonders to create an appetite for the Chinese poets in the West, in turn, inspired a later generation of West Coast American poets as well. Even the analogy of the axe handle has become an axe handle bequeathed from generation to generation across the globe. The title of Gary Snyder's 1983 collection *Axe Handles* reflects this globe-spanning network of connections, and the title poem describes Snyder's revelation about his indebtedness to those who came before, both Eastern and Western poets.

In the poem, while Snyder shows his son Kai how to throw an axe, Kai remembers the spare hatchet head in the shed and wants to make his own axe. They find a broken handle that they can cut to fit. Then Snyder recalls Pound's translation from the *Shi jing*: "The pattern is not far off" (l. 17).[20] He explains how to shape the new handle with the cutting axe. He then "hears again" Lu Ji's quotation of this same aphorism, which reminds him of his studies of Chinese and Japanese language, literature, and culture under the direction of Shih-hsiang Chen at the University of California, Berkeley, in the 1950s.[21] This second recall triggers an epiphany: both Pound and Chen were axes, from which Snyder shaped his own art and life. Snyder himself is an axe, and his son a handle about "to be shaping again, model / And tool, craft of culture, / How we go on" (ll. 34-36).

When we speak of literary "traditions," it is difficult to escape the suggestion that writing within a tradition is akin to obtaining membership in a club. One is either in or out of the tradition, in or out of the club, depending on one's adherence to the rules or one's cultural position or heritage. Some clubs are notoriously difficult to enter, depending on one's background. The axe handles analogy, however, localizes the transaction between one poem, one work, or one poet and another. It thereby is more open-ended and more promising in describing how a poet in one context finds inspiration in the work of another poet from a very different context. It requires no perceived club membership. A useful axe can come from any culture at any time for the one who seeks its use. It can be a poem or poet or a way of proceeding, whatever inspires the poet to commit words to a new poem in a new present.

Inaugural Washington State Poet Laureate Samuel Green speaks of this same axe handles way of shaping one's poetic craft as a matter of granting oneself permissions, not in an authoritative sense but in an invitational sense:

> It isn't as though we ask for something and are granted our request; it's that we enter into a contract with another writer that wouldn't be possible had the other writer not produced material that makes possible what we do ourselves. Levertov talked about "affinities of content," but I'd say it goes farther than that. We are talking about something greater than mere "influence." It's more personal. It's more like having someone walk through a door we didn't think was open to us, and so we walked through, as well. For example, I would argue that the personal nature of the blues actually had a direct effect on some poets taking certain risks with their content in their own poems—even Berryman. It is pretty easy to see that Snyder learned a whole way of seeing from his readings of Japanese and Chinese poetry—a habit of being, if you will. I took my own teacher's advice to heart: "You have to read everything!" Licking the glacier, I call it.[22]

"Licking the glacier" might seem a daunting task if your primary goal is to consume the whole mass, much as Eliot's discussion of mastering an impossibly vast tradition can seem daunting. But the important consideration is that every lick brings nourishment in itself. The door metaphor is also useful for describing Donne's relationship to Brown. Seen in its light, Donne's poetry—like the poetry of Randall Mann, Evie Shockley, Gwendolyn Brooks,

Langston Hughes, Countee Cullen, Claude McKay, Natasha Trethewey, and many others—opens a few of the many doors Brown has walked through in the making of himself as a poet. This is why certain moves he makes in his poems are reminiscent of Donne's.

Consider, for instance, the brash, even audacious treatment of Christianity to describe nonreligious subjects or phenomena. Donne's appropriations of specifically Catholic beliefs and practices to describe a religion of love must have seemed bold if not outrageous to the more severely devout Catholics of his time, even as the resulting poems delighted his friends, patrons, and fellow Inns of Court wits. Donne portrays himself and his mistress as two, perhaps the only two, saints in their personal religion of love. "The Canonization" defends their love against naysayers by fulfilling all the steps in the Catholic process for sainthood.[23] The most challenging stage of the process of becoming a saint is offering proof of miracles. Donne's proof? The miraculous sex he and his lover enjoy, figured in metaphors of transmutation

> Call us what you will, wee'are made such by love;
>   Call her one, mee another flye,
> We'are Tapers too, and at our owne cost die,
>   And wee in us finde the'Eagle and the dove.
>   The Phoenix ridle hath more wit
>   By us, we two being one, are it.
> So, to one neutrall thing both sexes fit.
>   Wee dye and rise the same, and prove
> Mysterious by this love. (ll. 19-27)

The puns in line twenty-six are especially bold. As Christ was believed to "dye and rise the same" through the miracle of resurrection, so do these lovers through the miracle of insatiable sexual appetite. Their deaths are the so-called "little deaths" of orgasm, their risings, subsequent physical arousals that prove them "Mysterious by this love." All "Divinity / Is love or wonder," Donne reminds us in "Valediction of the booke" (ll. 28-29). When he imagines the lover-saints dead in "The Relique," he predicts that their remains will serve as relics for future lovers. This time, he portrays these saint-lovers as chaste in life but not, perhaps, in death. Those who exhume their bodies with spy "A bracelet of bright hair about the bone" (l. 6)—the line Eliot loved so much, a line that is also likely a sexual joke.[24] In this same poem, the logic of the speaker's sainthood conceit playfully pushes him into positing himself as a Christ. After their bones are brought before the king, "then / Thou shalt be'a Mary Magdalen, and I / A something else thereby" (ll. 16-18). These are daring expressions. So prevalent is the logic of the religion of love in a decidedly Catholic vein that Donne can refer to it casually in poems that develop other conceits at much greater length. While trying to assuage the sadness of lovers parting in "A Valediction forbidding mourning," Donne tells his lover not to cry or carry on too loudly because doing so would be a "prophanation" of their "joyes / To tell the layetie" their "love"—love as a religious mystery again. Donne was neither the first person nor the last to appropriate Christianity for another discursive purpose. But one can see how Donne's example, made widely available in many a classroom, could open a door for others to walk through.

Brown does not fashion a religion of love in *The Tradition*. But anyone steeped in Donne can catch a whiff of resemblance in Brown's playful use of religion as a conceit in "Monotheism":

Some people need religion. Me?
I've got my long black hair. I twist
The roots and braid it tight. *You're*

My villain. You're a hard father, from
Behind, it whines, tied and tucked,
Untouchable.   (ll. 1-6)

Every night comes the ritual of untying the hair before the vanity mirror. And in this ritual, the presence of desire is like that of a saint's for the divine:

        Undo. Un-

Wind. *Finally your fingers*, it says
Near my ear, *Your fingers. Your
Whole hands. No one's but yours.* (ll. 9-12)

The hair's vehemence sounds like that of a Holy Sonneteer's.

Another door I can imagine Donne opening for Brown is the unapologetic assertion of self, of an identity center, even when the self-conveyed is suffering or unflattering. The misogynistic personae of several of Donne's poems touting promiscuity offer points of view that are far from flattering. When the speaker of "The Indifferent" advances the outrageous position that the only woman he cannot love is the one who insists on monogamy, he likely fails to win many fans among the wide range of women he seems to address. Likewise, when the speaker of the elegy "Nature's lay Ideot" complains about being thrown over by the woman he trained in the Ovidian arts of love, the terms through which he expresses his outrage reveal more about him than the "lay Ideot" in question:

Thy graces and good words my creatures bee,
I planted knowledg and lifes tree in thee
Which, Oh, shall Strangers tast? Must I alas
Frame and enamell plate, and drinke in glas?
Chafe waxe for others Seales; breake a Colts force
And leaue him then, beeing made a redy horse? (ll. 25-30).

The figurative commodification of his departing lover is far from endearing. The same can be said of his self-centeredness. Yet poems like these appear to value fidelity to perspectival truth despite its ugliness. We may not agree with or endorse this truth—likely not in the case of these two poems. Regardless, the effect is that we are being let in on a secret, what one tells oneself in private. Such fidelity carries a degree of risk.[25]

Brown's poems dealing with aspects of promiscuity adhere to a similar perspectival fidelity, often to foreground the pain and even self-loathing of the experience. "A.D." treats hook ups borne of undefined loneliness as "wounds": "Each wounds you badly, but no boy hurts / Like the first one / When you slept in a bed / Too narrow for two" (ll. 1-4). The second-person speaker recalls this first encounter while in a king-sized bed with another man a decade later:

Ten years, your feet hanging, tangled and long, and still
You're the victim

Of such nightmares. You breathe
Like he's been lying

                On top for the last decade.
A man goes to heaven, you suffocate below the weight. (ll. 11-16)

The "he" in line 14 is the first boy who seems to haunt the speaker in the weight of every subsequent lover. In contrast with the two previous Donne poems, the speaker of this poem seems much more sympathetic. Still, the central gesture—speaking a private truth—is similar. Despite the speaker's realization, escape from being used seems impossible, as if the speakers of Brown's poems of promiscuity are caught in an unbreakable cycle. In "Thighs and Ass," the speaker reports he "did not think / Of being divided or entered" as he built muscle through squats and lunges (ll. 1-4). But he also confesses he "knew meat would lure men" and sketches an image of himself as being mounted as if he were an animal carrying a rider "at a good speed for a long distance" (ll. 5, 10). The poem ends with the speaker snatching the "fruit of the tree / We pause to hide behind" and feeding this fruit to his rider (ll. 12-15). The poem delivers the force of an unwelcome admission, an unhappy realization about the self. While Brown's speaker describes himself and not his lover as a broken animal, both Brown and Donne in these poems perform distinctive selves voicing uncomfortable truths from their points of view. There is little sense of self-censorship in the face of an assumed readership. Indeed, the lack of censorship fosters a greater intimacy with readers.

Donne even foregrounds the speaking self in poems about the dissolution of the self. In "A nocturnall upon S. Lucies day," that poignant portrayal of interior devastation resulting from the death of Donne's beloved wife Anne, Donne spends more than thirty lines describing his deadness, his emptiness, his nothingness. Yet it is not enough to be merely dead, empty, or nothing; he must be the exemplar of all three. The deadness of all things in winter cannot compare to him because he is its "Epitaph" (l. 9). He is "every dead thing," a "quintessence even from nothingnesse, / From dull privations, and leane emptinesse" (ll. 12, 15-16). The grief of losing his wife "ruin'd" him, and he is "re-begot / Of absence, darknesse, death; things which are not" (ll. 17-18). He is the "grave / Of all," the "Elixir grown" from "the first nothing" (ll. 21-22, 29). Even in this painstaking description of the ultimate "None," Donne distinguishes himself from everyone and everything else, even plants and stones (l. 33). This anti-self is thus paradoxically still an assertion of self, a distinguishing of self from all others.

In "The Microscopes," Brown enacts a similar paradoxical self-assertion through an account of the self-reduced. This time, not grief but the experience of looking through microscopes in school triggers diminishment. Brown recalls hating microscopes for resembling "baby cannons, the real children of war" and for reducing "[o]ur actual selves" to a cell (ll. 3, 9). Under that microscopic gaze, he explains, a "piece of my coiled hair on one slide" was "[j]ust as unimportant as anyone else's / Growing in that science / Class where I learned what little difference / God saw if God saw me" (ll. 11-15). This "one fear" when combined with the microaggressions of being shoved in hallways and being expected to master the white narrative of American history continues the process of diminishment. "I'm a kind / Of camouflage," Brown explains,

> I never let on when scared
> Of conflicts so old they seem to amount
> To nothing really—dust particles left behind—
> Like the viral geography of an occupied territory,
> A region I imagine you imagine when you see
> A white woman walking with a speck like me. (ll. 32-38)

As with Donne's nocturnal, one cannot help but notice this self-reduced, this speck, so foregrounded in the poem that we cannot help but take it into account.

The voices of Donne and Brown are very different. So are their concerns, their preoccupations, their most frequently addressed subjects, their historical positions, and their cultural contexts. Yet their similarities in approach—which result in what I am calling Donnean notes—suggest that Brown's claim of indebtedness to Donne is not some offhand remark but a true acknowledgment, one of many he might have made about many other poets. The almost complete absence of allusions, echoes, and poetic answers—distinctive Donnean shadows—suggests Donne's influence did not derive from direct textual engagement, in which specific Donne poems enabled or spoke to new poems the way Vaughan's poems enabled or spoke to Anne Cluysenaar when she crafted her "Vaughan Variations." Instead, reading Donne seems to have granted new permissions or opened new possibilities in the way Green describes. Donne's poems, the axe handles he left behind, the doors he walked through and left open for others, offered new choices Brown could make while developing his distinctive style, just as other poets—Hughes, McKay, or even Milton, for example—offered other choices. Poets develop their individualized techniques by building a repertoire of choices that most closely accords with how they view the world and how they view themselves in the world. Such a view of craft acquisition stresses strong, enabling voices rather than narratives of literary history. It stresses access to a wide variety of voices from diverse cultures rather than an exclusionary focus on national canons. It necessitates a willingness to see poetry as its own end rather than as a means to some other end. Every poet's journey must be that poet's own. But no poet can make that journey without those who have come before. The challenge for educators today is how best to keep those prior poets available at a time when the humanities are under assault and when, increasingly, the teaching of literature is treated primarily as a means to nonliterary, noncreative ends.

NOTES

1. The others were Gwendolyn Brooks for *Annie Allen* (1950), Rita Dove for *Thomas and Beulah* (1987), Yusef Komunyakaa for *Neon Vernacular: New and Selected Poems* (1994), Natasha Trethewey for *Native Guard* (2007), Tracy K. Smith for *Life on Mars* (2012), Gregory Pardlo for *Digest* (2015), and Tyehimba Jess for *Olio* (2017).

2. *The Tradition* (Port Townsend, WA: Copper Canyon Press, 2019).

3. *Please* (Kalamazoo, MI: Western Michigan University, 2008); *The New Testament* (Port Townsend, WA: Copper Canyon Press, 2014).

4. Kara van de Graaf and Richie Hofman, "Jericho Brown." 6 January 2016. *Lightbox Poetry* lightboxpoetry.com/?p=516. Accessed 10 March 2020.

5. As it happens, "Prayer of the Backhanded" is included in Jay Hopler's and Kimberly Johnson's anthology *Before the Door of God: An Anthology of Devotional Poetry* (New Haven, CT and London: Yale University Press, 2013), 414.

6. "*Crucifying,*" l. 14; "As due by many titles," l. 14; "If poysonous minerals," l. 14; "Batter my heart," ll. 12–14; and "Oh, to vex me," l. 14.

7. "Jericho Brown in Conversation with Michael Dumanis," *Bennington Review*. Issue 6: Kissing the Future (www.benningtonreview.org/jericho-brown-interview). Brown credits his studies at the University of New Orleans with instilling an interest in poetic forms. From Murphy and Gery he learned not only specific forms but also the essential relationship between form and content. Each "informs" the other in a "conversation" that helps Brown see and follow the direction of a poem. Surely Donne's poems must have figured in these formative experiences.

8. Eliot, *The Sacred Wood: Essays on Poetry and Criticism.* Reprint ed. (Marsfield Centre, CT: Martino Publishing, 2015), 44–45.

9. Eliot, *The Sacred Wood*, 43.

10. Eliot, *The Sacred Wood*, 47.

11. Eliot, *The Sacred Wood*, 52–53. He adds, "But, of course, only those who have personality and emotions know what it means to escape these things."

12. Here I have in mind the poetry gathered in Carolyn Forché's anthology *Against Forgetting: Twentieth-Century Poetry of Witness* (New York: W. W. Norton & Company, 1993) as well as the work of those poets who, like Brown, draw attention to racial injustices in the United States and elsewhere.

13. Eliot, *The Sacred Wood*, 47.

14. Dumanis, "Jericho Brown in Conversation with Michael Dumanis," *Bennington Review*. Issue 6: Kissing the Future. www.benningtonreview.org/jericho-brown-interview.

15. Dumanis, "Jericho Brown in Conversation."

16. Dumanis, "Jericho Brown in Conversation."

17. "Axe-Handle," *The Book of Songs: The Ancient Chinese Classic of Poetry*, trans. Arthur Waley (New York: Grove Press, 1996). This edition reprints Waley's 1937 translations with additional translations by Joseph. R. Allen and a forward by Stephen Owen.

18. *Readings in Chinese Literary Thought*, trans. Stephen Owen (Cambridge, MA: Council on East Asian Studies, Harvard University Press, 1992), 86. Owen notes, "By Lu Chi's time, this aphorism had become common wisdom and was often cited in prose, with no direct reference to its source in the *Book of Songs*."

19. Pound, *The Classical Anthology* (Cambridge, MA: Harvard University Press, 1954). Pound translates these lines similarly: "To hack an axe-haft . . . the pattern's near" (l. 7, 10).

20. Snyder, *Axe Handles* (New York: North Point Press, 1983); rep. Shoemaker & Hoard, 2005.

21. Snyder's translations of twenty-one poems by the Ch'an Buddhist hermit poet Han Shan issued from this same period.

22. Private correspondence, February 23, 2021.

23. See John A. Clair, "Donne's 'The Canonization,'" *PMLA* 80 (1965): 300–302.

24. Eliot considered this line "an example of those things said by Donne which could not have been put equally well otherwise, or differently by a poet of any other school" (*The Varieties of Metaphysical Poetry*, 125). John T. Shawcross glosses the line this way:

> bracelet (thus placing it past the hand and at varying positions on the one of the arm) and "bright" hair suggest a phallic joke: though in life they "knew not . . . difference in sex," in death they have become a loving couple. (*The Complete Poetry of John Donne*, 402)

25. One could argue that the risks of such poems for Donne were less than they might be today, in the sense that Donne's contemporaries assumed, more often than not, that the speakers of poems were personae rather than the poets themselves. The reverse tends to be true in American poetry today. Nevertheless, Donne was self-conscious enough about how his poems *might* be viewed outside of his coterie readership to resist attempts to publish them. Meanwhile, Brown, by his own admission, often writes from the perspective of a fictional persona.

Shadow Instruction

An Afterword

One hundred years after the publication of Grierson's *Metaphysical Poems & Lyrics of the Seventeenth-Century: Donne to Butler*, several of the poets represented therein continue to inspire some of the finest poets writing in *this* century. Although Grierson's anthology is no longer in print, numerous other anthologies and editions allow new readers to encounter the poetry of Donne, Herbert, Crashaw, Vaughan, and Marvell for the first time. Much has changed in the world of Anglophone poetry since Grierson's time. The proliferation of poets publishing today from many walks of life argues against the easy classification of individuals into groups. Gone are the days when reviewers and critics gleefully proclaim new literary movements such as the "modern metaphysicals" or its twenty-first-century equivalent. Indeed, more than a few scholars today take issue with the term "metaphysical" as a descriptor for Donne, Herbert, Crashaw, Vaughan, and Marvell. The tremendous outpouring of contextual scholarship on the lives and work of each of these writers has demonstrated how each is so distinctive from the others as to render lumping them together as "metaphysical" problematic. "Do we still use that obsolete term?" one professor asked in response to a questionnaire Sidney Gottlieb distributed during the compilation of his *Approaches to Teaching the Metaphysical Poets* in 1990.[1] Certainly if we restrict the meaning of "metaphysical" to a prescribed content as if this poetry addressed nothing else, its value as a descriptor deserves to be questioned.

Yet the poetry of Donne, Herbert, Crashaw, Vaughan, and Marvell is much more than any narrowly defined content. It shares certain durable characteristics that distinguish it as a way of writing: its "felt thought," in Eliot's words; its dramatic intensity; its honest wrestling with received habits of thought and traditions; its minute examination of motives and behavior; its ready use of startling conceits; its resistance to perceived literary fashions in favor of authentic speech; and its fearlessness in addressing the uncomfortable. At least one of these characteristics may be said to issue from a preoccupation with the nature of reality and the self's relation to it. The rest concern habits of language use and matters of style. When poets today speak of Donne and the other metaphysicals, they highlight specific attributes of this style, usually with admiration. In his excellent book *How Poems Get Made*, for example, James Longenbach highlights "The Canonization" as a primary illustration of how the back and forth between parataxis and hypotaxis makes Donne's "conclusions simultaneously inevitable and unprecedented."[2] Here and elsewhere in Longenbach's book Donne's poems illustrate many of the finer points of making poems. Similarly, Robert Hass, in his book on poetic craft, *A Little Book on Form*, identifies Donne, Herbert, Crashaw, and Vaughan as exemplary inventors of difficult poetic forms somehow capable of conveying naturalness, energy, and intimacy.[3] In her list of her most frequent go-to poets "for sustenance," Kim Addonizio singles out "Donne and Herbert for their questioning and soul-searching."[4] At its heart, metaphysical poetry is a poetry of deep reflection and discernment. Humankind seldom has an adequate supply of either activity. Small wonder, then, that the metaphysical poets continue to fascinate contemporary poets, who still learn much from their seventeenth-century forbears.

As was true in the 1920s and afterward, poets, writers, publishers, and aficionados continue to celebrate the metaphysical poets and will keep doing so for the foreseeable future. Several fellowships and learned societies—the John Donne Society, the George Herbert in Bemerton Group, the George Herbert Society, the Vaughan Association, and the Andrew Marvell Society—exist primarily for this purpose.[5] Donne, Herbert, Vaughan, and Marvell all have journals devoted to their lives and work.[6] In addition, Donne especially enjoys the status of cultural icon not unlike Shakespeare or Milton. His statement "No man is an island" has entered the English language with the same force as Shakespeare's "To be, or not to be," "All that glitters is not gold," and "Brevity is the soul of wit." It has appeared in numerous cartoons, comic books, advertisements, and political speeches.[7] Moreover, Donne's poems have figured prominently in several novels as a well as a Pulitzer Prize–winning play.[8] When COVID-19 took hold in February 2020, it was no surprise that *Devotions upon Emergent Occasions* became the centerpiece of public lectures on coping with illness, or that a physician/poet like John Okrent would publish his own "Corona Sonnets," a crown of sonnets implicitly following the lead of Donne's *La Corona*, in response to emerging conditions.[9]

As vibrant as the presence of the metaphysical poets might seem in the wider culture, however, the classroom nevertheless remains the primary locale where the majority of readers are introduced to their poems. Many of the poets discussed throughout this book first read Donne's "The good-morrow," Herbert's "Love (III)," and Marvell's "To His Coy Mistress" as assigned reading in foundational courses often taken for granted as essential in literary education. But the sad truth in 2021 is that we no longer can assume these poets will be taught with their former frequency and prevalence, especially when the courses in which they typically appear themselves are vanishing. The media have declaimed the "crisis in the humanities" at length in recent years and the decline of English departments in particular. Indeed, in January 2020, on the eve of the pandemic, *The Chronicle of Higher Education* published an issue of *The Chronicle Review* on the question "Can literary studies survive?" That was the subtitle. The editors encoded their answer to this question in the title proper: "Endgame." Contributions gathered in this issue examine the dire straits of the academic job market, the horrific effects of austerity measures, dwindling enrollments in English departments, the collapse of disciplinary boundaries, the decline of culture, and pervasive befuddlement about what to do about it all. "The academic study of literature is no longer on the verge of collapse," the editors declare by way of introduction. "It's in the middle of it."[10] We are living in the aftermath of what Andrew Kay considers the "extinction event" in Academe—the 2008 recession—and the disaster capitalism that followed in the slashing of college and university budgets, the elimination of programs, and the nonrenewal of established tenure track lines.[11] The subsequent pandemic has exacerbated these trends.

The metaphysical poets are especially susceptible to disappearing from the curriculum in the current climate, as neoliberals question pursuits unsanctioned by the needs of the marketplace, and as what Simon During calls "emancipatory culturalism" condemns canonical European literature wholesale on the grounds that it was written by dead white men and therefore is of "little interest to those who are neither men nor white."[12] Yet the poetry of Donne, Herbert, Vaughan, and Marvell retains the uncanny ability to speak beyond itself and to reach a variety of readers who may have little in common with *these* dead white men, or, indeed, with each other. Poets and readers throughout the world today find in their work valuable insights into fundamental experiences of human existence: desiring, loving, aging, grieving, questioning, doubting, joy, sadness, wonder, and gratitude. Metaphysical poetry is equally valuable for *how it speaks* as much as for *what it says*. As the previous chapters have shown, it opens doors into new and rewarding uses of language that encourage thoughtfulness in consonance with feeling. In this sense, the admiration of Eliot, Brooke, Yeats, and others in the first half of the twentieth century for the "felt thought" of Donne still makes sense. The same can be said of other durable characteristics of his style of writing. The distinctive use of conceits and figures of speech, the indulgence in verbal relish, the willingness to dramatize precise states of thought and feeling, the dedication to argument with an eye toward understanding—all of these qualities and habits have much to teach those looking to discover and cultivate their own writing voices in the twenty-first century.

Michael Clune notes that the "capitulation of cultural education to consumer preference" supposedly in the cause of a valueless relativism—what he calls "dogmatic equality"—sacrifices a "possibility central to humanistic education": "The prospect you might be transformed, that you might discover new modes of thought, perception, and desire, has been foreclosed."[13] Others, too, in recent weeks have touted the paramount importance of a transformative education through deep encounters with the great voices of the past. Four weeks ago, in response to Howard University's decision to eliminate its classics department, Cornell West and Jeremy Tate condemned the decision in an opinion piece published in *The Washington Post*. They highlight the importance of reading Socrates, Cato, and Cicero for Frederick Douglass and the Rev. Martin Luther King Jr. "Academia's continual campaign to disregard or neglect the classics is a sign of spiritual decay, moral decline and a deep narrowness running amok in American culture," they explain.[14] They argue cogently for the centrality of the great voices of the past, wherever they originate, in educating for a better future. Professors dedicated to the cause of emancipatory culturalism often stress the importance of meeting students "where they are"; but if we leave them there, we cannot take them anyplace new. We cannot stretch their imaginations, or better still, show them how to do this themselves. The metaphysical poets are among the finest poets in the world for furthering this sort of growth and discovery.

In one of his essays, Seamus Heaney writes that the goal of teaching poetry should be to help students experience the "living nature of poetic tradition" more than anything else:

> Nowadays, undergraduates are being taught prematurely to regard the poetic heritage as an oppressive imposition and to suspect it for its latent discriminations in the realm of gender, its privilegings and marginalizations in the realms of class and power. All of this suspicion may be salutary enough when it is exercised by a mind informed by that which it is being taught to suspect, but it is a suspicion which is lamentably destructive of cultural memory when it is induced in minds without any cultural possessions whatever. On the other hand, when a poet quotes from memory or from prejudice or in sheer admiration, "the canon" is manifested in an educationally meaningful way. To put it simply, I believe that the life of society is better served by a quotation-bore who quotes out of professional love than by an "unmasking"-bore who subverts out of theory.[15]

Simply reading poetry can do wonders. The poet Samuel Green maintains what he calls his "rescue shelf," a shelf full of carefully chosen books of poems he turns to when the howling of the wolves gets too close. His poems are on my rescue shelf, along with volumes by several of the poets discussed in this book and many others as well. Some critics dismiss the study of literature as a wasteful indulgence in pleasure, a troubling oversimplification. But pleasure is not the reason why people sometimes recite Donne's "The good-morrow" at weddings or "Death be not proud" or "A Valediction forbidding mourning" at funerals. In such cases, living with a poem becomes a momentous event. The teaching of poetry, above all else, should honor the music of what happens in such encounters. It should foster them.

The contemporary poets discussed in this book responded to and drew energy from metaphysical poets as individuals, not from any larger narrative. Poems by Donne, Herbert, and the others became axe handles useful for these later poets in shaping their own craft. A curricular approach privileging this sort of interaction stresses not the defense or promulgation of any top-down narratives of literary history or critical dogmas but the juxtaposition of strong poetic voices capable of reaching people as only the best poets can. By "strong voices," I mean those poets whose poems have lodged into the collective consciousness of a community, who address profound urgencies in insightful ways, who push the boundaries of expressive possibilities, who expand or innovate the resources of genre, who offer a ready word-hoard of wisdom, and who inspire subsequent generations of writers to discover their own voices as well. Readers of poetry seek what enriches, what feeds, and what fosters new insights capable of adding value and meaning to their lives. The exclusion of voices that happen not to be mainstream or canonical can work against this search. Faced with the limitations of time and opportunity, those of us teaching must consider carefully the benefits of every voice and ask honestly whether its power can speak to current and future needs. Can it bestow wisdom? Can it illuminate the past for us and thereby provide new understanding? Can it help us to speak in ways that are as powerful and distinctive today as they were when it was written? Can it help us *find* our voices by giving us the models, techniques, and words to spark our imaginations? If the answer to most of these questions is "yes," then that voice belongs on a syllabus.

The metaphysical poets, some of the strongest voices of the seventeenth century, open quite a few doors if we have the wherewithal to follow them through. But it very well may be that keeping them in the classroom during the coming years will require creativity and flexibility, especially if we are to address concerns about the exclusion of marginalized voices while simultaneously avoiding reductionism and oversimplification. A course on the later seventeenth century, for example, could seize on the fact that Vaughan in Wales and Marvell in England lived and wrote at roughly the same time as Matsuo Basho in Japan and Sor Juana Inéz de la Cruz in New Spain. A course on mindfulness could juxtapose the meditative poems of Donne, Herbert, and Vaughan with poems arising from Buddhist and other practices and faith traditions. A course on the history of lyric could allow Donne to rub shoulders with Sappho, Li Ch'ing-chao, Langston Hughes, and many others. Students crave such comparative encounters. A student of Achsah Guibbory's at Barnard College recently suggested the creation of a course on comparative Renaissances in which English Renaissance poets appeared alongside poets from the Harlem Renaissance, say, or the San Francisco Renaissance. Piers Brown at Kenyon College teaches a course called "Moderns and Early Moderns," which examines how the metaphysical revival of the early twentieth century shaped the literary and interpretive sensibilities of the modernists, those next generation metaphysicals. A poetry writing course could ask students to learn from metaphysical poems how to write poems of their own. There is no shortage of possibilities if we substitute both/and thinking for either/or thinking. We can be creative in how we teach these poets. We can enable their great voices to continue to empower the great voices of the future. Though we may be walking in the afternoon of our time with them, the light is yet strong enough to cast a multitude of shadows.

May 19, 2021
Birthday of the Buddha
Dash Point, Washington
Sean H. McDowell

NOTES

1. Gottlieb, *Approaches to Teaching the Metaphysical Poets* (New York: The Modern Language Association of America, 1990), xi.
2. Longenbach, *How Poems Get Made* (New York: W. W. Norton, 2018), 35.
3. Hass, *A Little Book on Form* (New York: HarperCollins, 2017), 353-363.
4. Tod Marshall, *Range of the Possible: Conversations with Contemporary Poets* (Spokane, WA: Eastern Washington University Press, 2002), 5.
5. More information on these organizations can be found via these websites: John Donne Society (www.johndonnesociety.org), The George Herbert in Bemerton Group (www.georgeherbert.org.uk/about/ghb_group.html), George Herbert Society (english.uncg.edu/george-herbert-society/), Vaughan Association (www.vaughanassociation.org), and Andrew Marvell Society (marvell.wp.st-andrews.ac.uk).
6. See *John Donne Journal: Studies in the Age of Donne* (johndonnesociety.org/journal.html), *George Herbert Journal* (muse.jhu.edu/journal/349), *Scintilla: A Journal of Literary Criticism, Prose and New Poetry in the New Metaphysical Tradition* (www.vaughanassociation.org/about-scintilla), and *Marvell Studies* (marvell.wp.st-andrews.ac.uk/marvell-studies/).

7. See Robert G. Collmer, "Donne Redone: A Literary Descent into the Vernacular," *Texas Humanist* 6, no. 6 (1984): 37-38.

8. See, for example, Edward Docx, *The Calligrapher* (New York: HarperCollins, 2003) and Margaret Edson, *W;t* (London: Faber and Faber, 1999), which won the 1999 Pulitzer Prize for Drama.

9. The first five of Okrent's "Corona Sonnets" appeared in *Poetry Northwest* on 17 March 2020 (www.poetrynw.org/john-okrent-corona-sonnets/) and sonnets six through eight appeared on the website *Love's Executive Order* on 25 March 2020 (www.lovesexecutiveorder.com). See also David Gutman, "A Tacoma doctor treats patients and writes poems about coronavirus," *The Seattle Times* (10 April 2020): www.seattletimes.com/seattle-news/health/a-tacoma-doctor-treats-patients-and-writes-poems-about-coronavirus/ .

10. "Endgame: Can literary studies survive?" *The Chronicle Review* (2020): 3.

11. Kay, "Academe's Extinction Event," *The Chronicle Review* (January 2020): 47ff.

12. During, "Losing Faith in the Humanities," *The Chronicle Review* (January 2020): 21-22.

13. Clune, "The Humanities' Fear of Judgment," *The Chronicle Review* (January 2020): 39-40.

14. Cornell West and Jeremy Tate, "Howard University's removal of classics is a spiritual catastrophe," *The Washington Post*, April 19, 2021, https://www.washingtonpost.com/opinions/2021/04/19/cornel-west-howard-classics/?utm_medium=email&utm_source=newsletter&wpisrc=nl_opinions&utm_campaign=wp_opinions.

15. Heaney, "On Poetry and Professing," *Finders Keepers: Selected Prose, 1971-2001* (London: Faber and Faber, 2002), 71-72.

Works Cited

Abowitz, Richard. "The Traveller: On the Poetry of Alfred Corn," *The Kenyon Review* 15, no. 4 (Fall 1993): 201–216.
Baker-Smith, Dominic."John Donne and the Mysterium Crucis." *English Miscellany* 19 (1968): 62–85.
Bald, R. C. *Donne and Drurys.* Cambridge: Cambridge University Press, 1959.
———. *John Donne: A Life.* Oxford: Oxford University Press, 1970.
Ball, Philip. *Curiosity: How Science Became Interested in Everything.* Chicago and London: The University of Chicago Press, 2012.
Bassnett, Susan. "In Memoriam: Anne Cluysenaar 1936-2014." *Scintilla* 18 (2015): 179–184.
Beecher, Don. "Eye-Beams, Raptures, and Androgynes: Inverted Neoplatonism in Poems by Donne, Herbert of Cherbury, Overbury, and Carew." *Cahiers Elisabéthains: Late Medieval and Renaissance Studies* 65 (2004): 1–9.
Bellette, Anthony F. "'Little Worlds Made Cunningly': Significant Form in Donne's *Holy* Sonnets and 'Goodfriday, 1613. Riding Westward.'" *Studies in Philology* 72 (1975): 322–347.
Bennett, J. A. W. *Poetry of the Passion: Studies in Twelve Centuries of English Verse.* Oxford: Clarendon Press, 1982.
Bettridge, Joel, and Eric Murphy Selinger, eds. *Ronald Johnson: Life and Works.* Orono, Maine: The National Poetry Foundation, 2008.
Bloom, Harold. *The Western Canon: The Books and School of the Ages.* New York: Harcourt Brace & Co, 1994.
———. *Genius: A Mosaic of One Hundred Exemplary Creative Minds.* New York: Warner Books, 2002.
Boyle, Maureen. "The Nunwell Letter." *Poetry Ireland Review* 127 (April 2019): 36–40.
Bradford, Curtis B. *Yeats at Work.* New York: The Ecco Press, 1978.
Bristow, Joseph. "Rupert Brooke's Poetic Deaths." *English Literary History* 81, no. 2 (Summer 2014): 663–692.

Brooke, Rupert. "John Donne." *Poetry and Drama* 1 (June 1913): 185–188.
Brooks, Helen. B. "A 'Re-Vision' of Donne: Adrienne Rich's 'A Valediction Forbidding Mourning.'" *John Donne Journal* 26 (2007): 333–362.
Brown, Jericho. *Please*. Kalamazoo, MI: Western Michigan University, 2008.
———. *The New Testament*. Port Townsend, WA: Copper Canyon Press, 2014.
———. *The Tradition*. Port Townsend, WA: Copper Canyon Press, 2019.
Brown, Piers. "Donne's Hawkings." *Studies in English Literature* 49, no. 1 (2009): 67–86.
Bucciantini, Massimo, Michele Camerota, and Franco Giudice, *Galileo's Telescope: A European Story*, trans. Catherine Bolton. Cambridge and London: Harvard University Press, 2015.
Carey, John. *John Donne: Life, Mind & Art*. New York: Oxford University Press, 1981.
Carlyle, Thomas. *Oliver Cromwell's Letters and Speeches: With Elucidations*. 5 vols. London: Chapman and Hall, 1870.
Carpenter, Frederic Ives. *English Lyric Poetry 1500-1700*. London: Blackie and Son; New York: Charles Scribner's Sons, 1897.
Chambers, A. B. "'Goodfriday, 1613. Riding Westward': The Poem and the Tradition." *English Literary History* 28 (1961): 31–58.
———. "*La Corona*: Philosophic, Sacred, and Poetic Uses of Time." In *New Essays on Donne*, edited by Gary A. Stringer, 140–172. Salzburg: Institut für englische Sprache und Literatur, Universitat Salzburg, 1977.
———. "'Goodfriday, 1613. Riding Westward': Looking Back." *John Donne Journal* 6, no. 2 (1987): 185–201.
Chapman, Wayne K. *Yeats and English Renaissance Literature*. New York: Macmillan, 1991.
Clair, John A. "Donne's 'The Canonization.'" *PMLA* 80 (1965): 300–302.
Clune, Michael. "The Humanities' Fear of Judgment." *The Chronicle Review*, January 2020, 38–41.
Cluysenaar, Anne. "Rereading Henry Vaughan's 'Distraction.'" *Scintilla* 1 (1997): 93–108.
———. *Timeslips: New and Selected Poems*. Manchester: Carcanet, 1997.
———. *Batu-Angas: Envisioning Nature with Alfred Russell Wallace*. Brigend: Seren Books, 2008.
———. *Touching Distances: Diary Poems*. Cardiff: Cinnamon Press, 2014.
———. "Absence, Presence: Recalling Peter Thomas." *Scintilla* 18 (2015): 171–173.
Coffin, Charles M. *John Donne and the New Philosophy*. New York: Columbia University Press, 1937.
Collmer, Robert G. "Donne Redone: A Literary Descent into the Vernacular." *Texas Humanist* 6, no. 6 (1984): 37–38.
Corn, Alfred. *All Roads at Once*. New York: Viking, 1976
———. *A Call in the Midst of the Crowd*. New York: Viking, 1978.
———. *The Various Light*. New York: Viking, 1980.
———. *Notes from a Child of Paradise*. New York: Viking, 1984.
———. *The West Door*. New York: Viking, 1988.

———. *Incarnation: Contemporary Writers on the New Testament.* New York: Viking Penguin, 1990.

———. *Autobiographies.* New York: Viking, 1992.

———. *Present.* New York: Counterpoint, 1997.

———. *Stake: Selected Poems, 1972–1992.* New York: Counterpoint, 1999.

———. *The Poem's Heartbeat.* 3rd printing. Ashland, OR: Story Line Press, 2001.

———. *Contradictions.* Port Townsend: Copper Canyon Press, 2002.

———. *Tables.* Winston-Salem, NC: Press 53, 2013.

———. *Unions.* New York: Barrow Street Press, 2014.

———. with Joanne Wang. *The Bamboo Pavilion.* New York: Four Seasons Press, 2019.

Crowley, Lara M. *Manuscript Matters: Reading John Donne's Poetry & Prose in Early Modern England.* Oxford: Oxford University Press, 2018.

Cunnar, Eugene R. "Donne's Witty Theory of Atonement in 'The Baite.'" *SEL: Studies in English Literature, 1500-1900* 29 (1989): 77–98.

———. "Fantasizing a Sexual Golden Age in Seventeenth-Century Poetry." In *Renaissance Discourses of Desire*, edited by Claude J. Summers and Ted-Larry Pebworth, 179–205. Columbia: University of Missouri Press, 1993.

de la Mare, Walter. "An Elizabethan Poet and Modern Poetry." *The Edinburgh Review* ccxvii (April 1913): 385

DiPasquale, Theresa M. "Ambivalent Mourning in 'Since she whome I lovd.'" In *John Donne's "desire of more": The Subject of Anne More Donne in His Poetry*, edited by M. Thomas Hester, 183–195. Newark: University of Delaware Press, 1996.

———. *Literature and Sacrament: The Sacred and Secular in John Donne.* Medieval & Renaissance Literary Studies. Gen. ed. Albert C. Labriola. Pittsburgh: Duquesne University Press, 1999.

———. "Compared with Me: Four Nocturnals." MLA Convention, Seattle, Washington, January 2020.

Disch, Thomas M. Review of *Present*, by Alfred Corn. *Boston Review*, December 1997/January 1998.

Docx, Edward. *The Calligrapher.* New York: HarperCollins, 2003.

Donne, John. *The Complete Poems of John Donne*, edited by Alexander Grosart. London: The Fuller Worthies Library, 1872–1873.

———. *The Poems of John Donne from the Text of the Edition of 1633*, edited by James Russell Lowell, Mabel Burnett, and Charles Eliot Norton. New York: Grolier Club, 1895.

———. *Poems of John Donne*, The Muse's Library, 2 vols., edited by. E. K. Chambers. London: Lawrence and Bullen; George Routledge and Sons; New York: Charles Scribner's Sons; E. P. Dutton, 1896.

———. *The Poems of John Donne.* 2 vols., edited by Herbert J. C. Grierson. Oxford: Oxford University Press, 1912.

———. *The Love Poems of John Donne.* London: The Nonesuch Press, 1923.

———. *The Elegies and The Songs and Sonnets*, edited by Helen Gardner. Oxford: Clarendon Press, 1965.

———. *The Complete Poetry of John Donne*, edited by John T. Shawcross. Garden City, NY: Doubleday/Anchor, 1967.

———. *Devotions Upon Emergent Occasions*, edited by Anthony Raspa. Oxford and New York: Oxford University Press, 1987.

———. *The Variorum Edition of the Poetry of John Donne* Vol. 6: *The Anniversaries and the Epicedes and Obsequies*, edited by Gary A. Stringer et. al. Bloomington and Indianapolis: Indiana University Press, 1995.

———. *The Variorum Edition of the Poetry of John Donne* Vol. 8: *The Epigrams, Epithalamions, Epitaphs, Inscriptions, and Miscellaneous Poems*, edited by Gary A. Stringer et. al. Bloomington and Indianapolis: Indiana University Press, 1995.

———. *The Variorum Edition of the Poetry of John Donne* Vol. 2: *The Elegies*, edited by Gary A. Stringer et al. Bloomington and London: Indiana University Press, 2000.

———. *The Variorum Edition of the Poetry of John Donne* Vol. 7.1: *The Holy Sonnets*, edited by Gary A. Stringer et. al. Bloomington and Indianapolis: Indiana University Press, 2005.

———. *The Complete Poems of John Donne*, edited by Robin Robbins. London and New York: Routledge, 2010.

———. *John Donne Poems*, edited by Paul Muldoon, Poet to Poet Series. London: Faber and Faber, 2015.

———. *The Variorum Edition of the Poetry of John Donne* Vol. 3: *The Satyres*, edited by Gary A. Stringer et. al. Bloomington and Indianapolis: Indiana University Press, 2016.

———. *The Variorum Edition of the Poetry of John Donne* Vol. 5: *The Verse Letters*, edited by Jeffrey S. Johnson et. al. Bloomington and Indianapolis: Indiana University Press, 2019.

———. *The Variorum Edition of the Poetry of John Donne* Vol. 7.2: *The Divine Poems*, edited Jeffrey S. Johnson et. al. Bloomington and Indianapolis: Indiana University Press, 2020.

Donoghue, Denis. "Denis Donoghue Celebrates the Quatercentenary of John Donne," *Spectator* 229 (18 November 1972): 795.

Drew, Elizabeth. *Discovering Poetry*. New York: W. W. Norton & Company, 1933.

Dryden, John. *Of Dramatic Poesy and Other Critical Essays*, Vol. 2, edited by George Watson. London: J. M. Dent & Sons Ltd, 1962.

Dumanis, Michael. "Jericho Brown in Conversation with Michael Dumanis." *Bennington Review*. Issue 6: Kissing the Future, 2019. http://www.benningtonreview.org/jericho-brown-interview.

Duncan, Joseph E. "The Revival of Metaphysical Poetry, 1872-1912." *PMLA* 68 (1953): 658–671.

———. *The Revival of Metaphysical Poetry: The History of a Style*. Minneapolis: University of Minnesota Press, 1959.

During, Simon. "Losing Faith in the Humanities." *The Chronicle Review*, January 2020, 20–24.

Eckhardt, Joshua. *Religion Around John Donne*. University Park: The Pennsylvania State University Press, 2019.

Edson, Margaret. *W;t*. London: Faber and Faber, 1999.

Eliot, T. S. "Andrew Marvell." *Times Literary Supplement*, 20 January 1921, 43
———. "The Metaphysical Poets." *Times Literary Supplement*, 20 October 1921, 669–670.
———. "The Metaphysical Poets." *Times Literary Supplement*, 3 November 1921, 716.
———. "John Donne." *Nation and Athenaeum* 30 (9 June 1923): 331–332.
———. "The Prose of the Preacher: The Sermons of Donne." *The Listener* 2 (2 July 1929): 22–23.
———. "Thinking in Verse: A Survey of Early Seventeenth-Century Poetry." *The Listener* 3 (1930): 441–443.
———. "Rhyme and Reason: The Poetry of John Donne." *The Listener* 3 (19 March 1930): 502–503.
———. "The Devotional Poets of the Seventeenth Century: Donne, Herbert, Crashaw," *The Listener* 3 (26 March 1930): 552–553.
———. "Donne in Our Time." In *A Garland for John Donne 1631-1931*, edited by Theodore Spencer, 1–19. Gloucester, MA: Peter Smith, 1931; repr. 1958.
———. *The Varieties of Metaphysical Poetry*, edited by Ronald Schuchard. A Harvest Book. New York: Harcourt Brace & Company, 1993.
———. *The Sacred Wood: Essays on Poetry and Criticism*. London: Methuen & Co., Ltd., 1920; rep. Marsfield Centre, CT: Martino Publishing, 2015.
Englands Helicon. Printed by I. R. for John Flasket. London, 1602.
Firth, C. H. *Cromwell's Army: A History of the English Soldier During the Civil Wars, the Commonwealth, and the Protectorate*. London: Methuen & Co., 1902.
Flynn, Dennis. "Donne and a *Female* Coterie." *LIT: Literature Interpretation Theory* 1 (1989): 127–136.
———. *John Donne and the Ancient Catholic Nobility*. Bloomington: Indiana University Press, 1995.
Forché, Carolyn. *Against Forgetting: Twentieth-Century Poetry of Witness*. New York: W. W. Norton & Company, 1993.
Forsythe, R. S. "*The Passionate Shepherd*; And English Poetry." *PMLA* 40, no. 3 (Sept. 1925): 692–742.
Foster, R. F. *W. B. Yeats: A Life*. Vol. I: *The Apprentice Mage, 1865-1914*. Oxford: Oxford University Press, 1998.
Frontain, Raymond-Jean. "Registering Donne's Voiceprint: Additional Reverberations." *John Donne Journal* 26 (2007): 295–312.
Frost, Kate Gartner. "'Preparing towards her': Contexts of *A Nocturnall upon S. Lucies Day*." In *John Donne's "desire of more": The Subject of Anne More Donne in His Poetry*, edited by M. Thomas Hester, 149–171. Newark: University of Delaware Press, 1996.
Gimelli Martin, Catherine. "The Erotology of Donne's 'Extasie' and the Secret History of Voluptuous Rationalism." *SEL* 44, no. 1 (2004): 121–147.
Goldberg, Jonathan S. "Donne's Journey East: Aspects of a Seventeenth-Century Trope." *Studies in Philology* 68 (1971): 470–483.

Gosse, Edmund. "Donne, John." *Encyclopedia Britannica*. 9th ed. Boston, MA: Little Brown, 1877.

———. *The Life and Letters of John Donne Dean of St. Paul's*. 2 vols. London: Heinemann, 1899; repr. Gloucester, MA: Peter Smith, 1959.

Gottlieb, Sidney, ed. *Approaches to Teaching the Metaphysical Poets*. New York: The Modern Language Association of America, 1990.

Granqvist, Raoul. *The Reputation of John Donne 1779-1873*. Studia Universitatis Upsaliensia. 24 Stockholm: Almqvist and Wiksell, 1975.

———. "A 'Fashionable Poet' in New England in the 1890s: A Study of the Reception of John Donne." *John Donne Journal* 4 (1985): 337–349.

Graves, Robert. *The White Goddess*. New York: Farrar, Straus and Giroux, 1948; renewed 1975.

Grierson, Herbert J. C., ed. *Metaphysical Lyrics & Poems of The Seventeenth Century: Donne To Butler*. Oxford: Clarendon Press, 1921.

Guibbory, Achsah. "A Sense of the Future: Projected Audiences of Donne and Jonson." *John Donne Journal* 2, no. 2 (1983): 11–21.

———. "Donne, Milton, and Holy Sex." *Milton Studies* 32 (1995): 3–21.

———. "Fear of 'loving more': Death and the Loss of Sacramental Love." In *John Donne's "desire of more": The Subject of Anne More Donne in His Poetry*, edited by M. Thomas Hester, 204–227. Newark: University of Delaware Press, 1996:

Gutman, John. "A Tacoma Doctor Treats Patients and Writes Poems About Coronavirus." *The Seattle Times*, 10 April 2020. http//:www.seattletimes.com/seattle-news/health/a-tacoma-doctor-treats-patients-and-writes-poems-about-coronavirus/.

Hair, Ross. *Ronald Johnson's Modernist Collage*. New York: Palgrave Macmillan, 2010.

Hartnett, Michael. *Collected Poems*. Loughcrew, Ireland: The Gallery Press, 2001.

Haskin, Dayton. *John Donne in the Nineteenth Century*. Oxford: Oxford University Press, 2007.

Hass, Robert. *A Little Book on Form*. New York: HarperCollins, 2017.

Healy, Thomas. "Playing Seriously in Renaissance Writing." In *Renaissance Transformations: The Making of English Writing (1550-1650)*, edited by Margaret Healy and Thomas Healy, 15–31. Edinburgh: Edinburgh University Press, 2009.

Heaney, Seamus. *Death of a Naturalist*. London: Faber and Faber, 1966.

———. *Wintering Out*. London: Faber and Faber, 1972.

———. *Field Work*. London: Faber and Faber, 1979.

———. *Preoccupations: Selected Prose, 1968-1978*. New York: Farrar, Straus and Giroux, 1980.

———. *Station Island*. London: Faber and Faber, 1984.

———. *The Government of the Tongue*. New York: The Noonday Press, Farrar, Straus, and Giroux, 1988.

———. *The Redress of Poetry*. New York: Farrar, Straus and Giroux, 1995.

———. *Finders Keepers: Selected Prose, 1971–2001*. London: Faber and Faber, 2002.

———. *Spelling It Out*. Loughcrew, County Meath, Ireland: Gallery Books, 2009.

———. *Human Chain*. New York: Farrar, Straus and Giroux; London: Faber and Faber, 2010.

Hennessy, Christopher Matthew. "Corn, Alfred (b. 1943)." *Glbtq*. http://www.glbtq.com/literature/corn_a.html/.

Herbert, George. *The English Works of George Herbert*, edited by George Herbert Palmer. Vol. 1. Boston and New York: Houghton Mifflin, 1905.

———. *The Works of George Herbert*, edited by F. E Hutchinson. Oxford: Clarendon Press, 1941.

Herman, George. "Donne's 'Goodfriday, 1613. Riding Westward.'" *Explicator* 14 (1956): Item 60.

Herz, Judith Scherer. "Under the Sign of Donne." *Criticism* 43, no. 1 (2001): 28–58.

———. "Tracking the Voiceprint of Donne." *John Donne Journal* 26 (2007): 269–282.

———. ed. *John Donne and Contemporary Poetry: Essays and Poems*. London: Palgrave Macmillan, 2017.

Hesiod. *Theogony* and *Works and Days: A Bilingual Edition*, translated by Kimberly Johnson. Northwestern World Classics. Evanston: Northwestern University Press, 2017.

Hester, M. Thomas, ed. *John Donne's "desire of more": The Subject of Anne More Donne in His Poetry*. Newark: University of Delaware Press, 1996.

———. "'Like a spyed Spie': Donne's Baiting of Marlowe." In *Literary Circles and Cultural Communities in Renaissance England*, edited by Claude J. Summers and Ted-Larry Pebworth, 24–43. Columbia and London: University of Missouri Press, 2000.

Hill, Christopher. *God's Englishman: Oliver Cromwell and the English Revolution*. London: Weidenfeld & Nicholson, 1970.

Hodgkins, Christopher. "In a Serious House: Church-Going with George Herbert and Philip Larkin." In *George Herbert's Travels: International Print and Cultural Legacies*, edited by Christopher Hodgkins, 207–223. Newark, DE: University of Delaware Press, 2011.

Hooker, Jeremy. "'Vaughan Variations': Anne Cluysenaar in Conversation with Henry Vaughan." *Scintilla* 19 (2016): 92–108.

Hopler, Jay, and Kimberly Johnson, eds. *Before the Door of God: An Anthology of Devotional Poetry*. New Haven, CT and London: Yale University Press, 2013.

Hoskyns, John. *Directions for Speech and Style*, edited by Hoyt H. Hudson. Princeton: Princeton University Press, 1935.

Hughes, Ted, and Seamus Heaney, eds. *The Rattle Bag*. London: Faber and Faber, 1982.

———. *The School Bag*. London: Faber and Faber, 1997.

Hurley, Ann Hollinshead. "Donne's 'Good Friday, Riding Westward, 1613' and the Illustrated Meditative Tradition." *John Donne Journal* 12 (1987): 67–77

———. *John Donne's Poetry and Early Modern Visual Culture*. Selinsgrove: Susquehanna University Press, 2005.

Hutner, Gordon, and Madison Smart Bell, et. al. "Situation of American Writing." *American Literary History* 11, no. 2 (Summer 1999): 215–353.
Jessopp, Augustus. *John Donne Sometime Dean of St. Paul's 1621-1631.* London: Methuen, 1897.
Johnson, Jeffrey. *The Theology of John Donne.* Studies in Renaissance Literature. Woodbridge, Suffolk: D. S. Brewer, 1999.
Johnson, Kimberly. *Leviathan with a Hook.* Persea Books, 2002.
———. *A Metaphorical God.* Persea Books, 2008.
———. *Made Flesh: Sacrament and Flesh in Post-Reformation England.* Philadelphia: University of Pennsylvania Press, 2014.
———. *Uncommon Prayer.* Persea Books, 2014.
Johnson, Ronald. *RADI OS.* Chicago: Flood Editions, 2005.
———. *ARK.* Chicago: Flood Editions, 2013.
Kay, Andrew. "Academe's Extinction Event." *The Chronicle Review*, January 2020, 47–57.
Keats, John. *The Poetical Works of John Keats*, edited by H. W. Garrod. 2nd ed. Oxford: Clarendon Press, 1958.
Kennelly, Brendan. *Cromwell: A Poem.* Newcastle upon Tyne: Bloodaxe Books, 1983, 1987.
———. *Familiar Strangers: New & Selected Poems 1960-2004.* Newcastle upon Tyne: Bloodaxe Books, 2004.
Kittay, Eva Feder. *Metaphor: Its Cognitive Force and Linguistic Structure.* Oxford: Clarendon Press, 1987.
Kuin, Roger. "Sustainable Energy: Philip Sidney and John Donne." *John Donne Journal* 33 (2014): 63–93.
Leavis, F. R. "The Influence of Donne on Modern Poetry." *The Bookman* 79 (1931): 346–347.
Lecky, W. E. H. *A History of Ireland in the Eighteenth Century.* London: Longmans Green and Company, 1896.
Le Comte, Edward. *Grace to a Witty Sinner: A Life of Donne.* New York: Walker and Company, 1965.
Legouis, *Andrew Marvell: Poet, Puritan, Patriot.* Oxford: Oxford University Press, 1965.
Lewalski, Barbara K. *Protestant Poetics and the Seventeenth-Century Lyric.* Princeton: Princeton University Press, 1979.
Lobanov-Rostovsky, Sergei. "Taming the Basilisk." In *The Body in Parts: Fantasies of Corporeality in Early Modern Europe*, edited by David Hillman and Carla Mazzio, 195–217. New York and London: Routledge, 1997.
Longenbach, James. *Stone Cottage.* Oxford: Oxford University Press, 1988.
———. *How Poems Get Made.* New York: W. W. Norton, 2018.
Low, Anthony. "The Compleat Angler's 'Baite'; or, The Subverter Subverted." *John Donne Journal* 4, no. 4 (1985): 1–12.
MacArdle, Dorothy. *Tragedies of Kerry.* Dublin: The Emton Press, 1924.
MacLeish, Archibald. *New Found Land.* Boston, MA: Houghton Mifflin Company, 1930.

―――. *Collected Poems, 1917-1982.* Boston, MA: Houghton Mifflin Company, 1985.

Malpezzi, Frances M. "Love's Liquidity in 'Since she whome I lovd." In *John Donne's "desire of more": The Subject of Anne More Donne in His Poetry*, edited by M. Thomas Hester, 196–203. Newark: University of Delaware Press, 1996:

Marotti, Arthur F. *John Donne Coterie Poet.* Madison: University of Wisconsin Press, 1986.

Marshal, Tod. *Range of the Possible: Conversations with Contemporary Poets.* Spokane, WA: Eastern Washington University Press, 2002.

Martz, Louis L. *The Poetry of Meditation: A Study in English Religious Literature of the Seventeenth Century.* New Haven, CT and London: Yale University Press, 1954; rev. ed. 1962.

―――. *The Paradise Within: Studies in Vaughan, Traherne, and Milton.* New Haven, CT and London: Yale University Press, 1964.

Marvell, Andrew. *The Poems and Letters of Andrew Marvell*, edited by H. M. Margoliouth; revised edition edited by Pierre Legouis and E. E. Duncan-Jones. 3rd edition. 2 vols. Oxford: Clarendon Press, 1971.

―――. *The Rehearsal Transpros'd and The Rehearsal Transpros'd: The Second Part*, edited by D. I. B. Smith. Oxford: Oxford University Press, 1971.

―――. *The Poems of Andrew Marvell*, edited by Nigel Smith. London and New York: Routledge, 2013.

McAlpine, Katherine, and Gail White, ed. *The Muse Strikes Back: A Poetic Response by Women to Men.* Brownsville, OR: Story Line Press, Inc., 1997.

McDowell, Sean H. "From 'Lively' Art to 'Glitt'ring Expressions': Crashaw's Initial Reception Reconsidered." *John Donne Journal* 24 (2005): 229–262.

―――. "Cataloging, *Dinnseanchas*, and the Lyricism of Tony Curtis." *ANQ* 25, no. 1 (January-March 2012): 59–68.

―――. "Henry Vaughan's Welsh Bird." *Scintilla: A Journal of Literary Criticism, Prose, and New Poetry in the Metaphysical Tradition* 21 (2018): 61–81.

McNees, Eleanor J. "John Donne and the Anglican Doctrine of the Eucharist." *Texas Studies in Language and Literature* 29, no. 1 (1987): 94–114.

―――. *Eucharistic Poetry: The Search for Presence in the Writings of John Donne, Gerard Manley Hopkins, Dylan Thomas, and Geoffrey Hill.* Lewisburg, PA: Bucknell University Press, 1992.

Meljac, Eric. "Windows in George Herbert and Philip Larkin: A Study of Poetic Metaphor." *Journal of Language, Literature, and Culture* 65, no. 3 (2018): 187–199.

Merle D'Aubigné, J. H. *The Protector: A Vindication.* Edinburgh: Oliver and Boyd, 1847.

Miner, Earl. *The Metaphysical Mode from Donne to Cowley.* Princeton: Princeton University Press, 1969.

Minto, William. "John Donne," *The Nineteenth Century* 7 (May 1880): 435–451.

Montague, John. *The Faber and Faber Book of Irish Verse.* London: Faber and Faber, 1974.

Murphy, Denis. *Cromwell in Ireland: A History of Cromwell's Irish Campaign.* Dublin: M.H. Gill and Son, 1883.
Nicholson, Marjorie. "Kepler, the *Somnium*, and John Donne." *Journal of the History of Ideas* 1 (1940): 259–280.
O'Driscoll, Dennis. *Stepping Stones: Interviews with Seamus Heaney.* London: Faber and Faber, 2008.
Okrent, John. "Corona Sonnets." Sonnets 1–5. *Poetry Northwest*, 17 March 2020. www.poetrynw.org/john-okrent-corona-sonnets/.
———. "Corona Sonnets." Sonnets 6–8. *Love's Executive Order*, 25 March 2020. http://www.lovesexecutiveorder.com.
Ong, Walter J. *The Presence of the Word: Some Prolegomena for Cultural and Religious History.* Minneapolis: University of Minnesota Press, 1981.
Osborn, Andrew. "Skirmishes on the Border: The Evolution and Function of Paul Muldoon's Fuzzy Rhyme," *Contemporary Literature* 41, no. 2 (Summer 2000): 323–358.
Ostriker, "What's Done is Donne and How Can I Find God Now: Poems from *The Volcano Sequence*." In *John Donne and Contemporary Poetry*, edited by Judith Scherer Herz, 85–101. London: Palgrave Macmillan, 2017.
Owen, Fiona. "'Into all this': a tribute to Anne Cluysenaar." *Scintilla* 18 (2015): 174–178.
Owen, Stephen. *Readings in Chinese Literary Thought.* Cambridge, MA: Council on East Asian Studies, Harvard University Press, 1992.
Patterson, Anabel. *Marvell and the Civic Crown.* Princeton: Princeton University Press, 1978.
Pebworth, Ted-Larry. "John Donne, Coterie Poetry, and the Text as Performance." *SEL: Studies in English Literature, 1500-1900* 29 (1989): 61–75.
———. "The Early Audiences of Donne's Poetic Performances." *John Donne Journal* 15 (1996): 127–137.
Post, Jonathan F. S. "Donne, Discontinuity, and the Proto-Post Modern: The Case of Anthony Hecht." *John Donne Journal* 26 (2007): 283–294.
Pound, Ezra. *ABC of Reading.* New Haven, CT: Yale University Press, 1934.
———. *The Classical Anthology.* Cambridge, MA: Harvard University Press, 1954.
Powers-Beck, Jeffrey. "'Time to Plant Tears': Elizabeth Bishop's Seminary of Tears." *South Atlantic Review* 60, no. 4 (Nov. 1995): 69–87.
Raiziss, Sona. *The Metaphysical Passion: Seven Modern American Poets and the Seventeenth-Century Tradition.* Philadelphia: University of Pennsylvania Press, 1952.
Ransom, John Crowe. "Eliot and the Metaphysicals." *Accent* 1 (1941): 148–156.
Rexroth, Kenneth. *The Complete Poems of Kenneth Rexroth.* Ed. Sam Hamill and Bradford Morrow. Port Townsend: Copper Canyon Press, 2003.
Roberts, John R. *John Donne An Annotated Bibliography of Modern Criticism 1912-1967.* Columbia: University of Missouri Press, 1973.
———. *George Herbert An Annotated Bibliography, 1905-1974.* Columbia and London: University of Missouri Press, 1978.

———. *John Donne an Annotated Bibliography of Modern Criticism 1968-1978.* Columbia: University of Missouri Press, 1982.

———. "John Donne's Poetry: An Assessment of Modern Criticism," *John Donne Journal* 1 (1982): 55–67.

———. *Richard Crashaw: An Annotated Bibliography of Criticism 1632-1980.* Columbia: University of Missouri Press, 1985.

———. *George Herbert: An Annotated Bibliography of Modern Criticism 1905-1984,* rev. ed. Columbia: University of Missouri Press, 1988.

———, ed. *New Perspectives on the Life and Art of Richard Crashaw.* Columbia and London: University of Missouri Press, 1990.

———. "Recent Studies in Crashaw," *English Literary Renaissance* 21 (1991): 425–445.

———. "'Me Thoughts I Heard One Calling, Child!': Herbert's 'The Collar,'" *Renascence: Essays on Values in Literature* 45, no. 3 (Spring 1993): 197–204.

———. *John Donne An Annotated Bibliography of Modern Criticism 1979-1995.* Pittsburg, PA: Duquesne University Press, 2004.

———. "Richard Crashaw: An Annotated Bibliography of Criticism, 1981-2002," *John Donne Journal* 24 (2005): 1–228.

———. *John Donne An Annotated Bibliography of Modern Criticism 1996-2012. DigitalDonne: The Online Variorum,* 2017: http://donnevariorum.tamu.edu.

Robinson, Forrest G. *The Shape of Things Known: Sidney's* Apology *in Its Philosophical Tradition.* Cambridge: Harvard University Press, 1972.

Roebuck, Graham. "'Glimmering lights': Anne, Elizabeth, and the Poet's Practice." In *John Donne's "desire of more": The Subject of Anne More Donne in His Poetry*, edited by M. Thomas Hester, 172–182. Newark: University of Delaware Press, 1996.

Rude, Donald W. Rude, "Seamus Heaney and John Donne: An Echo of 'The Ecstasy.'" *John Donne Journal* 22 (2003): 255–257.

Rudenstine, Neil L. *Sidney's Poetic Development.* Cambridge: Harvard University Press, 1967.

Rutkin, Lance. "Paul Muldoon: An Interview" *The American Poetry Review* (May/June 2017): 19–22.

Sabine, Maureen. "No Marriage in Heaven: John Donne, Anne Donne, and the Kingdom Come." In *John Donne's "desire of more": The Subject of Anne More Donne in His Poetry*, edited by M. Thomas Hester, 228–255. Newark: University of Delaware Press, 1996.

Schelling, Felix E., ed. *A Book of Elizabethan Lyrics.* Boston, MA: Ginn, 1899.

Selinger, Eric Murphy. "*ARK* as Garden of Revelation." In *Ronald Johnson: Life and Works*, edited by Joel Bettridge and Eric Murphy Selinger, 323–342. Orono, Maine: The National Poetry Foundation, 2008.

Severance, Sibyl Lutz. "Soul, Sphere, and Structure in 'Goodfriday, 1613. Riding Westward.'" *Studies in Philology* 84, no. 1 (1987): 24–43.

Shaw, David W. "Masks of the Unconscious: Bad Faith and Casuistry in the Dramatic Monologue," *ELH* 66, no. 2 (1999): 439–460.

Shawcross, John T. *Intentionality and the New Traditionalism: Some Liminal Means to Literary Revisionism*. University Park, PA: The Pennsylvania State University Press, 1991.

Sherwood, Terry G. "Conversion Psychology in John Donne's Good Friday Poem." *Harvard Theological Review* 72 (1979): 101–122.

Sidney, Philip. *An Apology for Poetry*, edited by Forrest G. Robinson. Indianapolis, IN: Bobbs-Merrill Educational Publishing, 1970.

Sloane, Thomas. "The Poetry of Donne's Sermons." *Rhetorica* 29, no. 4 (2011): 403–428.

Smith, A. J., ed. *John Donne: The Critical Heritage*. London and Boston, MA: Routledge & Kegan Paul, 1975.

Snyder, Gary. *Axe Handles*. New York: North Point Press, 1983; rep. Shoemaker & Hoard, 2005.

Stallworthy, Jon. *Between the Lines: Yeats's Poetry in the Making*. Oxford: Oxford University Press, 1965.

Stanwood, P. G. *John Donne and the Line of Wit: From Metaphysical to Modernist*. The 2008 Garnett Sedgewick Memorial Lecture. Vancouver: Ronsdale Press, 2008.

Starza Smith, Daniel. *John Donne and the Conway Papers: Patronage and Manuscript Circulation in the Early Seventeenth Century*. Oxford: Oxford University Press, 2014.

Stephens, Meic. "Anne Cluysenaar: Writer and academic whose numinous poetry drew on her fascination with science as well as her spirituality." *The Independent*, Friday, 14 November 2014, https://www.independent.co.uk/news/obituaries/anne-cluysenaar-writer-and-academic-whose-numinous-poetry-drew-her-fascination-science-well-her-spirituality-9862395.html.

Stevens, Wallace. *Collected Poetry & Prose*, edited by Frank Kermode and Joan Richardson. New York: Library of America, 1997.

Stirling, Kirsten. "Liturgical Poetry." In *The Oxford Handbook of John Donne*, edited by Jeanne Shami, Dennis Flynn and M. Thomas Hester, 233–241. Oxford: Oxford University Press, 2011.

Stringer, Gary A. "The Composition and Dissemination of Donne's Writings." In *The Oxford Handbook of John Donne*, edited by Jeanne Shami, Dennis Flynn, and M. Thomas Hester, 12–25. Oxford: Oxford University Press, 2011.

Stubbs, John. *John Donne: The Reformed Soul*. New York and London: W. W. Norton & Company, 2006.

Sullivan, II, Ernest W. *The Influence of John Donne: His Uncollected Seventeenth-Century Printed Verse*. Columbia: University of Missouri Press, 1993.

———. "Donne's Epithalamion for Anne." In *John Donne's "desire of more": The Subject of Anne More Donne in His Poetry*, edited by M. Thomas Hester, 35–38. Newark: University of Delaware Press, 1996.

Summers, Joseph H. "George Herbert and Elizabeth Bishop," *George Herbert Journal* 18, nos. 1–2 (Fall 1994/Spring 1995): 48–58.

Taliesin. *The Book of Taliesin: Poems of Warfare and Praise in Enchanted Britain*, translated by Gwyneth Lewis and Rowan Williams. London: Penguin Classics, 2019.

Townsend, Ann. "The Problem of Sincerity: The Lyric Plain Style of George Herbert and Louise Glück," *Shenandoah* 46, no. 4 (Winter 1996): 43–61.
van de Graaf, Kara, and Richie Hofman, "Jericho Brown." 6 January 2016. *Lightbox Poetry* http//:lightboxpoetry.com/?p=516.
Vaughan, Henry. *Henry Vaughan: Selected Poems*, edited by Anne Cluysenaar. The Golden Age of Spiritual Writing. London: Society for Promoting Christian Knowledge, 2004.
———. *The Works of Henry Vaughan*, edited by Donald R. Dickson, Alan Rudrum, and Robert Wilcher. 3 vols. Oxford: Oxford University Press, 2018.
Vendler, Helen. *Seamus Heaney*. Cambridge: Harvard University Press, 1998.
Virgil. *The Georgics: A Poem of the Land*, translated by Kimberly Johnson. London: Penguin Books, 2009
von Maltzahn, Nicholas. *An Andrew Marvell Chronology*. New York: Palgrave Macmillan, 2005.
Waley, Arthur. *The Book of Songs: The Ancient Chinese Classic of Poetry*. New York: Grove Press, 1996.
Wallace, John Malcolm. *Destiny His Choice: The Loyalism of Andrew Marvell*. Cambridge: Cambridge University Press, 1969.
Walton, Izaak. *Walton's Lives*, edited by S. B. Carter. London: Falcon Educational Books, 1951.
West, Cornell, and Jeremy Tate. "Howard University's removal of classics is a spiritual catastrophe," *The Washington Post*, April 19, 2021, https://www.washingtonpost.com/opinions/2021/04/19/cornel-west-howard-classics/?utm_medium=email&utm_source=newsletter&wpisrc=nl_opinions&utm_campaign=wp_opinions.
White, James Boyd. "Reading One Poet in Light of Another: Herbert and Frost," *George Herbert Journal* 18, nos. 1 & 2 (Fall 1994/Spring 1995): 59–80.
Wiley, Margaret. "The Poetry of Donne: Its Interest and Influence Today." *Essays and Studies* 7 (1955): 78–104.
Williamson, George. *The Donne Tradition: A Study in English Poetry from Donne to the Death of Cowley*. New York: The Noonday Press, 1930.
Wolf, Philipp. "Early Modern to Romantic: The Secularization of Memory." In *Modernization and the Crisis of Memory: John Donne to Don DeLillo*, Costerus New Series, 139, edited by C. C. Barfoot, Theo D'haen, and Erik Kooper, 29–60. Amsterdam and New York: Rodopi, 2002.
Worden, Blair. *Literature and Politics in Cromwellian England*. Oxford: Oxford University Press, 2007.
Wootton, David. *The Invention of Science: A New History of the Scientific Revolution*. New York: Harper Perennial, 2015.
Yeats, W. B. *The Letters of W. B. Yeats*, edited by Allan Wade. New York: The Macmillan Company, 1955.
———. *The Collected Works of W. B. Yeats*. Vol. I: *The Poems*, edited by Richard J. Finneran, second ed. New York: Scribner, 1997.
———. *The Collected Works of W. B. Yeats*. Vol. III: *Autobiographies*, edited by William H. O'Donnell and Douglas N. Archibald. New York: Scriber, 1999.

———. *The Yeats Reader*, edited by Richard J. Finneran. New York: Scribner Poetry, 1997; rev. ed. 2002.

———. *The Tower (1928) Manuscript Materials*, edited by Richard J. Finneran with Jared Curtis and Ann Saddlemyer. Ithaca, NY and London: Cornell University Press, 2007.

———. *The Collected Works of W. B. Yeats*. Vol. XIII: *A Vision (1925)*, edited by Catherine E. Paul and Margaret Mills Harper. New York: Scribner, 2008.

———. *The Collected Works of W. B. Yeats*. Vol. XIV: *A Vision: The Revised 1937 Edition*, edited by Margaret Mills Harper and Catherine E. Paul. New York: Scribner, 2015.

Yenser, Stephen. "'Spontaneity': Herbert's Irruption in the Poetry of Elizabeth Bishop and James Merrill." In *George Herbert's Travels: International Print and Cultural Legacies*, edited by Christopher Hodgkins, 191–205. Newark, DE: University of Delaware Press, 2011.

Yezzi, David. "'Power of Some Sort or Other': On Poems & Prayers," *The New Criterion* 30, no. 8 (2012): 29–33.

Young, R. V. *Doctrine and Devotion in Seventeenth-Century Poetry: Studies in Donne, Herbert, Crashaw, and Vaughan*. Cambridge and Rochester, NY: Boydell and Brewer, 2000.

Zabel, Morton D. "Comment: The Mechanism of Sensibility," *Poetry: A Magazine of Verse* 34 (1929): 150–155.

Index

Abowitz, Richard, 140
Addonizio, Kim, 176
Allusion, 1, 9, 11, 21, 22, 24, 26, 27, 29, 30, 35, 48, 51, 57, 60–61, 73, 85, 112, 118, 129, 131, 159, 172
Amergin, 69
answer poem, 9–11, 30, 35–52, 57–60, 114, 172
Aubrey, John, 103
Auden, W. H., 112
axe handles, 166–67, 172, 179

Bacon, Francis, 6
Bald, R. C., 47
Bashō, Matsuo, 179
Bassnett, Susan, 107
Bedient, Calvin, 8
Beecher, Don, 32n20
Berryman, John, 167
Bingham, Kate, 8
Bishop, Elizabeth, 130
Blake, William, 83
Bloom, Harold, 21, 32n18, 131, 165
Bogan, Louise, 7
Boyle, Maureen, 2, 9, 36, 43, 45–52, 163
Brodsky, Joseph, 129
Brooke, Rupert, 4, 129, 177
Brookes, Edward, 39

Brooks, Gwendolyn, 167
Brown, Jericho, 2, 10, 12, 157–72; "A. D.", 170; "Another Elegy (1)", 161; "Cain", 161; "Cakewalk", 162–63; "Duplex (3)", 158; "The Microscopes", 171; "Monotheism", 169; "Morning", 161; "Prayer of the Backhanded", 159–60; "Scarecrow", 160; "Thighs and Ass", 170–71; "The Tradition", 157–58; "The Virus", 163
Brown, Mike, 157–58
Brown, Piers, 79–80, 180
Browning, Robert, 5
Burnett, Mabel, 2
Burt, Stephen (Stephanie), 8

Campana, Joseph, 8
Carey, John, 47, 146
Carpenter, Frederic Ives, 2
Cato, 178
Chambers, E. K., 2
Chapman, Wayne C., 110
The Charioteer of Delphi, 29–30
Charles I, King of England, 63–64
Chaucer, Geoffrey, 7
Cicero, 178
Clampett, Amy, 131
Clune, Michael, 178

Cluysenaar, Anne, 2, 10–11, 95–107, 172; *Batu-Angas: Envisioning Nature with Alfred Russell Wallace*, 98; "Open Ways", 97; "Poems on Visual Materials", 97–98; *Touching Distances*, 98; "Vaughan Variations", 97–107, 172
Cole, Henri, 131
Cooper, Jane, 131
Copernicus, Nicolaus, 79, 87
Corn, Alfred, 2, 10, 11, 130–39; "Easter Eucharist", 137–38; "Resources", 11, 131–36
Crane, Hart, 7
Crashaw, Richard, 175–76
Crawford, John, 157
Cromwell, Oliver, 10, 61–70, 73
Cullen, Countee, 168
Cunnar, Eugene R., 32n20

Davenport, Guy, 74
Day Lewis, C., 7
Dickinson, Emily, 80
DiPasquale, Theresa M., 155n8
Disch, Thomas M., 131
Donne, Anne, 9, 43, 45–52, 171
Donne, John, 2, 4–5, 12, 22–28, 35, 38–52, 73, 76–80, 83, 89, 111–26, 126n5, 126–27n15, 143–55, 158–72, 175–80; "The Anniversarie", 150; "The Apparition", 117–18; "The Baite", 35, 38–43, 45, 58, 112; *Biathanatos*, 50; "Breake of Day", 43, 106; "The broken heart", 117; "The Calme", 49; "The Canonization", 39, 51, 149, 168, 176; "Confined Love", 49; *Devotions Upon Emergent Occasions*, 12, 28, 143–45, 149, 152, 158–59, 162, 176; Elegy 6: "Natures lay Ideot", 169; Elegy 8: "To his Mistress going to bed", 49, 57, 150; "The Extasie, 9, 22–28, 35, 39, 40, 111, 114; "The Flea", 42, 84, 150; "Good friday/Made as I was Rideing westward, that daye" ("Goodfriday, 1613. Riding Westward"), 78–80, 86–87, 144–47; "The good-morrow", 39, 51, 52, 177, 179; Holy Sonnet 1: "As due by many titles", 154–55, 160; Holy Sonnet 3: "This is my Playes last Scene", 150; Holy Sonnet 4: "At the round Earths imagin'd corners", 77–78, 152; Holy Sonnet 5: "If poysonous minerals", 160; Holy Sonnet 7: "Spitt in my face yee Iewes", 77, 152; Holy Sonnet 10: "Batter my heart", 150–52, 160; Holy Sonnet 19: "Oh, to vex me", 160, 163; "Hyme to God, my God. In my Sicknes", 149; "The Indifferent", 124–25, 169; *La Corona*, 160, 176; "Lecture upon the Shadow", 1, 13; "The Legacie", 117; "Loves exchange", 150; "Loves infiniteness", 118; "To Mr. Henry Wotton ("Sir, More than kisses . . ."), 51; "To Mr. Henry Wotton. 2 Iuly. 1598. At Court." ("Here is no more newes"), 150; "A nocturnall upon S. Lucies day", 171; "The Prohibition", 150; "The Relique", 41, 168; "The Sunne Rising", 39–41, 43, 45, 117–18, 161; "The triple Foole", 149; "A Valediction forbidding Mourning", 9, 46, 51, 52, 112–14, 126–27n15, 169, 179; "Valediction of the booke", 168; "A Valediction of weeping", 150; "Woman's constancy", 117
Donnelly, Karen, 36, 44–45
Donoghue, Denis, 7
Douglass, Frederick, 178
Dow, Mark, 8
Drew, Elizabeth, 7
Drury, Sir Robert, 46–47
Dryden, John, 7, 74, 112, 160
Dubrow, Heather, 8
Dumanis, Michael, 165
Duncan, Joseph E., 2, 15n4, 74
During, Simon, 177

Index

echo, 1, 9, 11, 26, 30, 35, 43, 57, 59, 70, 73, 112, 129, 131, 135, 139, 159, 172
Eliot, T. S., 2, 4–7, 10, 12, 16n16, 16n23, 39, 57, 74, 111, 112, 130, 164–68, 174n24, 175, 177
Empson, William, 7, 74
energia, 116–20, 126, 127n18
Englands Helicon, 36–38

Fairfax, Sir Thomas, 61
felt thought, 5–6, 74, 175, 177
Floyd, George, 157
Fludd, Robert, 88
Ford, Katie, 8
Forsythe, R. S., 53n4
Friel, Brian, 109–10
Frontain, Raymond-Jean, 21, 130
Frost, Robert, 110
Fuller, R. Buckminster, 83

Galileo Galilei, 79, 87
Gardner, Helen, 53n6
Garner, Eric, 157–58
Gery, John, 164, 173n7
Gimelli Martin, Catherine, 32n18
Ginsberg, Allen, 8, 21
Glück, Louise, 130
Goodyer, Henry, 47
Gosse, Edmund W., 2
Gottlieb, Sidney, 175
Granqvist, Raoul, 2
Green, Samuel, 166, 172, 178–79
Gregory, Lady Augusta, 3
Grierson, Herbert J. C., 2–5, 42, 57, 110, 175
Grosart, Alexander B., 2
Guibbory, Achsah, 26, 180

Hartnett, Michael, 69
Haskin, Dayton, 2, 15n4
Hass, Robert, 176
Heaney, Seamus, 2, 9–11, 22–30, 31n9, 35, 39, 60, 98, 109–26, 130, 163, 178; "Bone Dreams", 98; "Chanson d'Aventure", 9, 11, 22–30, 111, 114, 115; "Glanmore Sonnets", 11, 24–25, 111, 115; "The Guttural Muse", 125; "La Toilette", 119; "Lovers on Aran", 115; "Mother of the Groom", 124; "The Otter", 122–23; "Poem", 118–19; "Polder", 119; "Scaffolding", 121–22; "The Skunk", 122; "Strange Fruit", 98; "Summer Home", 119; "Twice Shy", 119; "The Underground", 120–21; "Undine", 121; "Valediction", 113–64; "Viking Dublin: Trial Pieces", 98; "Wedding Day", 119
Hecht, Anthony, 127
Herbert, George, 7, 11, 22, 31n9, 111, 130–39, 159, 175–80; "The Collar", 11, 134; "Love (III)", 11, 135–36, 177; "The Thanksgiving", 11, 136–38
Herbert, Matthew, 103, 105–6
Herrick, Robert, 36
Herz, Judith Scherer, 8, 11, 21–22, 31n8, 115, 129–30, 163
Hester, M. Thomas, 39, 53n8, 54n10, 54n15, 54n18
Hill, Geoffrey, 112
Hillman, Brenda, 8
Holtby, Mary, 36, 43–45
Hooker, Jeremy, 96, 99, 106, 107
Hooker, Robert, 6
Hopkins, Gerard Manley, 75
Hopler, Jay, 148
Horace, 36, 62
Hoskyns, John, 116–17, 144
Hughes, Langston, 168, 172, 180
Hughes, Ted, 27, 110, 112

Ignatian meditation, 76–86, 103
Inéz de la Cruz, Sor Juana, 179
influence, 7–8, 10
intertextual engagement, 12, 73, 115

Jarman, Mark, 8, 21
Jessopp, Augustus, 2
Johnson, Kimberly, 2, 8, 10, 12, 143–55, 163; "Aubade", 148; "On

Divination by Filaments", 154; "Easter, Looking Westward", 144–46; "Exercises in Translation", 151; "Goodfriday", 146–48; "Love Song", 151; "The Melancholy of Anatomy", 152; "A Nocturnall Upon Saint Chuck Yeager's Day", 155n8; "Ode on Lanugo", 152; "Ode on My Appendix", 152; "Ode on My Belly Button", 152–54; "Ode on My Cancer", 152; "Ode on My Episiotomy", 151–52; "A Psalm of Ascents", 151; "The Story of My Calamities", 148; "Three Bouquets", 148–49
Johnson, Ronald, 2, 10, 73–75, 83–90; *ARK*, 10, 73–75, 83–90; *RADI OS*, 74–75
Johnson, Samuel, 1, 5, 120–21
Jonson, Ben, 110, 112

Kay, Andrew, 177
Keats, John, 7, 27–28
Kennedy, X. J., 149
Kennelly, Brendan, 2, 10, 60–61, 65–70, 73; *Cromwell: A Poem*, 10, 65–75
Kepler, Johannes, 79, 87
King, Jr., Martin Luther, 178
Kinsella, Thomas, 112
Kittay, Eva Feder, 42
Kuin, Roger, 117
Kunitz, Stanley, 13

Larkin, Philip, 130
Leavis, F. R., 6
Le Comte, Edward, 47
Legouis, Pierre, 61
Levertov, Denise, 167
Li Ch'ing-chao, 180
Lobanov-Rostovsky, Sergei, 26
Longenbach, James, 176
Low, Anthony, 42
Lowell, James Russell, 2
Lowell, Robert, 109
Lu Ji, 166

MacDiarmud, Hugh, 118
MacLeish, Archibald, 2, 7, 10, 57–60, 73
MacNiece, Louis, 7
Mann, Randall, 167
Marlowe, Christopher, 36–40, 48
Marotti, Arthur F., 52n1
Martz, Louis L., 10, 75–76, 78–79, 82, 83, 89, 96
Marvell, Andrew, 10, 36, 57–70, 73, 111, 175–80; "The Garden", 10, 58–60; "To His Coy Mistress", 10, 36, 58–60, 177; "An Horatian Ode upon Cromwell's Return from Ireland", 10, 60–65, 69, 73, 111; *The Last Instructions to the Painter*, 64; "The Nymph Complaining for the Death of her Fawn", 111
McAlpine, Katherine, 43–45
McCarthy, Cormac, 68
McKay, Claude, 168, 172
McNees, Eleanor J., 32n18
meditative poetry, 10, 75–90, 133
metaphysical conceit, 1, 4, 11, 48, 51, 74, 120–23, 144–45, 153, 160, 162, 168–69, 175, 177
metaphysical poetry, 4, 7, 13, 73–75, 107, 110–11, 163, 175–80
Meynell, Alice, 7
Miłosz, Czesław, 109, 111
Milton, John, 7, 74–75, 165–66, 172, 176
Miner, Earl, 74
Minto, William, 2
modal resemblance, 10, 73, 86–90, 159, 172
modern metaphysicals, 7, 38, 74, 175, 180
More, Sir Robert, 48
Morton, Angela, 11
Muldoon, Paul, 8, 21, 22, 31n8, 112, 129, 163
Murphy, Kay, 164, 173n7

Newton, Isaac, 88
Norton, Charles Eliot, 2

O'Driscoll, Dennis, 27, 109, 118
Okrent, John, 176
Olson, Charles, 73, 74, 83
Ong, Walter J., 21
Ostriker, Alicia, 8
Ovid, 36
Owen, Fiona, 107

Patterson, Anabel, 61–62
Peacock, Molly, 8
Petrarch (Francesco Petrarca), 114
Phillips, Carl, 8, 21
Phillips, Rowan Ricardo, 8
Pope, Alexander, 112
Post, Jonathan F. S., 8
Pound, Ezra, 30, 75, 83, 110, 166
Pythagoras, 97

Raiziss, Sona, 74
Ralegh, Sir Walter, 36–40
Ransom, John Crowe, 4, 7, 21, 74
Read, Herbert, 7
response poem. *See* answer poem
Rexroth, Kenneth, 58
Rhees, John David, 104
Rich, Adrienne, 8
Rickword, Edgell, 129
Roberts, John R., 3, 7–8
Robinson, Forrest G., 127n18
Rude, Donald W., 24–25

Saddlemyer, Ann, 24
Sappho, 180
Schuchard, Ronald, 6
shadows, 1–2, 57, 59, 73, 100–101, 144, 172, 180
Shakespeare, William, 176
Shaw, David W., 32n20
Shawcross, John T., 174n24
Shelling, Felix E., 2
Shi jing (Book of Odes), 166
Shockley, Evie, 167
Sidney, Sir Philip, 116–18
Sitwell, Edith, 7, 74
Snyder, Gary, 166–67

Socrates, 178
Southwell, Robert, SJ, 76
Spender, Stephen, 7
Spenser, Edmund, 60, 66, 110
Stevens, Wallace, 7, 75, 95
Stubbs, John, 47
Sullivan II, Ernest W., 54n16
Synge, J. M., 109, 112

Taliesin, 71n20
Tate, Allen, 7, 21
Tate, Jeremy, 178
Tennyson, Alfred, Lord, 5
Theocritus, 36
Thomas, Dylan, 7, 118
Thomas, Peter, 11, 96–97
Trethewey, Natasha, 168
Tu Fu (Du Fu), 36

unconscious influence, 11–12, 131, 135–39

Vaughan, Henry, 10–11, 95–107, 172, 175–80; "Affliction (I)", 99; *Daphnis. An Elegaic Eclogue*, 103; "The Garland", 98; "The Holy Communion", 102; "I Walkt the other day", 96; "Love-sick", 98–99; "Midnight", 103; "The Queer" ("The Query"), 105–6; "Rules and Lessons", 100; "The True Christmas", 100; "The Waterfall", 102; "The World", 107
Vaughan, Thomas, 97, 103, 106
Vendler, Helen, 24–25, 123
verbal relish, 12, 130, 145–53, 177
voiceprint, 11, 21, 115, 129–39, 159
von Maltzahn, Nicholas, 61

Wallace, John Malcolm, 63
Walton, Izaak, 46–47, 54n16
Warren, Robert Penn, 7
watermarking, 39–40, 45
West, Cornell, 178
White, James Boyd, 141

Wiley, Margaret, 7
Williams, Tennessee, 129
Williams, William Carlos, 83
Williamson, George, 6, 16n26
Winters, Yvor, 7
Worden, Blair, 61
Wordsworth, William, 7, 70, 111
Wylie, Elinor, 7, 74

Yeats, W. B., 3–5, 7, 10, 15n10, 61, 75, 80–83, 86, 109–11, 158, 177; "The Cold Heaven", 3; "Easter, 1916", 61; "Fallen Majesty", 3; "Leda and the Swan", 82; "Meditations in Time of Civil War", 81–82; "The Municipal Gallery Re-visited", 110; *The Playboy of the Western World*, 3; "Sailing to Byzantium", 82; "The Second Coming", 82; "To a Young Beauty", 3
Yenser, Stephen, 8

Zabel, Morton Dauwen, 7
Zevon, Warren, 129
Zukofsky, Louis, 73, 74, 83

About the Author

Sean H. McDowell is associate professor of English at Seattle University. A past president of the Andrew Marvell Society and of the South-Central Renaissance Conference, he is the executive director of the John Donne Society, a contributing editor of *The Variorum Edition of the Poems of John Donne*, and the editor of the *John Donne Journal: Studies in the Age of Donne*. The author of numerous essays on Shakespeare, Donne, Herbert, Crashaw, Vaughan, and Marvell, he also has published on modern Irish and American poets. His own poems have appeared in publications in Ireland, England, Wales, Australia, and the United States.

www.ingramcontent.com/pod-product-compliance
Lightning Source LLC
Chambersburg PA
CBHW020119010526
44115CB00008B/896